HOYLE'S *Simplified Guide to the Popular Card Games*

HOYLE'S Simplified Guide to the Popular Card Games

WITH COMPLETE EXPLANATION OF TERMS, RULES, AND PROCEDURES

NEWLY REVISED AND ENLARGED, WITH RECENT GAMES AND A GLOSSARY

by Walter B. Gibson

DOUBLEDAY & COMPANY, INC., *Garden City, New York*

Printed in the United States of America

Contents

Introduction to the Popular Card Games

Times have changed since Edmond Hoyle penned his famous works on whist and other games, two centuries ago, but the cards themselves have remained much the same. The majority of card games still utilize the standard pack of fifty-two cards, composed of four suits, spades (♠), hearts (♡), diamonds (◇), and clubs (♣).

Each suit has thirteen cards, usually valued in descending sequence: ace, king, queen, jack, ten, nine, eight, seven, six, five, four, three, two. In certain games, however, the ace is low, giving the king the status of top card and valuing the ace as one. There are other games in which the ace is either high or low according to the player's choice.

Sometimes the cards are valued in ascending sequence, as ace, two, three, etc. Many players refer to the two as the "deuce," and the term "trey" is occasionally applied to the three. Formerly, the jack was called the "knave," but this term is now obsolete, at least in American card circles.

Various games give special values to specific cards; these will be detailed in connection with the games themselves. In some instances this is simply a divergence from the usual sequence. In bridge and other widely-played games one suit may be designated as a "trump" suit, giving it precedence over the other suits. This will be discussed in the "Introduction to the Trump Games."

Kings, queens, and jacks are called face cards, picture cards, or court cards; the remainder of the pack are spot cards. Technically, the ace is a spot card, though when it is high, many players incorrectly class it as a court card.

In whist the ace, king, queen, and jack of trumps are termed "honors" and this term can be applied to other suits as well; but it is complicated by the fact that in bridge, which has largely supplanted whist, the ten also is a trump honor. The term "high cards" is sometimes used to designate aces and face cards.

A thirty-two-card pack is used in the French game of piquet, the eight cards of each suit being valued **A K Q J 10 9 8 7**. The same pack is used in écarté, a now outmoded game, but the values run **K Q J A 10 9 8 7**. The same thirty-two cards form the modern euchre pack, to which the joker has been added, making thirty-three.

Two piquet packs make up the sixty-four-card pack used in the once popular game of bezique, the cards of each suit ranking **A A 10 10 K K Q Q J J 9 9 8 8 7 7**. Still played in Europe, bezique has been largely supplanted in America by the similar game of pinochle, in which the bezique pack is sometimes used. The standard pinochle pack, however, consists of forty-eight cards, running in the same sequence, but with the eights and sevens omitted.

A more modern trend is to add more cards to existing packs. In six-handed five hundred the joker is included along with additional spot cards in the form of elevens, twelves, and thirteens. Packs with a fifth suit–called royals or eagles–once enjoyed a run of popularity, only to decline.

With the appearance of canasta, a 108-card pack came into vogue, consisting of two regulation fifty-two-card packs, each with a pair of jokers. Further developments of that popular and exciting South American game have led to the introduction of triple packs containing 162 cards in all.

In modern parlance a "pack" is called a "deck," and the terms may be used interchangeably. There is no difference between a bridge deck and a poker deck so far as make-up is concerned; each contains the fifty-two regular cards with two jokers as extras for games in which they may be used. But bridge cards are cut one-quarter-inch narrower than so-called poker cards, so that they can be spread more easily when held in the hand.

In most card games the opening procedure is the shuffling or mixing of the pack. This may be done by dividing the pack in two portions and riffling the ends together in dovetail fashion. The portions are then pushed together, the pack is squared, divided, and the process repeated.

An overhand shuffle is also used, the pack being held in the right hand, thumb at one end, fingers at the other. The left thumb then pulls away clusters of cards from the top of the face-down pack; then a few more, letting them fall on those already drawn away, until the shuffle is completed.

Before the game starts, anyone may shuffle the pack and spread it face down on the table. Players then draw cards and turn them face up, to decide who is to be the first dealer in the game. Highest card wins the deal, unless otherwise specified, some persons preferring the lowest card, with ace low.

Another way is for the person who shuffled the pack to announce, "First jack is the dealer" (or some other card than the jack). He then deals the cards himself, turning them face up from the top of the pack and placing them in front of the players, one by one, beginning at the left and continuing in clockwise fashion until a jack (or another specified card) appears.

Positions at the card table can be decided in a similar manner. Players may also draw for partners, the two high cards playing against the two low, or high and low being partners. A tie can be settled by another draw, or cards may be valued by suits in the order spades, hearts, diamonds, clubs, the ♡**9** taking precedence over the ◇**9** in a draw for high.

Rules of certain card games sometimes include exacting provisions where the draw for deal and partners is concerned, but there is no reason to bother about them, particularly in sociable play, as they have actually no bearing on the game itself. Such choices could just as well be made by the toss of a coin, and it is up to the players to decide upon the method.

Generally, the game begins with the dealer shuffling the pack, one notable exception being in bridge, when two packs are used. Then, the player at the dealer's left shuffles the first pack and gives it to the dealer. While the pack is being dealt, the dealer's partner shuffles the second pack and places it at his right, in readiness for the next deal.

In any game any player may demand the right to shuffle the pack before a deal, and the dealer can always claim the privilege of shuffling last.

After the shuffle the dealer lays the pack face down in front of the player on his right, or toward his opponent in a two-player game. That player cuts the pack by lifting off an upper portion and placing it beside the lower. The dealer completes the cut by placing the lower portion on the upper. The cut may be unequal, but if a player leaves at least a half-dozen cards in the smaller packet, he will meet the rulings of all games.

In dealing, the usual procedure is to hold the pack face down in the left hand and draw cards from the top with the right, the left thumb aiding the process. The dealer places these cards face down in front of the players, beginning at his left and continuing around to himself.

In some games certain cards are dealt as an extra hand, or in a special group called a widow. Also, there are games in which cards are dealt face up, either to different players, or in the center of the table. These and other exceptions to normal dealing are detailed in games where they occur.

Just as the number of players varies in different games, so does the number of cards dealt and their distribution. In bridge there are four players and the entire pack of fifty-two cards is dealt singly, thirteen cards to each. In draw poker there are usually four to six players, and each is dealt five cards, singly. In two-handed pinochle twelve cards are dealt to each player, either in threes or fours, as the dealer may prefer.

Here again we encounter rules that too often have no direct bearing on the game itself. If a pack has been properly shuffled, the dealer should have the right to distribute the cards as he pleases, provided he gives the correct number to each player and everyone agrees. In short, dealing is a matter of custom or convenience, more than of hard or fast rule. In a social game any group is free to prescribe its own dealing procedure.

Any violation of an agreed ruling is a misdeal. It is also a misdeal if the face of a card is exposed in dealing, except in games where certain cards are dealt face up. If the dealer turns up a wrong card, he may deal another face down in its place if circumstances allow and other players agree.

It is a misdeal to give too many or too few cards to a player. It is also a misdeal if the wrong number of hands is dealt. If no one objects to a misdeal and the dealer corrects it, the deal stands.

However, a player may demand that the cards be gathered, shuffled, and dealt again.

The new deal is usually made by the same dealer, except in games where the deal is definitely an advantage, or when specific rules call for the deal to go on to the next player.

After the deal, procedure varies according to individual games. In some, more cards are drawn from the pack; in others, bids are made before proceeding with the play. Except when certain cards are dealt face up, it is customary for each player to hold his cards toward himself so that the other players cannot see their faces. Such cards are shown later as playing rules demand.

Some games, like poker, involve matching hands to determine the winner. Others, like rummy–and to some extent pinochle–depend upon drawing cards from the pack to form certain desired combinations. In many games, players place cards face up on the table, where higher cards capture those of lesser value. A player taking such "tricks," as they are termed, places them face down in a trick pile. Such piles are later checked for total tricks or cards with special point value, to determine the winner. All trump games fall into the trick-taking group.

Rules of many card games require that certain cards be played when possible. Failure to comply with this is termed a "renege" or "revoke" and usually carries a penalty unless corrected. In casual games such infractions are often condoned.

In more complex games, like canasta and its offshoots, penalties are more frequent and to some degree form a part of the scoring schedule, with which they are listed.

The object of many card games is for one player or team to score sufficient points to win over the opponents. Sometimes the margin of victory is important, the losers being charged with the difference. Other games are played on a deal-by-deal basis, settlement being made in chips or tokens during the course of play or at the finish of each deal.

HOYLE'S *Simplified Guide to the Popular Card Games*

Cassino

Cassino is a unique game, even to its peculiar spelling, which distinguishes it from "casino" (gaming place), the word from which it is derived. Through its long and uncheckered history the rules of cassino have remained practically unchanged, a tribute to its intriguing features.

Though a grand game for all ages, cassino is by no means a childish pastime, unless the purpose is to instill true card sense into the younger generation. In that case the lessons learned through cassino may prove invaluable, for the game encourages quick thinking under rapidly changing circumstances.

Oddly, cassino is one game in which the entire pack of fifty-two cards can be dealt out evenly to two, three, or four players.

Four cards are dealt face down to each player, and four more cards are dealt face up in the center of the table. Plays are made with the cards held by the players; after that, each player is dealt four more cards. This continues until the pack is exhausted.

No cards are dealt in the center of the table beyond the original four. Thus the players themselves are dealt a total of forty-eight cards, a number divisible by two, three, or four. The game varies somewhat according to the number of players, and for convenience we shall first describe the two-handed game, then cover the others.

The primary object of the game is to pick up cards from the board by matching them with single cards played from the hand. These are placed face down in front of the player and become his trick pile. Suits have no significance in the actual play, nor do the values of the cards, except as they may be added to form a total for taking further tricks.

Thus, if there is a seven on the board, you may pair it with a seven from your hand and take it; or you may combine a five and two on the board, adding their values (five and two) and taking them with the seven.

Similarly, you could combine a six and ace (six and one) on the board, or a four and three (four and three), to take them with your seven. Two aces (two) could be combined with a deuce (two) and a three (three) to add up to that same seven.

Also you may build to a required total by adding a card from your hand. Suppose you saw a four and a two on the board. In your hand you hold an ace along with your seven. You put the four and two together and add your ace to complete the pile, announcing "Seven."

That constitutes your play. On the next play you take your "build" with your seven. Provided, of course, that your build is still there. Your opponent has his turn between your turns. If he holds a seven of his own, he can play it and pick up your build for himself.

A player can add to his opponent's build if he holds the necessary cards. If one player adds a two from his hand to a three on the board and says "Five," his opponent can add an ace from his hand and make it six. He must have a six in his hand to take the build later. But he cannot use a card from the table to increase a build.

Just as you can take two "combines" with a single card, so can you place a combine with a build. Suppose a two, three, and four are face up on the board. In your hand you hold an ace and a five. You can put the two and three together, saying "Five." Then add the ace to the four, saying "Five." Putting one set on the other, you have a pile which you term "fives."

You take the "double build" with your five on a later play. Meanwhile, your opponent can take the build–if he holds a five –but he cannot add to it because it consists of two sets of cards (two and three; ace and four). Thus, doubling a build is a form of protection.

In announcing such a double build as fives you also prevent the other player from giving it a different value. He is not allowed to add up your fives as "one, two, three, four," call the total ten, and take the pile with a card of that denomination.

A common form of double build is placing a card, say a four, from the hand upon a four on the table and calling it fours. Even in that case the build cannot be treated as an eight. Only another four from a player's hand can take the double build.

Face cards can be built in this fashion. A jack on the table can be covered with a jack from the hand and called jacks. The player must have another jack in his hand to take the build. The same applies with queens and kings.

The purpose of this combining, building, and taking tricks is to acquire cards that count toward an individual score, according to the following table:

For the most *cards* taken	3 points
For the most *spades* taken	1 point
For taking the ♢**10** or *big cassino*	2 points
For taking the ♠**2** or *little cassino*	1 point
For each *ace* taken	1 point
For a *sweep* of the board (described below)	1 point

If cards come out equal, they do not count. Hence the smallest number of points in a round of cassino is eight, consisting of spades (one), big cassino (two), little cassino (one), and the aces (four). Generally, however, there are eleven points scored in a two-handed game and frequently more, when sweeps are allowed.

Here is an example of a sweep:

On the board a player sees the ♠**4**, ♠**3**, ♣**2**, and ♡**A**. In his hand he has the ♢**10**, or big cassino. He adds the board cards up to ten and takes them all with the ten of diamonds. In that one play he gains five cards toward a score in cards, and two spades toward a score in spades.

He also gains two immediate points for big cassino (♢**10**), and one such point for an ace (♡**A**). In addition, his sweep gives him another point. To indicate this, he turns a card face up in the pile that he has taken, so that the sweep can be counted when he looks through the pile to check his score.

There is an element of luck in the sweep just described, and often the play becomes still more one-sided after a sweep has been made. Whenever a player is unable to take a card or make a build, he must play a card face up on the board, so that it becomes available for combines, builds, or takes, like any others that are lying there.

Suppose you have opened the game with a sweep of the sort just described. Your opponent is then forced to make a blind play, say with a jack. If you happen to have a jack, you can immediately take it, gaining another sweep. In fact, you might make three such sweeps, particularly if the cards had been poorly shuffled prior to the deal. All this would be sheer luck, however, without a modicum of skill on your part.

Cassino addicts often eliminate sweeps from the game, therefore, particularly in two-handed play. Still, the luck holds for one as much as for the other. Besides, sweeps provide more fun, and their inclusion is recommended. Often, a few sweeps will enable a player to stage a surprise comeback.

After the last deal of four cards has been played out, cards left on the table are awarded to the person who took the final trick. Gathering in such surplus cards does not constitute a sweep, but it gives the player taking the final trick that many more cards toward cards or spades, together with any actual counters that he might be lucky enough to pick up.

For that reason, a player often holds back a face card that he receives in the final deal, since by matching it with one on the table he can take the last trick and with it those extra cards. But if two face cards of different value–say, a king and a jack–are showing in the final round, there is little use in holding back the king if the other player is the dealer and has the jack in his hand. By holding back the jack he can take the last trick in spite of you.

In modern cassino a rule is often introduced prohibiting a player from taking two face cards with one of the same denomination. Thus, if the ♢**J** and ♣**J** are on the board, only one can be taken with the ♠**J**. Similarly, if the ♠**Q** is on the board, a player cannot build the ♡**Q** on it, then take both with the ♢**Q**. However, if all three are on the board, as ♡**K** ♢**K** ♣**K**, he is usually allowed to take them with the fourth, in this case the ♠**K**.

Such a rule is not part of the original game; if used, it should be specified beforehand. Its purpose is to make the face cards come out evenly, so that sweeps are always possible. Unless this rule is included, there will occasionally be an "odd" face card at the end of the hand. Players must keep this in mind when planning to take the last trick.

Equally important is the fact that if three jacks (or other face cards) are taken as a single trick, the fourth card will later become a "blocker," preventing any sweeps from then on. This adds a defensive factor to the play, enabling the player with the high score to lessen his opponent's chance of lucky gains.

Some cassino players regard each complete hand as a game, but the more customary procedure is to play for a total score of twenty-one. This means that the two-player game will run from two to four hands. If both players reach twenty-one, the simplest and most satisfactory system is to declare high score as game.

There is another method, known as "counting out," in which a player announces when his score has reached twenty-one and play is stopped at that juncture. If he is right, he wins; if wrong, he loses. Should both players go over twenty-one without announcing it, they count their points in this order:

Cards, spades, big cassino (♢**10**), little cassino (♠**2**), aces (♠ ♣ ♡ ♢, in that order), and sweeps. The first to reach twenty-one in that manner is the winner.

Skilled cassino players make a fetish of the game, keeping close check of every card played. This obviously can pay off in very close scores; also it is an advantage when counting out, which experts prefer to the high-score system.

In casual play the simplest plan is to go after cards and spades, something that the beginner is apt to overlook because of the lure of taking big or little cassino and the aces. Naturally, those should not be neglected, but the player who consistently bags cards and spades will be the long-run winner.

Thus, suppose the board shows:

♣**3** ♡**5** ♠**5**

Your hand contains the ♡**3** and the ♣**8**. Rather than take the ♣**3** with the ♡**3**, you can take the ♣**3** and ♡**5** with the ♣**8**, thus gaining one more card. Better than that, the ♣**3** should be combined with the ♠**5** (instead of the ♡**5**), so as to catch a spade as part of the bargain.

However, if you feel you can risk it, you can combine the ♣**3** and ♡**5**, then place the ♡**3** on the ♠**5** as a build, putting the two sets together and calling them eights. On the next play you would take the lot with the ♣**8**.

The question of "risk" is answered thus:

Early in the hand you can afford to take chances, as the odds are against your opponent's holding an eight. But later, if no eights have been played, the odds will be in his favor and your risk too great. On the contrary, if all the remaining eights have been used, your build is a sure thing near the finish of the hand.

Often you can use a preliminary build as a "straw in the wind" for a better build to follow. For example, the board shows ♣**4** ♡**8**. In your hand, you have ♡**5** ◊**A** ♣**9**. By placing the ♡**5** on the ♣**4** and announcing "Nine," you provide a perfect decoy if you think a nine is in your opponent's hand.

He plays his nine and takes your build (♡**5** and ♣**4**), whereupon you place the ◊**A** on the ♡**8** and announce another build of nine. In taking the trick on the next play you gain the ◊**A** as a counter. If your opponent has no nine, you simply add your second build to the first and take them both together.

In short, test your opponent with expendable cards and save the choice ones. Sometimes it is better to let your opponent make a build while you trail along with a face card. This is particularly true if you are holding a card like ♣**10** and suspect that the big cassino (◊**10**) is in your opponent's hand.

Suppose the board showed ♡**3** ♣**4** ♠**8** ◊**9**.

You might have a suitable card (say, ♠**6**) to make a build of ten. But it would be better to play a ♡**J** and see what the other player is about. If he should build a ten, you could take it, stopping him from using his big cassino.

You'd have to hope for a chance to use your ♠**6** in some other way and also hope that he couldn't make another ten build. But you run such risks anyway. The more you lessen your chances of a loss, the bigger your opportunity to win at cassino. If you hold two face cards, such as ♡**J** ♠**J**, it is preferable to lay the ♡**J** on the board, hoping to take it with the ♠**J** later.

If someone takes the ♡**J** with another jack, you still will have a chance of picking up the ♠**J** in a later hand; but if you play the ♠**J** first, your opponent will get it. That could mean the difference of a winning count in spades.

Handle the little cassino (♠**2**) blandly, not blindly. Don't risk it with a hasty build or lay it among a lot of spot cards so that your opponent can use it. If he trails along with an odd deuce of his own, you can snap it up as a quick trick with the little cassino rather than bother with a build at all.

The same applies to aces. Always take an ace with an ace when you can, unless you are positive that a build is safe. It is also good business to clinch a trick when the big cassino (♢**10**) is involved. Only when the quest for cards or spades is very close and extremely vital should you take chances with cards that are counters in their own right.

Many odd situations develop in cassino, and it is well to be prepared for them. Here are some:

When you make a build and your opponent does not take it, you cannot "trail" on your next play, that is, simply lay an odd card face up on the table and let the build wait. You must take the build that you have made unless:

You can form a duplicate build to go with it.

You can raise that build to a higher one.

You can make a separate bona-fide build.

You can take a trick in its own right.

Here, all these situations are shown in a single hand, yet it is the very sort of thing that may develop at any time in cassino play and therefore adds zest to the game.

On the table are:	♢**2**	♣**3**		
You are holding:	♢**A**	♣**2**	♣**4**	♡**10**

It is your play. You place the ♣**2** on the ♢**2** and say "Four."

Why not take the ♢**2** with the ♣**2**? Because you really want to build the ♢**A** on the ♣**3**, but you are first finding out if it is safe. Let us suppose it is. Your opponent trails by playing a jack or some other face card.

So you form a duplicate build by placing the ♢**A** on the ♣**3** and piling it on the first build with the declaration "Fours!" On your next play you can pick up the works with your ♣**4**.

That is, provided your adversary wasn't sitting back with a four of his own, waiting for that very thing to happen.

Taking the same setup, suppose that your opponent holds the following cards:

♠**5** ♠**9** ♣**J** ♢**K**

You begin by building a four (♣**2** on ♢**2**). He places his ♠**5** on it and announces "Nine." This is quite legitimate on his part, as his holding of the ♠**9** gives him that privilege.

You also have the privilege of raising the build. So you plank your ♢**A** on top and say "Ten." On your next play you use the ♡**10** to take it.

Again, taking the same setup so far as the board and your hand are concerned, but giving your opponent different cards, the situation is this:

Opponent:	♡**6**	♣**J**	♠**5**	♢**6**
On table:	♢**2**	♣**3**		
Your hand:	♢**A**	♣**2**	♣**4**	♡**10**

It is your play first. You build the ♣**2** on the ♢**2**, four.

Your opponent lays down the ♡**6** thinking that by trailing it, he can take it with the ♢**6** later. But rather than let the ♡**6** go to waste, you place it on the ♣**3**, add the ♢**A** from your hand, and announce "Ten."

You now have two builds in operation, a four and a ten, while in your hand you have the required cards (♣**4** and ♡**10**) to take them both. That makes each a separate, bona-fide build. You take one with the ♣**4** and the other with the ♡**10** in separate plays.

Suppose your opponent happened to be holding other cards, as:

♢**Q** ♡**K** ♠**10** ♢**10**

You begin by building a four (♣**2** on ♢**2**).

Your opponent trails with the ♠**10** by simply laying it on the table. His laying down of a high card indicates that he may have another ten in his hand and very probably the big cassino (♢**10**). Otherwise, why would he trail with a card that is a potential trick taker, as all tens are? He would be smarter to hold it and try to build up lesser cards that you might play.

So you spike the potential threat by taking the ♠**10** with your ♡**10**. Whether or not he holds the ♢**10** does not matter. On your next play you can take the four that you have already built.

There is one thing you can't do. If you put the ♣**2** on the ♢**2** and say "Four" and your opponent should lay down a card like the ♡**2** by itself, you can't put the ♡**2** on your four build, saying "Six," and then add your ♣**4** with the announcement "Ten."

The reason is, you can't build from the board when you raise either your opponent's build or your own. Anything added must come directly from your hand.

THREE-HANDED CASSINO

Three-handed cassino is a fast, intriguing game that presents an interesting problem. In it, two of the players have a distinct advantage. One is the man "under the gun"–the first player–as the lead is always his and there are twelve cards in each deal.

The other is the dealer, who plays last and therefore occupies the "cleanup" spot. He has the strongest chance of coming out ahead in cards and spades.

The unfortunate player is the "middleman"; although the deal moves along after every hand, he is liable to fill that same slot twice in a twenty-one-point game, which makes his defeat practically a foregone conclusion.

The simple way to offset that is to play for a higher total, preferably forty-nine points. Then, three-handed cassino acquires a fascination all its own, which can only be appreciated after the game has been played many times. In the long run it is surprising to see how often skill will tell. The difficulties of the middle player are ironed out until they are almost nil.

Two factors work toward the middleman's advantage. Whenever there is a tie for cards–usually between the first and third players–the three points for cards are nullified. The middleman profits thereby.

Even more frequently there may be a tie in spades, which nullifies one point. That means there can be a seven-point hand, and even if the first and third man take all the counters, the middleman doesn't fare too badly. Sweeps are an accepted part of the three-handed game and they, too, may work occasionally to the middleman's advantage.

The principal thing to remember in three-handed cassino is that any build you make has less chance of getting by than in the two-handed game. You must allow for that and at the same time snap up any opportunity that comes your way. A few sizable takes at the start of the game may give you enough cards or spades to win on both counts.

You can also profit by throwing opportunities to a player whose score is lagging, in preference to the top man. Here, indeed, is a "sleeper" among card games that can only be extolled by those who have experienced its spell.

FOUR-HANDED CASSINO

Here is another dandy that combines card sense with team play. In four-handed cassino you deal four cards to each player and four more to the board, as in the other versions of the game. On each succeeding deal, each player is given four more cards, right through to the finish.

The difference is that the players sitting opposite each other are partners, forming two teams: North-South and East-West, as in bridge. The players on a team put all their tricks together and add their total at the finish. As in two-handed cassino, game is usually twenty-one points.

Each player is strictly on his own, however, where builds are concerned. To build them, you "have to have them," as the slogan goes. Suppose you, as South, build a four and a three and call it seven. West comes along and knocks it off with a seven of his own.

On the board is a two, and your partner, North, holds a five. But he can't put his two on the five and call it seven unless he holds a card of that denomination. He can, however, play his two face up on the board in the hope that it will trail along to you, so that you can take the two and five as a combine.

Of course, East, the intervening player, may have something to say about it, as he will recognize exactly what your partner is trying to do to help you. But this—as with most things in cassino—is a situation that may work two ways. Wittingly or unwittingly, the intervening opponent may be forced to play to your advantage.

Sweeps are an important feature of the four-handed game, adding a surprise element that is duly appreciated by those who play it. Otherwise, the game follows the pattern already outlined, but with the proviso that you should always keep your partner's needs in mind and fill them as you can.

ROYAL CASSINO

In this simple but obvious expansion of standard cassino, the face cards are given values according to their rank: jack, 11; queen, 12; king, 13. Thus, "builds" can be made accordingly: if the board should show ♡**6** ♣**4** ◇**2**, all three cards could be taken by the ♡**Q**. For players who are mathematically inclined, this adds new zest to the game, which otherwise remains the same where playing and scoring are involved.

SPADE CASSINO

In this game, every spade in the pack is counted as a point in its own right. The ♠**2** (little cassino), therefore, is two points; the ♠**A** counts two; and the ♠**J** counts two, being given the point that is usually credited to the entire spade suit. The total value of points normally taken in a single hand thus becomes 24, as follows: cards, 3; big cassino, 2; little cassino, 2; ♠**J**, 2; ♠**A**, 2; three aces, 3 (1 point each); ten spades, 10 (1 point each). Game is set at 49 points to allow for the heavier scoring.

ROYAL SPADE CASSINO

Here, royal cassino and spade cassino are combined, allowing bigger builds along with higher scores. As in all forms of cassino, "sweeps" may be included by agreement, adding that much more excitement. Game is 49 points.

Fan-tan

This is a simple yet intriguing game that provides surprises and an occasional tense finish in which a keen or lucky play can change the outcome. It derives its name from a Chinese game of the same name that is played with buttons, beans, or other tokens. Chips or counters are used in the present game, as their use is preferable to keeping a record on a score sheet, though the latter course may be adopted if desired.

Three, four, five, or more players participate in Fan-tan, each being provided with an equal number of chips. A fifty-two-card pack is dealt around, and odd cards go singly to persons at the dealer's left. Players arrange their hands in suits, from king down to ace, which is low in this game. Play then starts with the man at the dealer's left.

If the player holds a seven, he puts it face up on the table. If he has more than one seven, he can play whichever one he prefers. If he lacks a seven, he must put a chip into a pot. The pot grows as the game progresses.

The second player may have various choices. If the first man fails to come up with a seven, the second player must provide one, or chip in. But if a seven has been played, he may add an eight of the same suit, placing it at one side of the seven to begin a series that builds up to the king.

Or he may add a six of the same suit, as the starter of a series that goes down to the ace. If he holds a seven, he can open a new suit if he wants. The only restrictions are that only one card can be laid down on each play and that a player must lay down a card if he can. Otherwise, he has to chip in.

So it continues around the board, with the option of adding a card to each new series as it develops, a nine going on an eight, a ten on a nine; or a five on a six, a four on a five, and so on. When one player declares "out" by adding a final card, the others must add one chip to the pot for each card they are caught with and are still holding in their hands.

Now let us run through a sample hand and from it draw a few conclusions. Assume that four players hold the following:

A

♠ **J 7 6 4** ♡ **10 7 6** ♣ **K 10 5 3** ◇ **10 2**

B

♠ **Q 10 3** ♡ **9 5 3 A** ♣ **J 8 2** ◇ **8 6 A**

C

♠ **K 2** ♡ **K Q J 8** ♣ **9 7 4** ◇ **K J 9 3**

D

♠ **9 8 5 A** ♡ **4 2** ♣ **Q 6 A** ◇ **Q 7 5 4**

A plays ♠**7** (in preference to ♡**7**).

B chips in, being unable to make a play.

C plays ♣**7**, as his only play.

D plays ◇**7**, hoping to push series to ◇**Q**.

A plays ♠**6**, still having ♠**4** as stopper.

B plays ◇**6**, hoping to push series to ◇**A**.

C chips in, being unable to make a play.

D plays ♠**5**, hoping to push series to ♠**A**.

A plays ♡**7**, as he still has hearts stopped, thus keeping ♠**4** as a stopper.

B plays ♣**8** rather than ◇**8**, which is a stopper.

C plays ♡**8** to open way to his high hearts.

D plays ♣**6**, hoping to push series to ♣**A**.

A plays ♣**5**, still having ♣**3** as stopper.

B plays ♡**9** rather than ◇**8**, which is a better stopper.

C plays ♣**4**, as the ♣**9** is a better stopper.

D plays ◇**5**, as he still has ◇**4** for a stopper.

A plays ♣**3**, his least valuable stopper.

B plays ♣**2** for the same reason.

C plays ♣**9**, his best stopper, having no other play.

D plays ♠**8**, still having ♠**9** as stopper.

A plays ♣**10**, to push series to ♣**K**.

B plays ♣**J**, having no other choice, except the more valuable ◇**8**.

C chips in, being unable to play.

D plays ♣**Q**, his least valuable stopper.

A plays ♣**K**, a worthless card, thus saving stoppers.

B plays ◇**8**, his only play.

C plays ♢**9**, a valuable stopper but his only play.

D plays ♣**A**, a worthless card, thus saving stoppers.

A plays ♠**4**, an equal choice with the ♢**10** and ♡**10**.

B plays ♠**3**, as his only play.

C plays ♠**2** for the same reason.

D plays ♠**A**, a worthless card, thus saving stoppers.

A plays ♢**10**, an equal choice with ♡**10**.

B chips in, as he has no possible play.

C plays ♢**J**, as his only possible play.

D plays ♢**Q**, his least valuable stopper.

A plays ♡**10**, as less valuable than ♡**6**.

B chips in, having no possible play.

C plays ♡**J**, beginning an end sequence.

D plays ♢**4**, as less valuable than ♠**9**.

A plays ♡**6**, a valuable stopper but the only play.

B plays ♡**5**, hoping to work down to ♡**A**.

C plays ♡**Q**, continuing end sequence.

D plays ♡**4**, in order to reach ♡**2**.

A chips in, having no possible play.

B plays ♡**3**, as his only possible play.

C plays ♡**K**, completing end sequence.

D plays ♡**2**, as much less valuable than ♠**9**.

A chips in, having no possible play.

B plays ♡**A**, a worthless card, but his only play, as well.

C plays ♢**K**, a worthless card, rather than his stopper ♢**3**.

D plays ♠**9**, his last card, and declares "out."

A is caught with two cards (♠**J** ♢**2**) and must put two chips in the pot. *B* has three cards (♠**Q** ♠**10** ♢**A**) and contributes three chips. *C* has two cards left (♠**K** ♢**3**) and puts in two chips. *D* collects those with the chips already there.

In this hand *A* had a good chance going in, but ran into trouble with the ♠**J**, though he tried to work toward it with his opening play of ♠**7**. Though *D,* the winner, followed an obvious line of play, he could have held back on spades because *A* followed with the ♡**7**. That indicated that *A* was more anxious to draw out spades.

When a player holds a long suit, he should move into it early, as it gives him many playing chances compared to those of his opponents. But he should not revel in such early luxury if it means neglecting suits in which he holds remote cards like queen-king or two aces. Otherwise he may be caught with them at the climax.

In the game illustrated there are no long suits, and the players were able to concentrate chiefly on retaining cards as stoppers. An eight with nothing above or a six with nothing below makes the most attractive stopper, other than a lone seven, but these prizes are very hard to hold.

However, experienced players do not worry when they see them go. Often, another player has a stopper a notch or two higher (or lower) and uses it to block the others himself. As an example in the game shown, if player *B* had put down his ◇**8** almost at the start, player *A* would have blocked the suit with the ◇**10** as his stopper.

Sometimes it is smart to take chances on such plays rather than to give away the general pattern of your hand by adhering to too deadly a style. In short, Fan-tan can be turned into a game replete with bluffing angles, according to the company involved. Generally speaking, few of the possibilities have been explored.

It is a temptation to "play out" a sequence like the ♡**J** ♡**Q** ♡**K** shown in hand *C*, while the other players fume. But don't feel too secure with holdings of that long-suit type. One of the other players may get into an "end run" of his own and block you in some other suit with a secondary stopper like a jack, leaving you helpless with an odd queen.

SIXTY-CARD FAN-TAN

This is the regular game, but played with sixty cards from the sixty-three-card pack described under six-handed five hundred. The pack includes elevens and twelves in all four suits, those values ranking between the ten and jack.

In such a game, eights are used as the base cards from which the up and down series are built, to king and ace respectively. The advantage of the larger pack is that more players can participate in the game.

Special Penalty

In all forms of Fan-tan, failure to play a card when one is able to do so costs a player a penalty of three chips, put into the pot. Failure to play a seven when no other play is possible costs five chips to the pot. Also, whoever holds the six and eight of that suit collects five chips from the offender, because of the importance of those stoppers.

Similar penalties may be applied in a variation of the game known as

FIVE-OR-NINE FAN-TAN

Here, instead of opening a new suit with a seven, players are allowed to use a five or nine. Whichever is used, it then stands. If a player lays down the five of clubs, for instance, the upward series begins with the six and runs clear up to the king, while the downward series will run from four down to ace.

With the nine of clubs the upward series would run ten to king; the downward, eight to ace. Sevens are never used as base cards in this version of the game. Failure to play either a five or nine when no other play is possible carries the five-chip penalty to the pot, plus another five chips to anyone holding a stopper just above or below the unplayed card.

In five-or-nine fan-tan there is less chance of being balked on the initial play, as there are eight possible base cards instead of only four, though these are reduced by two each time a suit is opened.

More important is the fact that a player holding both a five and a nine may improve his chances by playing one in preference to the other. With a holding such as **K 9 8 6 5** a play of the nine may open an immediate path to the isolated king, while the five is preserved as an effective stopper. This adds an element of skill not found in the older game.

This game, as regularly played, includes the strict rule that whichever is used as starter for the first suit, a five or a nine, must also be used to start the remaining suits during that deal. This keeps the game simple, but sometimes too much so. If, as often happens, the first player has only a five or a nine, he has no choice of a starter and the succeeding players are automatically restricted, thus reducing the game to the status of ordinary Fan-tan.

However, if players so desire, they can agree beforehand that any sequence may begin with a five or a nine, thus increasing the scope of the game and adding to its interest.

Michigan

This modern game emerged from a medley of old English card games. Its immediate progenitor was a form called boodle, a term still used to designate certain pay-off cards which appear on a special layout and are appropriately called boodle cards. Another variant, Saratoga, has to do with the placing of the chips on the boodle cards and has been incorporated into michigan as generally played.

The layout, which is most conveniently formed by using four cards from a spare pack, consists of an ace, king, queen, and jack of different suits, as:

♡**A** ◇**K** ♠**Q** ♣**J**

On these boodle cards each player puts a required number of chips, sometimes in hit-or-miss fashion, as one on the ace, three on the king, none on the queen and jack, or however he prefers. But in Saratoga it is customary for each player to put one chip on each card, with the exception of the dealer, who must put two chips on each card.

The cards are dealt singly to each player, but an extra hand is included as a widow, this being the first hand on the dealer's left. This continues until the entire pack of fifty-two cards has been dealt face down. With three players the deal comes out even; but with more players–anywhere up to eight–the deal will end part way around, so that players up to that point will each have one more card than the rest.

Players look at their hands, and if the dealer does not like his, he may exchange it for the widow, laying his own hand face down as a "dead hand" in its place. Or, as an alternative, he can keep his own hand and offer the widow to the highest bidder. Taking or buying the widow has a double advantage. It may turn out to be a better playing hand, and the player acquiring the widow also knows the contents of the extra hand that he discarded, which may help him in his play.

Take this sample of a four-handed game, in which the cards are shown. Note that duplicates of the boodle cards are underlined, as they have a special value:

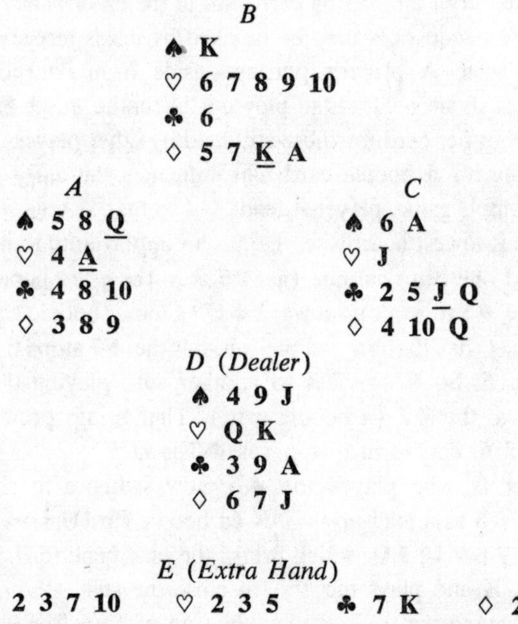

In this case the dealer (*D*) discarded his original hand and took the widow, because the original did not contain any boodle cards to match those in the layout. However, he failed to acquire any by the switch.

Holding a boodle card is valuable, because whenever a player lays down a boodle card from his hand, he wins the chips that are on the corresponding boodle card of the layout. This, however, is restricted by the playing rules that follow.

The player on the dealer's left (*A*) starts by laying his lowest card in any suit face up in the center of the table. He follows that by playing others of the suit, if he has them, up to the ace, which is the highest card. If he is stopped in such a run, another player continues the sequence if he can, and the play continues thus. The original player can pick up where another leaves off.

When play is stopped by a missing card, or when the top of a sequence is reached, the player is allowed to play his lowest card in another suit. If he has no other suit, the play moves to his left, until it reaches a player who can begin a sequence with a new suit. If it passes clear around to the original player, he can play his lowest card in the lone suit.

At the outset all missing cards are in the extra hand, but as play progresses, sequences may be blocked by cards already played, as will be seen. A player's purpose–aside from collecting on any boodle cards he holds–is to play out his entire hand. He then collects a chip per card for those still held by other players.

Aiming for a boodle card may influence the early play. Thus, in the sample game, player *A* leads ♡**4** so that ♡**A** (a boodle card) will be his lowest heart when he has an opportunity to make a later lead. No one can continue (as ♡**5** is in the extra hand, *E*), so *A* plays the ♠**5** to work up toward ♠**Q** (another boodle card).

Player *C* has the ♠**6** and plays it, but the ♠**7** stops the sequence, being in *E*. So *C* switches to another suit, playing the ♣**2** as a lead-up to the ♣**J** (a boodle card). That brings prompt plays of ♣ **3 4 5 6**, ending in a stop (as ♣**7** is in *E*).

Player *B*, who played the ♣**6**, now switches to another suit, playing ♢**5** as a lead-up to ♢**K** (a boodle card). That is followed by ♢ **6 7 8 9 10 J Q**, which brings the play back to *B*, who cashes in the ♢**K** and plays the ♢**A** to close the suit.

Still having the lead, *B* plays his run of ♡ **6 7 8 9 10**, hoping that the ♡**J** is in the extra hand, *E*, to stop the sequence. In that case *B* could switch to the ♠**K** and go out. But *C* holds the ♡**J** and plays it. *D* follows with ♡ **Q K** and *A* cashes in the ♡**A** to close the suit.

A switches to the ♠**8**, hoping for a run to follow, but when *D* plays the ♠**9** the sequence is blocked (by ♠**10** in *E*). *D* has to play ♣**9** as the lowest card in his only other suit. *A* plays ♣**10**, and *C* cashes in the ♣**J**, which he follows with the ♣**Q**. Another stopper is encountered in the ♣**K** (in hand *E*), which pleases *C* immensely.

C switches to ♠**A** and closes the suit, enabling him to make another switch to ♢**4** and go out. He collects three chips from *A*, one chip from *B*, and three chips from *D*, all representing leftover cards. *A* is the most disappointed, since he was caught with the ♠**Q** and was unable to cash it as a boodle card. So the chips stay on the ♠**Q** for the next round.

One argument in favor of letting players ante chips on the cards they want is that it enables them to equalize the boodle cards when chips remain on one from the preceding round. But Saratoga specialists insist that the chance building up of one particular boodle pile adds the peculiar piquancy that luck alone can supply.

In reviewing this sample round, these points might be noted:

When *B* played the ♣**6** and was stopped, he passed up a chance of getting rid of a five-card run in hearts in order to go after the ♢**K** as a boodle card. This proved good policy, as he eventually attained his aim.

Later, however, he ran the ♡ **6 7 8 9 10** when he had the chance, rather than lead the lone ♠**K**. As a result, he was stuck with only one card instead of five. What's more, he would have been surely stuck, for this reason:

When *A* led the ♡**4** at the very start, it was stopped, proving that the ♡**5** was in hand *E*. Thus player *B* would never have had a chance to get into his heart run if he had played the ♠**K** first.

Other factors being equal, the play of a card like ♠**K** has merit, because it is higher than the boodle card of that suit (♠**Q**) and therefore doesn't lead up to it. When *B* led his ♡**6** and ran it up to ♡**10**, he made it easy for *A* to cash his ♡**A**. Still, *B* had no other play, and one stopper could have spoiled it for *A*.

Should the dealer (*D*) have swapped the widow for his own hand, as he did? The answer is "yes." Study the discarded hand, *E,* and you will note that its load of low cards would have given *D* a hard time getting into three suits. That, more than the fact that his original hand lacked boodle cards, prompted the dealer to make the exchange.

Picking up boodle cards in the widow is an inducement, but it should not be overstressed. It's better to keep a hand with high cards, as other players must lead up to them. Sell the widow if you are the dealer, and don't bid for it if your own hand looks good enough.

Holding boodle cards doesn't mean that a player will cash them. In the round shown, *A* was caught with the ♠**Q** because *C* was able to play above it with the ♠**A**; this had become the only spade that *C* held and therefore was the lowest in his hand.

To make the game a little tougher, sometimes a rule is introduced that a player must switch to a suit of the opposite color; that is, from a red suit (♡ or ◇) to a black suit (♠ or ♣) or vice versa. Thus, in the game shown, *C* could not have gone to the **♠A** following his play of the **♣Q**, as both were black suits.

Instead, he would have had to play the **◇4** as a red suit, but since diamonds were stopped (because *B* played the **◇5** earlier), it would have been easy for *C* to switch to the **♠A** from the **◇4**. There are times, however, when this could wreck a player's chances of going out.

As already stated, when a player is unable to switch suit, the play moves to his left. If the next player cannot meet the required change of suit, the play moves along. If it finally comes back to the original player–as frequently happens under the "red-and-black" rule–he is allowed to resume play with the lowest card in whatever suit (or suits) he holds.

The cards may be piled in sequences as they are played, then turned down when the stop arrives. But it is preferable for each player to show his cards as he plays them, then turn them down in front of himself so they can be checked later in case of errors. These occur when a player starts a suit with a wrong card, overlooking his lowest. For that, he must pay one chip to each opponent and forego collecting on a boodle card.

Another penalty is invoked if a player overlooks a card he should have played during a sequence, thus causing an artificial stop. In that case he must make good the amount on the boodle card in that suit if the player holding it fails to cash it, but the chips on the boodle card remain there. The penalized player continues to play the hand, but cannot collect on boodle cards or from the other players if he goes out. They simply continue until some player wins the hand.

There are many variations of michigan, with even more names, some of which are interchangeable. Players should decide beforehand regarding minor differences between variations. One interesting innovation is the introduction of a wild card–usually the ace of diamonds–under the title of

Spinado. This card may be played as part of a sequence, becoming an automatic stopper which enables the player to switch to another suit. For example: the player holding the wild **◇A** has just played the ♣**10** and is reasonably sure that someone else holds the ♣**J**. Rather than let the other player cash in on the boodle card (♣**J**), he announces "Spinado" and plays the ♢**A**.

This ends the sequence. Another use for the wild card is to switch to another suit in which the player can cash a boodle card of his own, or go out, thus completing the hand and collecting accordingly.

Technically, spinado is a special feature that belongs to the older game of boodle–or newmarket, as it is also called–rather than to the modern form of michigan. But it has carried over into the present-day game. Occasionally, the joker has been put into the pack to serve as the wild card instead of the ace of diamonds, which then remains an ordinary card with no special function.

Additional Boodle Cards: Another way of punching up the staid old game of michigan is to use extra boodle cards, taken from the spare pack and added to the layout, as the ♢**10**, ♡**J**, or both. Such cards call for the usual ante and are played exactly like the other boodle cards.

Another plan is to place a pair of cards from the spare pack together on the layout, as ♠**Q** and ♠**K**. To collect the boodle from this combination, a player must hold *both* those cards in his hand and play them accordingly. This may be made easier by putting three cards from the spare pack in the layout sequence, say ♠**J**, ♠**Q**, and ♠**K**, with the rule that if a player holds and plays *two* of these *in order*–either ♠**J**, ♠**Q**; or ♠**Q**, ♠**K**–he collects the boodle from the layout.

A sequence of three cards in *any suit*–as **8**, **9**, **10**–may be used as a boodle combination. To represent this, cards of those values but of different suits are taken from the spare pack and placed in overlapping form on the layout. The sequence applies to all suits, and the first player lucky enough to hold all three values in any one suit picks up the chips, if he is also lucky enough to play them.

All such boodles carry over, if uncollected, and new chips are added with each succeeding hand, stepping up the competition proportionately.

In michigan it is customary for each player to keep his cards separate from the others as he plays them, so that the hands can be checked later for any irregularities in the play.

Rummy

Rummy was derived from cooncan, a rudimentary game played with a forty-card pack, which consisted of forming cards into specialized groups by a simple matching process. Adapted to the fifty-two-card pack with slight variations, it became rummy and spread like wildfire. Today, the various forms of rummy rank among the most popular card games of all time, and many more elaborate card games have emerged from the rummy pattern.

So simple is the basic game of rummy that the best way to learn it is to play it. You don't even need a pack of cards. Just note what happens with the following hands, which are dealt ten cards to a person, in a two-handed game. The pack itself is laid face down on the table, and the top card, turned up beside the pack after the deal is made, becomes known as the upcard–which is also shown:

FIRST PLAYER

♡K ♣Q ♠Q ◊Q ♡9 ♡7 ♡5 ♠4 ♣4 ♡3

♠J

(*Pack*) (*Upcard*)

SECOND PLAYER

◊J ◊9 ♣9 ♠8 ♠6 ◊7 ◊6 ◊5 ♡4 ♣2

This odd arrangement varies from most other games, but it isn't odd to the rummy player. He groups his cards into three (or four) of the same value, or three (or more) of one suit in sequence. These are the groups that he can "lay down" to clear the hand and "go out."

The first player already has a group of three queens (**♣Q ♠Q ◊Q**) and some cards toward a run in hearts. But before he can lay down or "meld" anything, he must add another card to his hand, either drawing the top card of the pack or taking the upcard.

Does he want the upcard, the **♠J**? No, because it would go only with the **♠Q** toward a run, and he already intends to meld the

♠Q with two other queens. Instead of taking the upcard, then, the first player draws the top card from the pack.

He gets the **♠9**. It goes with the ♡**9** and he places it there. Then he melds the group of three: **♣Q ♠Q** ◇**Q**. After that he discards the ♡**K**, placing it face up on the **♠J**, so that the ♡**K** now becomes the upcard.

He discards the ♡**K**, because it is a high card which can count heavily against him, and because he has nothing to go with it.

It is now the second player's turn. He has a nice meld ready in the form of a three-card sequence (◇ **7 6 5**), but he must draw first. He doesn't want the ♡**K**, so he draws the top card of the pack.

He gets the **♣A**. This is a good card for two reasons. Aces are low in rummy and low cards are good to hold. Also, the **♣A** goes with the **♣2** toward a sequence. So the second player melds the sequence he already holds (◇ **7 6 5**) and discards the ♡**4**.

Why the ♡**4**, a low card? Because he has nothing to go with it. His ◇**J** is high, but if he should draw a ◇**10** it would link with the ◇**9** in his hand, so he has sequence prospects there.

As chance has it, the second player's discard of the ♡**4** works against him, for when it becomes the upcard, the first player picks it up and fills three fours (**♠4 ♣4** ♡**4**), which he promptly lays down.

Note that the first player could have melded a sequence, ♡ **5 4 3**, but that would allow the second player to add either the ♡**6** or the ♡**2** to the end of the run. Such adding of cards to an opponent's meld is called "laying off" and is an important feature of rummy. By melding three fours the first player limited the second player to only one possible layoff, the ◇**4**.

The second player draws from the pack, gets the **♣3**, and lays down **♣ 3 2 A** as a sequence. He now discards the ◇**J**.

The first player draws the **♣6** and discards it.

The second player snaps up the **♣6**, thinking that he will do better with sixes than with nines. He keeps the ◇**9**, in case he should get the ◇**8** to fit into his sequence (◇ **7 6 5**) and he discards the **♣9**.

The first player takes the **♣9** as the upcard and lays down the ♡**9 ♠9 ♣9** as a meld. He discards the ♡**7**.

The second player draws the **♠5** from the pack. He lays off the

◇**9** on the three nines which the first player just melded. The second player then discards the ♠**8**.

The first player draws the ♡**6** and discards it.

The second player takes the ♡**6** as the upcard, adds it to the sixes he already holds, and lays down ♠**6** ♣**6** ♡**6**. He then discards the ♠**5** and goes out, winning the hand.

He then scores the number of points represented by the cards in the loser's hand. In this instance the loser (first player) has only five points, represented by a single card, the ♡**5**. So the winner (second player) scores five points to his credit.

This explains why players prefer to discard high cards. Face cards (**K Q J**) count ten each, and the rest count according to the number of their spots. If the first player had been caught with a jack instead of a five, it would have cost him ten points instead of only five.

Now you know how to play rummy, but there is a lot more to the game than can be shown in a single hand, particularly one that was run through much faster than most, in order to demonstrate it more compactly.

Sometimes, players working to fill three kings or a high sequence are caught with thirty or forty points in a hand. If you ask why they should be holding on to all those big cards, the answer is simple: it is often easier to fill the high-card "openings" because opponents are inclined to throw the very cards you want.

This is especially true when three, four, or more players are in the game, which then continues around the table. In three- and four-hand rummy each player receives only seven cards; in five- and six-hand, they usually are dealt five or six cards each. In such games many players hold on to low cards rather than be caught with high ones should someone else "call out."

So high cards are an attraction to a player who is willing to gamble on a quick out, especially when the game includes a now general rule that if a player can lay down his entire hand at once, melding it in a complete "spread," he is said to "go rummy" and can collect double from each of the other players. This is explained more fully in the next section, "Block Rummy."

Score may be kept with chips or tokens, which are handed over to the winner. Or he may simply be credited with points which are written on a score pad and added, hand by hand, the first player to reach one hundred winning the game.

Beginners constantly ask this question: if a player is down to two cards in his hand, say ♡**2** ♠**2**, can he add a third card from the draw–as ◇**2**–and lay them down to go out? Or does he have to make a discard to "legalize" this final meld?

In the standard game of rummy the discard is not required. You can go out on the meld or lay down, making a discard only if you have an extra. Confusion has arisen over this because a variation was introduced years ago, demanding a final discard. In that case it would be necessary to lay off the last two cards on an existing meld and discard the third.

Such a rule, if introduced into the game, should be specified and clearly recognized beforehand; it is not part of basic rummy.

BLOCK RUMMY

In regular rummy, if the entire pack has been drawn and no player has melded out, the discard pile is still available for the next player's draw. If he does not want to draw from it, he simply turns the entire pack face down, draws the top card, and discards in the usual fashion, beginning a new discard pile. Thus, play continues.

This is varied in block rummy, in which the round ends when no one is willing to draw the final discard. Hands are shown and the player caught with the lowest number of points is winner. The losers are allowed to deduct that many from the cards they still hold.

Example: A three-player game is blocked, with players holding:

X	*Y*	*Z*
♠**2** ♣**2**	◇**A** ♡**A**	♠**7** ♠**6** ♡**2** ♠**A**

Player *Y* is winner, with two points against him. So *X*'s four points are reduced to two points; and *Z*'s sixteen points are reduced to fourteen points.

Going Rummy: Frequently, a canny player will hold back his melds, thus keeping opponents in ignorance as to the status of his hand. This also handicaps the opponent, because it prevents him from laying off any odd cards that might go with such melds.

If a player holds back so long that he can meld his entire hand at once, he is said to "go rummy." In some circles a special scoring rule is introduced, whereby a player who goes rummy is paid double by his opponents. This rule, though in common usage, should be stipulated before the game. In going rummy a player is allowed to discard one odd card, just as in going out normally.

In another version a player is required to go rummy in order to go out. With such a rule there is no double scoring, but all scores run higher because the losing players are caught with full hands of cards.

Even in the early days of rummy a variant was included in which the ace was counted high as well as low, where melding was concerned, thus making it allowable to lay down either **♣ A K Q** or **♣ 3 2 A**. Later, the innovation of a "round-the-corner" meld was introduced, with the ace counting both high and low, if so required, so that it could be melded in a sequence of **♣ 2 A K**.

This feature is included in the more modern game of:

BOATHOUSE RUMMY

Here the play is the same as in standard rummy, except for the draw, which is stepped up to add excitement to the game. Each player, as usual, may draw the top card of the pack, or pick up the card that is showing on the discard pile.

But if he takes the latter, he is immediately penalized. For the privilege, he must draw another card–either from the top of the pack or the discard pile–but he is only allowed to discard one card in the customary way.

Thus, in order to fill a meld, he must load his hand as well. It is worth it if it helps him to go out faster, but he runs the risk of having someone else go out in the meantime. All this adds that much more excitement to the game.

Two modes of scoring are used in boathouse rummy. One is the usual count, but with an ace counting eleven instead of only one, should a player be caught with such a card; this is because an ace ranks either high or low.

The other form of scoring is to count all cards as one each, regardless of their value. The practice dates back to the very early days of rummy, when it was played as a juvenile game called nosy. If a player found himself left with, say, three cards, his opponent squared them into a little packet and thwacked the loser three strokes back and forth across the tip of the nose. It was good fun, except when you were caught with a thick packet of seven cards and took as many raps. There were a lot of red noses after the game was over and perhaps that is how the childish pastime of nosy gained the adult title of rummy. Certainly this tracing of its etymology is as good as any.

But rummy has gone a long way during the years between, as will be recognized by a study of the games that follow.

Gin Rummy

Early in the days of rummy a game was devised called poker rum, which differs from the original game in one important detail, namely: no melds are allowed until the unmatched cards in a player's hand total fifteen points or less. He can then lay down his entire hand, forcing the other players to do the same.

Each player then counts the pip value of his unmatched cards, or "deadwood," as they are popularly termed. The winner scores the difference in his favor, exactly as in a hand of rummy in which no further plays are possible. In poker rum, however, the player who calls for the showdown loses ten extra points to another player who shows the same count or less.

That is the risk of calling out or "knocking," as it came to be known, because it was customary to knock on the table to terminate the hand. From poker rum was derived a variant called poker gin and later simply gin, which lay latent for some three decades. Then suddenly it turned rampant and under the name of "gin rummy" it surged to popularity just before World War II, gaining fame as one of the best and most exciting of all two-handed card games.

The added feature of gin rummy which gives the game its powerful punch consists of the laying off of deadwood on the other player's meld. This can be easily understood by considering in brief the play of a sample hand.

In gin rummy each player is dealt ten cards singly, as in rummy, and the next card is turned face up beside the pack to start the discard pile. The nondealer, as first player, may pick up the upcard if he wants it, discarding another in its place. If he refuses to take the upcard, he foregoes his first play and the privilege goes to the dealer, who, as second player, can either take the upcard or forego his play.

From then on, play proceeds as in regular rummy. The first and second players draw alternately either from the face-down pack or by taking the upcard, then discarding from the hand. Each player forms his hand into meldable groups of three or four cards of the same value (as ♢**Q** ♡**Q** ♣**Q**) or sequences of three or more cards in a suit from king down to ace (as ♢ **10 9 8 7**) in the usual rummy style.

But neither player is allowed to meld until he has reduced the value of his unmatched deadwood to ten points or less. Then, if he wishes, he may knock. In modern gin a player may signify the knock by making a discard face down, thus ending the play. As an example, suppose the hands have reached the following state:

First Player: ♣**J** ♡**J** ♠**J** ♠**10** ♠**9** ♡**5** ♡**4** ♡**3** ♡**2** ♣**2**
Second Player: ♢**9** ♣**9** ♡**9** ♣**6** ♣**5** ♣**4** ♣**3** ♢**3** ♡**A** ♣**A**

The first player, at this juncture, has a count of twenty-one in deadwood (♠**10** ♠**9** ♣**2**) and therefore cannot knock.

The second player, however, has a deadwood count of only five points (♢**3** ♡**A** ♣**A**), so he knocks and lays down his hand:

♢**9** ♣**9** ♡**9** ♣ **6 5 4 3** ♢**3** ♡**A** ♣**A**

He may also announce "Down for five," referring to his deadwood. The first player then proceeds to meld his hand as follows:

♣**J** ♡**J** ♠**J** ♡ **5 4 3 2**

But the first player does not stop there. He is still holding ♠**10** ♠**9** ♣**2** as deadwood, and he adds two of these cards to the second player's meld, putting the ♠**9** with the ♢**9** ♣**9** ♡**9** and the ♣**2** on the lower end of the ♣ **6 5 4 3** sequence. That leaves the first player with only the ♠**10** as deadwood, for a count of ten against him.

So the second player wins by a margin of a mere five points, even though he had a much bigger edge when he knocked. Note also that as "knocker" his original meld is final. He cannot dispose of any of his deadwood on his opponent's meld. He is caught with both the ♡**A** and the ♣**A**. He cannot tack them on to the sequences now represented by the ♡**2** and ♣**2**.

In scoring, the winner of the hand credits himself with the difference between his count and the loser's. Thus in the hand illustrated, the second player, *Y,* picks up five points, while the first player, *X,* gets nothing. A running score is kept, hand by hand, with one hundred as the game.

There are ways in which the score of an individual hand can

be increased. In one a player knocks so quickly that he catches his opponent with a lot of losing cards that can't be laid off. Another way is to undercut your opponent when he knocks. For example:

Player X: ♡**KQJ** ♠**987** ♣**543** ◇**8**
Player Y: ♡**654** ♡**10** ♠**10** ♣**6** ♣**2** ◇**2** ◇**A** ♣**A**

This looks nice for player *X,* who knocks and lays down three sequences, with only the ◇**8** as deadwood, counting eight points against him. In contrast, all that player *Y* can meld is one sequence, consisting of ♡ **6 5 4**, leaving him stuck with seven other cards that add up to a thirty-two-point pip total.

But do they? Not quite! Player *Y* lays off the ♡**10** on *X*'s ♡ **K Q J** sequence. *Y* also puts the ♠**10** on *X*'s ♠ **9 8 7**. *Y* then adds his ♣**6** and ♣**2** to their respective ends of *X*'s last sequence, ♣ **5 4 3**. That leaves *Y* with the ◇**2** ◇**A** ♣**A** as deadwood, totaling four points.

This undercuts *X*'s eight points by four. For merely tying *X, Y* receives a bonus of twenty-five points. To this is added the undercut points, in this case four, giving *Y* twenty-nine for the hand to *X*'s nothing.

In contrast, the player who knocks also has the chance of "going gin," which means that he melds his entire hand, with no deadwood. For this he gains a special bonus of twenty-five points, plus the total of his opponent's deadwood, because the opponent is not allowed to lay off when a player goes gin.

As an example:

Player X: ♡**J** ◇**J** ♣**J** ♠**J** ♡**987** ◇**432**
Player Y: ♣ **10 9 8** ♡**10** ♡**6** ♡**5** ◇**6** ◇**5** ◇**A** ♠**A**

Here player *X* might have been holding the ♡**2**, but instead of knocking, he went for gin, and drew the jacks to complete his meld, whereupon he discarded the ♡**2.**

Note the plight of player *Y*. He can meld one sequence, ♣ **10 9 8**. Ordinarily, he could put the ♡**10** on one end of *X*'s ♡ **987** and the ♡ **6 5** on the other. He could also add ◇ **6 5** to the top of *X*'s ◇ **4 3 2** and the ◇**A** to the bottom. Then *Y* would only have one point (the ♠**A**) against him.

But those layoffs are not allowable, since *X* went gin. *Y* can only meld his ♣ **10 9 8** and take a thirty-four-point beating for the rest, giving *X* a total score of fifty-nine points for the hand, thanks to the twenty-five-point bonus for going gin.

The player who wins the game by first making one hundred points or more also receives one hundred points as bonus. He doubles his score, including the bonus, if his opponent fails to win a hand. In scoring such a shutout the winner is said to have "skunked" the loser.

The winner of each hand is also credited with twenty-five points. Thus, if *X* should reach one hundred by winning five hands as opposed to *Y*'s four, *X* would be credited with the difference of twenty-five points. Sometimes the player who loses the game wins more individual hands. In that case he is credited accordingly, as will be noted in sample scores.

In some gin circles only ten or twenty points are given for undercutting an opponent, and only twenty points are allowed for going gin or winning a hand. These scores should be decided upon beforehand; otherwise the scoring should stand as already given.

There is more strategy in the play of gin than in ordinary rummy. It is usually good policy to hold at least three low cards, as they make it possible to knock sooner, and they cost you less if you are stuck with them. Occasionally, too, they will enable you to undercut your opponent.

However, aces and deuces, like kings and queens, fit the ends of sequences only. Also, it is often hard to fit these low cards into groups of the same value, as your opponent, too, may be holding them.

So it often pays to keep high cards that are already paired or in sequence, on the chance that you will fill a high combination quickly. This applies particularly to the early stages of the play, for as it progresses, unmatched high cards become more of a liability.

In discarding, it may prove good policy to dispose of cards of the same approximate value as those which your opponent is discarding, since he apparently doesn't want them. But that is where gin rummy can prove itself quite tricky.

A player holding two unneeded cards, say the ♡**9** and the ♠**5**, may deliberately discard the ♠**5**, hoping to coax his opponent into throwing cards of lower values, thus making it more difficult for the opponent to reduce his count. A discard of the ♡**9**, in contrast, would have encouraged the opponent to discard his higher values instead.

In short, gin rummy is a game of wits, in which outguessing or bluffing the opponent plays an interesting and exciting part. It is vital to note and remember every card that an opponent takes from the discard pile, as well as to judge whether he intends to use it in a group or sequence.

Your own holdings may help with this. Suppose that you have just filled a group of three jacks with the ♣**J**. You discard the ♣**Q** and your opponent picks it up. It is highly likely that he is using it to fill a set of queens, as the only other card he could hold toward a sequence is the ♣**K**.

Most cases are less obvious than this, but by studying your own draws and keeping track of the opponent's discards, you can often figure further as the game proceeds. In gin rummy it is allowable to look back through the discard pile, provided both players so agree. Otherwise the cards must be remembered closely.

The more quickly a player lays down his hand, the more points he is likely to collect, since his opponent will have fewer draws in which to match up his own hand. So the very essence of gin is to knock as soon as possible.

It is worth knocking with any count of ten or less during the first half-dozen draws. From then on, a lower count is necessary to avoid being undercut by the opponent, who may be laying back, awaiting that very opportunity. To be safe, the count should be down to five points or less.

If play continues until only about a dozen cards remain in the pack, it is best to go for gin, as the point margin may be very low. Care must be taken not to discard anything that the opponent wants; and in some instances, the best course is simply to block him by holding back the cards that he probably is after.

In gin the hand becomes dead when all but two cards have been drawn from the pack. There is no further draw, either from the pack or discard pile, and there is no score in that hand. The pack is simply gathered, shuffled, and dealt over again by the same dealer.

HOLLYWOOD GIN

This is gin rummy played in the form of three overlapping games. Each player's *first* winning hand is scored in Game 1 only, his *second* winning hand in Games 1 and 2, his *third* winning hand in Games 1, 2, and 3.

Suppose that player *X* scores twenty-three points in the first hand, against player *Y*. It would be scored thus on the sheet:

Game 1		*Game 2*		*Game 3*	
X	*Y*	*X*	*Y*	*X*	*Y*
23	–				

In the next hand *X* scores fifteen points. That is added to his score in Game 1 and is also entered in Game 2. He actually scores double, but the points are divided into two games.

Game 1		*Game 2*		*Game 3*	
X	*Y*	*X*	*Y*	*X*	*Y*
23	–	15	–		
38	–				

Now, *Y* wins a hand, scoring twenty-seven points, but since it is his first win, it goes in Game 1 only, thus:

Game 1		*Game 2*		*Game 3*	
X	*Y*	*X*	*Y*	*X*	*Y*
23	–	15	–		
38	–				
–	27				

In the next hand *X* wins with a mere two points. Being his third win, it is credited in all three games, actually tripling his score for that hand:

Game 1		*Game 2*		*Game 3*	
X	*Y*	*X*	*Y*	*X*	*Y*
23	–	15	–	2	–
38	–	17	–		
–	27				
40	–				

Assuming that *Y* scores eighteen points in the next hand, he would score it, as his second winning hand, in Games 1 and 2:

Game 1		*Game 2*		*Game 3*	
X	*Y*	*X*	*Y*	*X*	*Y*
23	–	15	–	2	–
38	–	17	–		
–	27	–	18		
40	–				
–	45				

In the next hand *Y* scores thirty-two points; since it is his third winning hand, he is credited for it in all three games:

Game 1		*Game 2*		*Game 3*	
X	*Y*	*X*	*Y*	*X*	*Y*
23	–	15	–	2	–
38	–	17	–	–	32
–	27	–	18		
40	–	–	50		
–	45				
–	77				

From there on, each player scores in all three games until one player wins Game 1, which is therewith ended and totaled. Further hands are scored in Games 2 and 3 until Game 2 is finished and totaled; additional hands are scored only in Game 3 until it is won and totaled.

Here are all three games carried through to their completion, with the final totals:

	Game 1			*Game 2*		*Game 3*		
	X	*Y*		*X*	*Y*	*X*	*Y*	
	23	–		15	–	2	–	
	38	–		17	–	–	32	
	–	27		–	18	23	–	
	40	–		–	50	–	56	
	–	45		38	–	31	–	
	–	77		–	74	43	–	
	61	–		46	–	63	–	
	–	101		58	–	–	84	
Bonus		+100		78	–	90	–	
		201		–	102	–	87	
Opponent's			Bonus		+100	104	–	
score		−61			202	+100		Bonus
		140	Opponent's			204		
Hand			score		−78			Opponent's
bonuses		0			124	−87		score
Score		140	Hand			117		
			bonuses		−50			Hand
			Score		74	+75		bonuses
						192		Score

If desired, further games can be played as part of the overlapping sequence, so that four, five, or more games are in progress at once.

OKLAHOMA GIN

In this stepped-up form of gin rummy the value of the first upcard establishes the knocking requirement, for that deal only. If a king, queen, jack, or ten is turned up, the play follows the pattern of a regular gin hand. With a nine or an eight there is not too much difference, but when the value gets down into the lower brackets, competition becomes keen indeed. If an ace is turned up, the usual rule is that a player must go for gin to win the hand.

To give the game still more punch, spades are customarily

scored double. This includes everything, so far as that hand is concerned, doubling the bonuses for gin, undercutting, and winning the hand. So even when a ten or a face card is turned up as the first upcard, there may be extra action, if the suit happens to be spades.

In Oklahoma gin, because of the high scores, game is usually placed at two hundred points instead of the customary one hundred of regular gin. The bonus for winning game is also put at two hundred instead of one hundred. These figures are optional, players being privileged to set other marks if they so choose. Oklahoma gin can also be played in overlapping games, Hollywood style.

KNOCK RUMMY

A fast, popular cross between standard and gin rummy, usually with more than two players. No melds are made until a player knocks, which is allowable any time he draws. He then discards, and all players meld what they can, but with no laying off on rival melds. The knocker collects the difference in points between his unmatched deadwood and that of each opponent, plus 25 if he goes rummy.

A player who ties the knocker, collects instead. If the knocker is beaten for low, he pays the difference in count, plus 10 points. No knock is allowed if the pack is reduced to the same number of cards as players. Draws simply continue until all cards are gone, when hands are melded and the one with lowest unmatched count is winner.

Multiple Klondike

For more fun than the old game of slapjack, try multiple Klondike. In its simple form Klondike is a game of solitaire, sometimes confused with Canfield. It is played as follows:

Deal seven cards in a cross-row, left to right, first card face up, the rest face down.

Now, deal a card face up on the second card; then single face-down cards on those to the right. Then deal a card face up on the third card, and singles face down on those to the right, and so on. Thus each pile will have one more card than the pile preceding it; and a card is face up on each pile.

You then move face-up cards by placing them on others that are one point higher in value but of the opposite color, as a red five on a black six; those two could go on a red seven, and so on.

Whenever you come to a face-down card, turn it up and place it elsewhere if you can. Whenever you eliminate a pile, the space can be supplanted by a face-up king, if available, and all the face-up cards descending from it.

An ace is removed and put in the center of the table, as the base on which to build a suit. The two of the suit goes on it, and so on clear up to the king.

You still have cards to help your builds. Go through the "stock," the remainder of the pack, turning three cards face up in a group. If you can use the card that shows, do so. Continue dealing through by threes, and when you have finished, turn the stock face down and go through again, as needed.

In regular Klondike the stock is gone through singly, only once; but in this game, threes are allowable, and when the stock is down to fewer than six cards, they may be gone through one at a time, repeatedly.

The reason is this: two or more players are in the game. If two, it is called double Klondike and the players are seated opposite. If three or four, it is triple or quadruple Klondike, or simply multiple Klondike. Each player has a full pack of cards.

It differs from the lone hand in this way:

You are allowed to put cards on the suit piles that some other player has begun to build. If he has got his spades up to the six and can't find a seven, slap yours on if you have it available!

There is no taking turns in this. Each player goes through his cards as fast as he can, looking for a play. The double game is speedy in its own right; but with three or four players, it becomes a madhouse.

With four, the opposite players are usually partners, calling each other's attention to possible plays, helping each other with builds, and–sometimes most important–keeping track of slips by the opposing team.

The idea is to get rid of your whole pack first; the player, or team, that is clear first is declared the winner. Sometimes one goes out while the opponents are still blocked, but often it is a slam-bang finish.

To help toward that desired result, two special privileges are allowed, not usual in Klondike. The first is this: to get at a needed or helpful card, a player may transfer a portion of a run from one higher card to another.

For example, he wants the ♡**8**, so that he can put it on a suit build. The red ♡**8** is attached to the black ♠**9**, and running down from the ♡**8** are the ♣**7** ♢**6** ♣**5**. None of those is playable at the moment.

On another pile the player has a descending run consisting of the ♣**J** ♡**10** ♣**9** ♢**8**. He cannot play the ♢**8**. But he can transfer the run below the ♡**8** to the ♢**8** without violating the alternate color rule. That frees the ♡**8** so that it can be played as desired.

The other privilege is to take back cards from a suit build and replace them singly, upon suitable face-up cards, in the original piles. Because recalled cards must be from the player's own pack, it is advisable to have different backs on all packs so that they can be easily distinguished.

Packs of different widths are also recommended–as bridge cards and poker cards–so that the mixed packs can be shaken apart, so to speak, when the suit builds are sorted following a game.

If all players or both teams fail to go out during one of these hectic hands, the one who has placed the most cards in the various suit builds is declared the winner.

Canasta

This South American game was still in the formative state when it skyrocketed to international popularity shortly after World War II. From then on, innovations were so frequent and radical that canasta developed as many variations as rummy, from which it was derived.

Though the game has gone beyond most efforts to stabilize it, the simplest and perhaps best approach to it is through a description of two-handed canasta in its somewhat basic form. The game is, of course, more generally played by four persons, with other modifications that will be detailed as we proceed.

In canasta a double pack, each with two jokers, is used, making 108 cards in all. In the two-handed game each player is dealt fifteen cards. The next card is turned up beside the pack and becomes the upcard. This represents a discard pile, which canasta players refer to as the pack, though its true name is *el pozo,* or "the pot."

To avoid confusion, we shall refer to the discard as the pot, to distinguish it from the original pack–or stock, as this is better termed, because it forms a stockpile of undrawn cards.

Each player's aim is to meld or lay down cards from his hand, placing them face up on the table, where they count as points toward his score. A meld must contain three or more cards of the same rank or value, as three kings, four tens, three queens. Jokers and deuces are wild and may be used in forming such groups, but only one wild card may be included in a group of three, or two in a group of four; in a group of five or more, three wild cards are the limit.

Thus, allowable combinations are:

K K K **Joker J J** **2 Q Q 2**

Joker A A 2 2 **2 8 8 8 2 2**

But these combinations are not allowed:

Joker 2 K **Joker 2 2**

Joker Q Q 2 2 2

Sequences (such as **Q J 10 9 8 7**) do not figure in ordinary canasta, hence a player can disregard suits and even colors. Red threes are an exception; they have a special bonus value, though they do not figure in the actual play.

The meldable cards count as follows:

Each joker	50 points
Each deuce	20 "
Each ace	20 "
Each king, queen, jack, ten, nine, eight	10 "
Each seven, six, five, four	5 "
Each black three	5 "

But the scoring does not stop there; this is just the beginning in the wildly exciting game of canasta. In making melds and adding to them, a player has a more important goal, which is essential to the game. That goal is to form a canasta, or "basket," consisting of seven cards of one variety. Wild cards may be included in such a combination (as **2 2 2 J J J J**), which then becomes known as a mixed canasta; a group made up entirely of "natural" cards (as **8 8 8 8 8 8 8**) is styled a natural canasta. Either type can serve a vital purpose: a player, to meld out, or bring a hand to its completion, must include a canasta (mixed or natural) in his meld. In the two-handed game two canastas are required nowadays, but with more players the "one" rule usually holds.

However, the purpose is the same; it is to compel each player to go after a canasta, thus livening up the game. In addition, canastas carry special bonus scores, which make them worth the try. Here are the bonus counts:

Each natural canasta	500 points
Each mixed canasta	300 "
Melding out	100 "
Melding out with a hidden or concealed hand	100 "
Each red three	100 "

(Values of red threes double if player holds all four)

When one player melds out, thus disposing of all cards from his hand, the other player is left, or "caught," with unmelded cards in his hand. These count against his score. As an example:

2 A A K K K 10 10 6 6 Black **3**

That would mean a loss of 125 points, to be deducted from the player's score. But when a player is building for canastas with 300- and 500-point bonuses, he can afford to take the risk, particularly when it might be helpful to his cause to retain certain cards in his hand.

Red threes are simply weeded from a player's hand before his turn and laid face up for a bonus score. No skill or judgment is required in this, but red threes involve one risk: if a player fails to make a meld before his opponent goes out, his red threes count against his score instead of toward it.

This may occasionally force a player into a hasty or unwise meld, especially if he has drawn all the red threes and stands to lose 800 points instead of making them. Usually, by that time he has managed to make an initial meld. Yet, making a first meld can prove difficult, as it requires a minimum of 50 points at the outset of the game; and this is increased to 90 points when a player's score reaches the 1500 mark; then to 120 points at the 3000 level.

These and other factors can best be understood by studying the hands dealt in a sample game and considering their potential play:

OPPONENT

2 2 A Q Q J J 10 9 6 6 6 6 5 Red **3**

Upcard: **10**

DEALER

Joker K K Q 10 10 9 8 8 8 5 5 5 4 Black **3**

To start the play, the opponent shows his red three and places it face up on the table. He draws a card from the stock as replacement. This turns out to be a nine, giving him two nines. That preliminary over, the opponent is ready for his actual play. He will draw a card, probably from the stock.

Before drawing he studies his hand for possibilities. As it

stands, the opponent can make an initial meld of 50 points, or more. For example:

A wild deuce and a pair of queens (or jacks) would give him 20 + 10 + 10 for 40 points, and three sixes (5 + 5 + 5) would add 15 more for a total of 55. But that would deplete his hand and would be unwise so early in the game.

A meld of two deuces and two queens (20 + 20 + 10 + 10) would exceed opening requirements with a total of 60 points, but it is better to save at least one wild card for later play. So the opponent would prefer to bank on a helpful draw from the stock, either in the form of a wild card or an ace, queen, or jack.

With an ace he could meld a deuce and two aces (20 + 20 + 20) for a total of 60 points. With a queen he could meld a deuce and three queens (20 + 10 + 10 + 10) for a total of 50. The same would apply to a deuce and three jacks.

Let us assume, however, that the opponent draws a seven, which is of no help. He discards it on the pot as the new upcard. He might have discarded the five instead, but any other discard would be unwise. All other cards either are already paired or, as in the case of the ace (worth 20 points) and the ten (worth 10 points), are more valuable than a seven or a five (worth only 5 points each).

The hands now stand:

OPPONENT

2 2 A Q Q J J 10 9 9 6 6 6 6 5

Melded: Red **3**

Pot: **10**

Upcard: **7**

DEALER

Joker K K Q 10 10 9 8 8 8 5 5 5 4   Black **3**

It is now the dealer's turn. He can make an initial meld of the joker and a pair of kings (50 + 10 + 10) for a total of 70 points. The same would apply with the joker and a pair of tens or eights. He, too, reserves decision until the draw.

With a poor draw the dealer might pass up his opening meld, as he can make 50 points at any time with the joker and any pair that he holds. But suppose he draws a deuce, giving him two wild cards. He can very well meld the joker and a pair—say, the kings—to meet the opening requirement. He makes that meld and discards his unneeded four. The hands then stand:

OPPONENT

2 2 A Q Q J J 10 9 9 6 6 6 6 5

Melded: Red **3**

Pot: **10**

7

Upcard: **4**

DEALER

2 Q 10 10 9 8 8 8 5 5 5 Black **3**

Melded: **Joker K K**

From now on the dealer can make any meld he wants, even as small as **5 5 5** (which, at 5 points each, count for only 15), because he has met his initial requirement. But there is still another factor that makes the opening meld important.

To run up a big score in canasta, a player must add more cards —and a lot more!—to his hand. Now, it is obvious that if he draws a card from the stock and discards one from his hand, all in the same play, he is not going to increase the number of cards he holds.

How, then, could he acquire more cards?

By picking up the entire pot or discard pile instead of drawing from the stock. To do this, he must be able to match the upcard with a pair from his own hand, or be able to add the upcard to a meld that he has already made.

Now, at the beginning of the game, the pot is said to be "frozen" against each player, which means that to draw the upcard, and the pot with it, he must match the upcard with a natural pair, consisting of two cards exactly like it.

That is, if the upcard happened to be a queen, he would have to show two queens in order to take the pot. After that, the pot is unfrozen and he can pick it up with a pair that includes a wild card, or by simply adding it to an existing meld.

Let us suppose, for instance, that the opponent proceeds

with a draw and gets a five; he discards his cheapest odd card, namely, his ten, which becomes the upcard.

OPPONENT

2 2 A Q Q J J 9 9 6 6 6 6 5 5

Melded: Red **3**

Pot: **10**

7

4

Upcard: **10**

DEALER

2 Q 10 10 9 8 8 8 5 5 5 Black **3**

Melded: **Joker K K**

The dealer wants that ten, so he shows his natural pair of tens and places the upcard with them as a meld. He then takes the rest of the pot—which includes another ten—into his hand and continues to meld as much as he wants. In this case, that would simply mean adding the fourth ten to the three on the board, as there is no need to make other melds this soon. The dealer would then discard an odd card, say the four.

The hands would then stand:

OPPONENT

2 2 A Q Q J J 9 9 6 6 6 6 5 5

Melded: Red **3**

Upcard: **4**

DEALER

2 Q 9 8 8 8 7 5 5 5 Black **3**

Melded: **Joker K K**

10 10 10 10

Now the pot is no longer frozen against the dealer. If the opponent should make a draw and discard a queen, the dealer could pick up the queen (as upcard) by showing a deuce and queen to go with it, melding them as three queens. He would also take the rest of the pot into his hand, as usual.

But the opponent probably would not discard a queen. So let us suppose that he and the dealer make three unsatisfactory draws in a row, discarding whatever they get from the stock, until the dealer, on his last draw, gets a nine and discards his queen instead. Now the hands stand:

OPPONENT

2 2 A Q Q J J 9 9 6 6 6 6 5 5

Melded: Red **3**

Pot: **4**
7
7
5
4
7
Q

DEALER

2 9 9 8 8 8 7 5 5 5 Black **3**

Melded: **Joker K K**
10 10 10 10

The opponent wants that queen. But he has not yet made an initial meld, with its 50 points. Also, the pot is still frozen against him. So he proceeds to lay down a deuce and his two queens (20 + 10 + 10) and places the upcard, the queen, with them for 10 points more, meeting the opening requirement. He then picks up the six cards from the pot and adds them to his hand.

Note that although he used the wild card (deuce) as part of the meld of four queens, he actually matched the upcard with a natural pair. He also is allowed to count its 10 points as part of the initial requirement.

So the hands now stand:

OPPONENT

2 A J J 9 9 7 7 7 6 6 6 6 5 5 5 4

Melded: Red **3**
2 Q Q Q

Upcard: **4**

DEALER

2 9 9 8 8 8 7 5 5 5 Black **3**

Melded: **Joker K K**

10 10 10 10

The four (as upcard) represents the opponent's discard after his meld. If he had needed 90 points for an initial meld, he could have put down his other deuce and the pair of jacks (20 + 10 + 10) for an additional 40.

As his hand now stands, the opponent could meld sevens, sixes, and fives, if he so chose. Or the dealer could lay down nines, eights, or fives.

But they still have to go after canastas, and it would be unwise to show their holdings so soon. Also, they may decide to throw some of their meldable cards—like fives—in favor of something better that they happen to draw from the stock.

The more cards a player gets in a pot the better his chance of running up a big score. So it is often expedient to prevent your opponent from taking a pot, since you want it for yourself. You can do that only by throwing away cards that your opponent cannot match with a pair in his hand or use on one of his melds.

It is not always easy to block the foe in that fashion. You may have discarded two or three jacks; but when you discard another, thinking it safe, you may find that your opponent has meanwhile drawn one from the stock. By matching your discarded jack with a mixed pair—wild card and jack—he takes the pot. That's one big reason for retaining wild cards.

Or you may have reached an impasse, where your only unwanted card—say, a five—goes with a group already melded by your opponent, and all he has to do is tack it on and take the pot with it. In short, there are times when the discard of *any* meldable card may seem unsafe.

In that case a black three is a good discard, if you have one. Black threes can be melded *only* when a player is melding out, and then they must form either a natural trio or a set of four. They *cannot* be made into a mixed canasta; and, most important, when a black three is the upcard, a player *cannot* match it in any way.

So, by discarding a black three, you block the other player from taking the pot. He must draw from the stock and make a regular discard. That covers the black three, and it is no longer a blocker insofar as taking the pot is concerned; but it is now your play. Your next draw from the stock may be a card that you can safely discard.

A still stronger measure is to discard a wild card, either a joker or a deuce but preferably a deuce, as a joker is too valuable. A wild card cannot be taken as an upcard, and if you discard a deuce, it blocks your opponent just as a black three would. But it does more.

Once a wild card is discarded, the pot is again frozen, just as at the start of the play. Now, if your next discard is a jack, your opponent will need a *natural pair* of jacks to take the upcard and the pot; he can't use a wild card and a jack. Also, you can safely discard a card of a value that he has already melded, which may give you considerable leeway.

Of course, the pack is frozen against you, too, but you may have a good chance of matching a future upcard with a natural pair, perhaps a better chance than your opponent, particularly if he knows less about your hand than you know about his. That is the calculated risk that you take, and it all adds interest to canasta.

If you manage to take the pot after a blocker has been discarded, you get the black three or wild card with it. Any such discard can be repeated, so you may pick up a couple of black threes along with a wild card.

Let us continue the play of the sample hand and see how such things work out in practice.

As already stated, the hands stand:

OPPONENT

2 A J J 9 9 7 7 7 6 6 6 6 5 5 5 4

Melded: Red **3**

2 Q Q Q

Upcard: **4**

DEALER

2 9 9 8 8 8 7 5 5 5 Black **3**
Melded: **Joker K K**
10 10 10 10

The opponent has just discarded a four to form a new pot or discard pile.

Dealer draws a ten, adds it to meld, discards a seven.

Opponent draws a joker, keeps it, discards a four.

Dealer draws a *red three* and melds it as a bonus card.

Dealer draws a seven, rejects it, so discards a seven.

Opponent draws a jack, keeps it, discards a five.

(Here, the opponent has decided to sacrifice the low-value fives, not knowing that the dealer can use them.)

Dealer draws an eight, keeps it, discards a nine.

(The dealer would have discarded a five, but now wants the opponent to throw more. So the dealer is sacrificing nines, not knowing that the opponent wants them.)

Opponent draws a king, holds it, discards a five.

Dealer draws a two, keeps it, discards a nine.

Opponent draws a queen, adds it to meld, discards a five.

Dealer draws a *red three* and melds it as a bonus card.

Dealer draws a queen, holds it, discards *black three.*

(Here, if the dealer had discarded the queen, the opponent could have taken the pot, by adding the queen to his meld. Having nothing to sacrifice, the dealer uses the black three as blocker.)

Opponent draws a king, holds it, and freezes pack by discarding a two.

(This shows the value of the freeze. The opponent has nothing he can sacrifice; if he puts kings in the pot, the dealer will try to take it in order to get them.)

Dealer draws a ten, melds it, discards a queen.

(Here, the dealer takes advantage of the freeze by discarding a queen which the opponent would like to pick up, but cannot, as he does not have two cards in hand to match it.)

Opponent draws a six, keeps it, discards a king.

(The opponent has used the same device. The dealer wants that king, but can't match it from his hand since his pair of kings are already melded.)

Dealer draws a nine, rejects it, discards the nine.

(That is what the opponent awaited. He is waiting with two nines, the very cards that the dealer is throwing off. The opponent wanted this to happen, and it did.)

Opponent matches discarded nine with two from hand and takes the entire pot.

Opponent then proceeds to meld his hand thus:

2 Q Q Q Q Q 2 **Joker 9 9 9 9 9** Red **3**
7 7 7 7 7 **6 6 6 6 6** **J J J** **5 5 5**

In his hand he holds: **A** **K K** **4 4** Black **3**

He discards the *black three.*

Dealer at this point is holding: **2 2** **8 8 8 8** **5 5 5**

Meld: **10 10 10 10 10 10** **Joker K K** Red **3** Red **3**

Dealer draws a black three and discards it.

Opponent draws an eight, but not knowing dealer wants it, he discards the eight.

Dealer matches the eight with those in hand and melds a mixed canasta, **2 2 8 8 8 8 8**. Having picked up two black threes, he discards a black three.

Opponent draws a jack, adds it to meld, discards a four.

Dealer draws a ten and adds it to meld, forming a second canasta, **10 10 10 10 10 10 10**. He also melds **5 5 5**. He discards a black three and goes out.

Now, the players stand:

OPPONENT

Melds:	**2 2 Q Q Q Q Q**	= 90 +	300	Mixed canasta
	Joker 9 9 9 9 9	= 100	100	Bonus for red **3**
	7 7 7 7 7	= 25	400	
	6 6 6 6 6	= 25		
	J J J J	= 40		*Total* 645
	5 5 5	= 15		
		270		
Holds in hand:	**A 4**	= −25		
		245		

Note that the opponent rates a minus score for the cards he still holds. This is because anyone holding cards after a meld has been made has the cards charged against him.

DEALER

Melds:	**10 10 10 10 10 10 10**	= 70 +	500	Natural canasta
	2 2 8 8 8 8 8	= 90 +	300	Mixed canasta
	Joker K K	= 70	100	For going out
	5 5 5	= 15	200	Bonus for two red threes
		245	1100	
				Total 1345

The discard pile consists of black three, four, black three. These cards are out of play, but it should be noted that a player holding one or two black threes must discard them to meld out. If he has three or four, he can meld them in a group, but only on the final meld. Canastas cannot be formed with black threes.

Cards may be added to a meld to form a canasta; also an eighth card can be added to a seven-card canasta. But if a wild card is tacked on to a natural canasta, it is reduced to a mixed canasta. For that reason, it is customary to square a completed canasta into a pile and place a red card on top to show that it is natural, or a black card to mark it as mixed. Added cards are placed beside canastas as play proceeds.

Not many canasta hands are finished as quickly as the example given, which was chosen for its brevity. The more the pot is built up, the more cards a player can pick up to form canastas, which are the big scoring factor. You need a lot of points to win a canasta game; the mark is 5000.

When a player's score reaches 1500, he requires 90 points for an opening in the next hand. When he reaches 3000 the requirement jumps to 120 points. If we study the following hand, we see graphically how this may influence the play:

Joker K K 10 10 10 9 9 9 9 8 7 5 5   Black **3**

An opening meld of **Joker K K** (or joker and any other pair) would exceed the 50-point opening requirement when the player's score is below 1500. But even **Joker 10 10 10** would not be enough for an opening meld of 90 points at 1500 or over. The player would have to meld **Joker 9 9 9 9** to make 90 with the fewest number of cards.

At 3000 and up, the most economical meld where cards are concerned would be **Joker 10 10 10** and **9 9 9 9**, which hits the necessary 120 exactly, using just eight cards.

A player holding a pair of aces instead of the two fives would be nicely off, as he could meld **Joker A A** and **10 10 10**, making his 120 points with only six cards.

Lacking a joker, there are problems with the higher brackets, though deuces can be helpful, as in this hand:

2 2 K K Q Q J J J J 9 8 5 5 3

Here, a meld of **2 K K 2 Q Q J J J J** would use up ten cards, but would still leave five for playing purposes. By waiting, however, a player might draw a joker, another deuce, or a pair of aces, all helpful toward the required 120.

Waiting would be almost imperative with a hand like:

K K K J J J 9 9 9 8 8 8 7 6 4

An initial meld of 120 would use all but the three odd cards (**7 6 4**) and the player would find it difficult to pick up the pot and gain cards for canastas. If he should draw a joker or deuce, the opponent could thwart him by freezing the pack, making it all the more difficult.

When a player's score goes into the minus column, as it may if an opponent melds out quickly in the first hand, the requirement for an opening meld is reduced. If the player's score is below zero, he needs only 15 points for his first meld.

The Two-Card Draw: This innovation has become a generally accepted part of two-handed canasta as commonly played today. Each player draws two cards from the stock, but discards only one, thus constantly increasing the total number of cards in his hand.

This eases the problem of the 90 and 120 opening melds, as a player can use a majority of his original cards and still have a chance to replenish his hand. It prevents one player from getting a lucky jump on the other and puts more emphasis on skill.

When the two-card draw is utilized, two canastas are always the requirement for a player to meld out. In a close game, where both players go over 5000, the one with the higher total is the winner, regardless of which one made the final meld out. The players are credited with 1 point for each 100, the nearest 100 being the determining factor.

Thus, a player winning with 5370 would be rated at 54; while his opponent, with 3945, would get 39, the first player having a victory margin of 15.

Canasta with Partners

The most famous form of canasta, and possibly the best, is the four-handed, two-team contest, from which many new versions have stemmed. Basically, it resembles the two-handed game just described, but with special rulings because there are two players on a side. Partners sit opposite each other, the play alternating from team to team.

The 108-card pack is used, but each player is dealt only eleven cards. Starting on the dealer's left, each player first shows and declares any red threes; he lays down his red threes toward a future bonus and replaces them by drawing from the stock. He then draws from the stock again to replenish his hand or takes the upcard.

The opening meld requirements are the same: 50 points when the team score is below 1500, 90 points when above 1500 and below 3000, 120 points for 3000 or more. When one player has met the requirements of the opening meld, the pack is unfrozen for his partner as well.

In making melds a player is allowed to lay off on his partner's melds. He can do this with the upcard, once the pack is no longer frozen. He can also pick up the upcard to add it as an extra card on a canasta which his team has melded.

All this hinges on whether the opponents are sufficiently unwary to make discards that will be treated in such cavalier fashion. They may be forced into situations of the kind by problems of their own. These must be seen to be appreciated, and you will see them in plenty when you play canasta.

Two new rules have been introduced to make it more difficult to pick up the upcard and the pot that goes with it. One rule is that a player cannot take the upcard to add to a completed canasta. He can add it only to a lesser group, toward the forming of a canasta.

If an eight is the upcard, he can add it to:

2 8 8 or **2 8 8 8** or even **2 2 2 8 8 8**

But he cannot add it to:

8 8 8 8 8 8 8 or **2 2 2 8 8 8 8**

The other rule is that a natural pair is needed when matching the upcard, just as if the pack were still frozen. Put both these rules into effect and the pack is almost frozen. The only loophole left is to add the upcard to a meld already on the table but still short of a canasta.

In making a meld involving the upcard, a player must go through a definite procedure. He first matches the upcard with a natural pair if the pack is frozen. As an opening meld, the meld is part of the required count, along with any meld made from his hand as it then stands. He then takes the discard pile into his hand and can meld anything from it, all in the same play. But this additional meld cannot be included as part of the opening count.

Since only eleven cards are dealt to each player, to come up with an opening meld of 120 points requires wild cards. But there are two players on each side, with twenty-two cards in all; one or the other has a good chance of catching a joker or some deuces.

However, if a team can meld out just short of the 3000 mark, it is strategically fixed for the next hand, as a meld of 90 points rather than 120 will put it in business. That little difference may speed its race for canastas in what the players hope will be the final hand, their purpose being to hop the hurdle by gathering more than 2000 points, thus making game.

Black threes serve as temporary blockers and wild cards freeze the pack, as in the two-handed game. But once a team acquires a canasta, it is free to meld out. Thus one player can surprise the opponents by melding out on the strength of his partner's canasta.

However, to do this with a "concealed" hand, a player must have a canasta of his own. He cannot have made a previous meld, not even by adding anything to his partner's meld. Nor can he add anything to his partner's meld in the act of melding out.

In return for all those difficulties, he has one compensation. He does not need a minimum count where an opening meld is concerned. Suppose he nurses his hand into the following:

7 7 7 7 7 7 7 4 4 4 4 Black **3**

This is just after a draw from the stock. He melds the sevens as a canasta and the fours as a smaller group; then he discards the black three. That's only 55 points in card values, not enough for a 90- or 120-point opener. But it suffices when melding out with a concealed hand.

The player gets 500 bonus points for a natural canasta and 200 for going out in this fashion, making 755 in all, plus points for any red threes that his team has declared. While the total is not big, as scoring goes in canasta, going out in this quick fashion may surprise the other team, catching it with a lot of unmelded cards before it can form canastas.

Thus it serves as a defensive measure against strong opposition. If a player has a score already above 3000 points, it gives him a chance to cash in quickly with a hand that would otherwise be hopeless, possibly scoring enough to make game, but in any case taking the opponents unaware. But that brings up another problem frequent in canasta:

Where will your partner stand if you decide to meld out on your own, with a concealed hand or otherwise?

The way to find out is to ask him. That is allowable in canasta. On any play, before or after you have made your draw, you can put the question, "Can I meld out?" If your partner answers "Yes," you must then meld out. If he answers "No," you can't meld out on that play.

You do not have to ask your partner if you can meld out, but if you do ask him and he says "Yes," you must be able to go through with it or take a penalty of 100 points.

Many penalties may be imposed in canasta, particularly in the four-handed game, where even minor infractions of the rules, at the expense of the other team, may have a strong bearing on a partner's play. The penalties are listed at the end of the chapter for easy reference.

IMPORTANT VARIATIONS

One simple way of punching up the game of canasta is to allow wild cards to be melded in groups of three or more, with the aim of making them into a natural canasta of their own. They are scored according to their customary points–joker 50 and deuce 20–with a bonus of 2000 for a canasta of seven wild cards.

Since there are twelve wild cards to work with, a wild canasta is easier to form than any other; but in going after a wild canasta, a player is forced to curtail his operations where mixed canastas are concerned. Often a few draws one way or another can cause a switch in purpose.

The game is simplified by keeping the pack frozen all the time. Only by matching the upcard with a natural pair can the pot be taken. This ruling is introduced almost automatically, because of wild cards having attained their independent status. But that status, in turn, has led to a differentiation in the wild cards themselves.

A canasta of seven deuces may be promoted to the rank of a natural wild canasta, with a 4000-point bonus. A special wild canasta of four jokers and three deuces is worth 3000. A mixed job of jokers and deuces stays at 2000 points.

Since these variations offer new scoring vistas, it is usual to jump the total score for game to 7500 points, with an opening meld of 150 points required when a team reaches the 5000 level. To provide for that necessary difference, players are dealt two extra cards each, or thirteen per player, beginning with the first deal.

The scoring is speeded somewhat in the early stages and gives a player a reasonable chance at nailing down an opening meld toward the end of the game.

Red threes are increased in value to keep pace with the stepped-up score. They are rated at 100 bonus points each, with an added bonus of 100 for the second, 100 for the third, and 400 for the fourth, making a total bonus of 1000 for holding all the red threes.

Black threes come in for special treatment in this stepped-up form of canasta. They may be discarded as blockers in the usual fashion, but they cannot be used over again by a player who acquires a black three in picking up the pack. In such a case the player simply weeds out black threes and lays them down as he would a red three. At the end of the hand each black three counts 5 points for the player who declared it; but if his team has laid down all four black threes, the lot is worth a bonus of 100 rather than a mere 20.

A simpler procedure, more in keeping with the wilder variants of canasta and a great deal more fun for those who like it, is the following:

Treat black threes exactly as you would red threes, but keep them in a separate category. Weed them from your hand as you find them, and lay them on the table at 100 points each, with an added bonus of 100 for the second, 100 for the third, and 400 for the fourth, making a total bonus of 1000 for holding all the black threes.

In both cases, threes count plus unless a team has failed to meld a canasta before the opposing team melds out. Failure to form a canasta switches the threes to the minus column.

CANASTA PENALTIES

Red Threes: Usually these count 100 points for a player or team, when declared and laid down in the course of play. But if the player or team fails to make a regular meld before the other side goes out, each red three counts 100 points against the melder.

All four red threes ordinarily count 800 points; this becomes 800 points against the holder in the absence of a meld. Where red threes are given higher values, as in the variation mentioned on pages 62–63, these apply as penalty counts as well.

If a player fails to declare a red three when he has an opportunity to do so, and is caught with such a card in his hand after the opposing player or team has melded out, he is penalized 500 points.

Black Threes: In the regular game these simply count as 5 points each against a player, unless he melds a group of three or four black threes when he melds out. In games where they are rated as red threes, black threes come under the same penalty rulings.

Drawing Cards: If a player draws out of turn, he must give the card to the player who should have drawn it. That player may either keep it as his next draw, or may bury it in the pack, which may be shuffled.

This applies only to opponents; if it happened that the player's partner was supposed to draw, the partner must keep the card as his draw.

However, if a player draws out of turn and puts the card in his own hand before the mistake is noted, he must keep it there until his turn to draw, when he is allowed to make his discard. As penalty, 100 points are deducted from his score.

This applies if the player picks up the discard pile when melding out of turn and adds it to his hand. He must then show his entire hand, so that the discard pile may be rearranged as closely as possible to its proper order. He then picks up his hand and awaits his turn. Penalty, 100 points deduction.

If the player melds illegally in his proper turn and picks up the discard pile, he must immediately make the correct meld. If he cannot do so to the full satisfaction of the other players, he must show his hand and rearrange the discard pile. He then picks up his hand and draws from the pack. Here a penalty is optional, but it is usually fixed at 100 points.

Mistakes in Melding: These sometimes occur in the opening meld, particularly when a player forgets that extra points are needed. If he is short, he may add another card or cards and form the meld to meet requirements, without penalty. If he takes back all the cards and does not meld, 10 points are added to his side's requirement for an opening meld.

Thus, if the team score happened to be 1600, the needed opening meld would be raised from 90 to 100 for that hand.

The player here has another choice; namely, to take back some of his cards and use others to make the proper meld. For that privilege, he (or his team) is penalized 100 points.

Similar rulings apply to other mistakes in melds. If a player uses too many wild cards or lays down wrong cards in a meld, he can add other cards from his hand to change or expand the meld and complete the discard. Any cards shown can be used to such purpose, but if any are taken back into the hand, the player is penalized 100 points.

If a player tries to go out before his team has formed a canasta –or before he has two canastas when so required–the penalty is 100 points.

As already stated, a player who asks his partner "Can I meld out?" and receives the answer "Yes" must then meld out his entire hand, or be penalized 100 points.

Similarly, if he starts to meld and then puts such a question, or begins melding before receiving a reply, or tries to meld out after his partner says "No," the penalty is 100 points.

Most minor infractions carry no penalty. If a player draws too many cards, he simply waits for further turns in which to discard them. If he sees extra cards during the draw, he must show them to the other players and allow the cards to be shuffled into the pack.

If a player lets cards in his hand be seen, he can be required to place them face up on the table and discard them at the first opportunity. This applies to the four-handed game, where the chance showing of a card might help a player's partner.

All penalties are optional, to the extent that when opponents allow play to proceed without enforcing them, the penalties cannot be demanded later.

Samba and Bolivia

With the urge for bigger and better melds in canasta, a three-pack version of the game came into vogue, utilizing 162 cards, including six jokers. A new scoring combination was introduced in the form of sequences, which could be built up from three cards to seven, provided all were in the same suit.

Such a sequence was called a samba, and other rules were incorporated with it to produce the game of samba.

The cards are dealt to two teams of partners as in four-handed canasta, but each player receives fifteen cards. To speed the game still further, each player draws two cards from the stock but discards only one as upcard on the discard pile.

To pick up the pot, you must match the upcard with a natural pair from your hand, unless the pack is no longer frozen. If it is no longer frozen, you may pick it up if you can add the upcard to any of your team's existing melds, short of a completed canasta.

In forming a mixed canasta only *two* wild cards may be included, instead of the *three* allowable in canasta. Thus, in canasta you can build to:

Joker 2 2 K K K K

In samba you can only build to:

Joker 2 K K K K K

You are restricted, too, when you have completed a canasta. While you may add cards to it, you can't pick up the upcard (and pot) for that purpose. However, that difficulty can often be avoided by building toward two canastas of the same denomination, as follows:

2 J J 2 J J J

This is allowable in samba because there are *twelve* cards of each and every value, with eighteen wild cards to help. So a team can be going after two canastas in jacks, as shown above, but when the game gets tight or chances of making "separates" begin to dwindle, the two can be merged into a canasta of the mixed type.

Those extra cards allow leeway toward the forming of sequences, the really individual feature of samba. Three cards (or more) of the same suit, when laid down in a meld, are scored according to the standard canasta count.

As an example:

♡ A K Q ♣ 6 5 4

The three hearts, representing top members of a sequence, would count 15, 10, 10, for a total of 35. The three clubs, as the lowest group, would count 5, 5, 5, for a total of 15. However, wild cards cannot be used in forming sequences.

Extend a sequence to seven-card length and you have a samba, as follows:

♡ A K Q J 10 9 8
♣ 10 9 8 7 6 5 4

You may add more cards to either end if you are able to form a samba in the first place. That's rather difficult, as there are only three cards of each type. Because of its comparative rarity, a samba–or sequence canasta, as it may be called–gains a bonus of 1500 points.

Two canastas are needed to go out, and a samba may be counted as one of them. In going out, a team receives a bonus of 200 points (compared to only 100 in canasta), but there is no extra bonus for going out all at once by keeping the hand concealed.

Game in samba is 10,000 points, and because of the higher scoring possibilities, initial melds are more exacting than in canasta. When the score is 0, you need 50 points; at 1500 you need 90 points; at 3000 you need 120 points; at 7000 you need 150 points.

These levels and their required counts differ in various versions of the game. The same applies to scoring red threes–and sometimes black threes–but in standard samba, red threes have the usual bonus of 100 points each, with a jump to 1000 for holding all six.

Those are plus scores, provided the team has melded two canastas–sambas allowable as such–but otherwise the red threes result in a minus score.

Sets of wild cards (jokers and deuces) cannot be melded. Melding of that type is utilized in the game of bolivia.

BOLIVIA

This development of samba includes the sequence valuation, but a run of seven cards in a suit is simply termed an *escalera,* or "ladder," instead of a samba, although it counts for the same 1500 points.

Looming still larger is a bolivia; the title is given to a canasta of wild cards, whether composed of deuces and jokers or simply deuces alone. A bolivia is valued at 2500 points. To encourage scoring further, game is 15,000 points; but the opening count needed at the various score levels (0, 1500, etc.) is the same as in samba.

What adds zest to bolivia is a going-out requirement. A team must meld not only a canasta or better to go out; it must meld at least one *escalera*–or one bolivia–in addition.

This requirement brings out important factors in the play of samba and bolivia, in contrast to that of ordinary canasta: in samba the triple pack and high count for a samba encourage players to go for bigger scores than in the simpler canasta.

However, there is a defensive element that may crop up strongly in samba: that of melding three of a kind and more to block the building of opposing sequences. Suppose you meld the sequence ♡ **8 9 10 J** as an encouragement for your partner to add whatever he can at either end. An opponent might counter by melding ♣**Q** ♡**Q** ♡**Q** in the hope that his partner will tack on the third ♡**Q** and block your ladder at the top. Or he might lay down the ♣**7** ♡**7** ♡**7** to chop off the lower end of the ladder. Actual melding would not even be necessary, as long as your opponents held such blockers, though once they showed them, your chance for an *escalera* would fade.

In samba such blocking tactics not only may curtail sequences, they can bring in lucky canastas that may win a hand. But in bolivia, a team that goes after "threes" and begins building them into canastas may be ruining chances for an *escalera,* which it might need in order to go out at all.

Still stronger is the inducement to go after a bolivia, which reduces the chances for mixed canastas, or causes players to disregard them until they size up the wild-card prospects. This, in turn, furnishes new incentive toward forming *escaleras,* which are less likely to be blocked and do not use wild cards at all.

Other rules have been introduced to speed up competition in bolivia and various offshoots of the canasta-samba clan. One is to raise the opening-meld requirements in bolivia, by making it necessary to meld a complete canasta or a higher combination (*escalera* or bolivia) when the score has reached 7000.

At the 8000 level an opening meld of 200 points is necessary; at the 9000 mark a player must lay down a natural canasta (not just a mixed type) or a higher combination, as his opening meld.

With such rules, game is usually set at 10,000 and is by no means easy to attain, for this reason: a penalty rule is invoked whereby a three- or four-card sequence takes 1000 points from a team's score if the partners have actually melded it and are caught with it when the hand ends. That means it isn't safe to lay down such a sequence, as your opponents may block it before your partner can add to it.

Maybe it's worth the risk if the discards indicate that your partner can tack on a card or two–to give the sequence a five-card length–or if you desperately need an added card so that you can put on more to complete an *escalera.* It all makes the game the more exciting.

In this version a bolivia is usually scored at 2000 points instead of 2500, so that it will not be given too much margin over an *escalera,* which loses some of its value because of the "minus" hazard.

Red threes are also given an added count. Five of them double in value from 500 to 1000 if held by one team, with 200 more for holding the sixth red three. But to put that bonus on the plus side, a team must manage to meld a single canasta or better. Otherwise, the red threes are scored in the minus column.

In all forms of bolivia black threes can be laid down at a mere 5 points each when a side is melding out, just as in canasta or samba. But if any black threes show up in another player's hand, 100 points are deducted from his team's score for each black three he holds. It is good policy, therefore, to get rid of such "stoppers" in a hurry, toward the late stages of a hand.

Cribbage

This game was described in the *Compleat Gamester,* published in 1674, under the name of "cribbidge," and during three centuries its most radical change has been in spelling. While the modern game calls for a deal of six cards to a hand instead of the original five, the five-card game is still a recognized form. So cribbage is still cribbidge.

Basically a two-player game, cribbage requires a standard fifty-two-card pack, with cards ranking in value from king down to ace, which is low. Each face card (king, queen, jack) has a value or count of ten, while the other cards are valued according to their spots, ten, nine, eight, and so on down to one for the ace.

The game begins with one player, the dealer, dealing six cards to his opponent and six cards to himself. Each player studies his hand and then discards two of the six cards without showing them to the other player. These four cards are laid face down together, forming an extra hand known as the crib.

Thus there are now three hands of four cards each: The opponent's, the dealer's, and the crib.

In retaining cards each player considers those that may be used in forming certain combinations that give him points toward game. These combinations are as follows:

A PAIR or two cards of the same kind   2 points

As ♡**K** ♣**K**, ♣**J** ◇**J**, ♡**5** ♠**5**

PAIRS ROYAL or three of a kind   6 points

As ◇**9** ♣**9** ♡**9**. These can be paired three ways: ◇**9** ♣**9**, ◇**9** ♡**9**, ♣**9** ♡**9**, hence the triple rating.

DOUBLE PAIRS ROYAL or four of a kind   12 points

Here ◇**A** ♣**A** ♡**A** ♠**A** will allow six pairings: ◇**A** ♣**A**, ◇**A** ♡**A**, ◇**A** ♠**A**, ♣**A** ♡**A**, ♣**A** ♠**A**, ♡**A** ♠**A**, giving a six-fold rating.

A SEQUENCE OF THREE CARDS   3 points

As **Q J 10** or **6 5 4**

AN ADDITIONAL SEQUENCE CARD 1 point

As **Q J 10** with **9** added

FIFTEENS—cards adding to fifteen in value 2 points

These include such combinations as **K 5**, **8 7**, **9 4 2**, **5 4 3 3**.

A FLUSH OF FOUR CARDS OF THE SAME SUIT 4 points

As ♢**Q** ♢**8** ♢**5** ♢**2**, which also includes two fifteens, **Q 5** and **8 5 2**. A hand such as ♠**J** ♠**10** ♠**9** ♠**8** would be worth four points for a flush and four points for a four-card sequence.

After each player has discarded two cards to form the crib, the pack is cut and a card turned up. This card is termed the "starter" and it serves as a wild card in each player's hand, so that each hand has five cards in all.

Special types of scores may be registered with the aid of the starter, as follows:

A FIFTH CARD in sequence 1 point

The starter can account for a third or fourth card in a sequence as well as the fifth.

A FIFTH CARD in a flush 1 point

The hand must already contain a four-card flush for the extra card to count.

HIS NOBS—a jack in a player's hand that is matched in suit by the starter 1 point

A player holding the ♡**J** would score for His Nobs if a heart —as the ♡**9**—should turn up.

In some cases the starter may add heavily to a player's score. Suppose his hand contains ♢**8** ♣**8** and ♢**6** ♡**6**. As it stands, he has only four points (two for each pair). But if a seven (say, the ♣**7**) should be turned up as the starter, it would give the player *four* distinct three-card sequences, rating three points each or twelve in all.

Also, the player would have two fifteens (♢**8** ♣**7** and ♣**8** ♣**7**), making four points more. So the total score of his hand, with starter, would be twenty points.

With pairs royal (as ♡**3** ♣**3** ♢**3**), the fourth card of that denomination (in this case the ♠**3**) as the starter would automatically give him double pairs royal, increasing his points from six to twelve.

In the original game of cribbage, players announced these totals before playing the hands. That meant that the hands had to be verified later. In the modern game the points are not counted until afterward. In the play the player keeps his own cards in front of him as he lays them face up on the table.

After the play the crib goes to the dealer, who turns it up and adds its contents to his score as if it were an extra hand, which it is. He counts the starter as part of it, just as with his own hand. There is just one limitation where the crib is concerned. No score is allowed for a four-card flush in the crib, unless it is matched in suit by the starter. In that case it becomes a five-card flush and is scored as such, giving the dealer five points.

Thanks to the crib, the dealer naturally has an advantage toward the attainment of game, which is sixty-one or preferably 121 points, but this is counterbalanced by the fact that the next deal goes to his opponent, who then has a chance to pick up extra points from the crib.

The play of the hand is important as a means of adding to each individual score. It follows the scoring pattern already described, but involves some new and intriguing factors and is subject to certain modifications that become apparent during the play.

If the dealer turns up a jack as starter, that card is termed "His Heels" and the dealer scores two points. Otherwise, the starter is not counted in connection with the play, its purpose being simply to start the action.

The opponent begins the actual play by placing one of his cards face up on the table. It is then the dealer's play, and if he can pair the card laid down by the opponent, the dealer scores two points, for a pair.

For example: if the opponent lays down a seven, the dealer might match it with another seven. But the opponent, on his next play, could lay down a third seven, if he has it, and score six points for pairs royal.

By laying down a fourth seven the dealer could score twelve for double pairs royal, but in every case the cards must be played in immediate succession. If two sevens were followed by an ace, another seven would not count toward pairs royal, as the chain has been broken.

Players can score full value for completed sequences. Suppose the opponent lays down a three and the dealer follows with a four. The opponent may then play either a two or a five, calling it a three-card sequence, which gives him three points.

Suppose the opponent played the two. The dealer could then play an ace or a five, forming a four-card sequence, for which he would score four points, not merely one additional point. In the play, full credit is given for each completed combination.

It is possible to score as high as seven points by the play of a single card that completes a seven-card sequence consisting of such cards as ♢**A** ♡**2** ♡**3** ♠**4** ♣**5** ♢**6** ♡**7**. But these do not have to be played for the sequence to be completed and thereby scored. Take the following example:

Opponent:	♡**8**	♣**4**	♢**5**
Dealer:	♢**6**	♠**7**	

In this case there is no sequence during the play of the first four cards. True, the ♠**7** goes with the ♢**6** and ♡**8** played earlier, but the intervening ♣**4** spoils the run. But the *fifth card,* the ♢**5**, puts five on the board that form a complete sequence, although the cards were not played in actual rotation or consecutive order. No points are scored until the play of the ♢**5**. By laying down that card the opponent gains five points.

During play, both the opponent and the dealer announce the values of the cards by totaling the spots—or count—up to that stage of the play. In the example shown above, the opponent would lay down the ♡**8** and say "Eight." The dealer, following with the ♡**6**, would announce "Fourteen." The opponent would play the ♣**4** and say "Eighteen." The dealer would play the ♠**7** and say "Twenty-five." The opponent would then lay down the ♢**5** and announce "Thirty, with a run of five."

Thus, a game between experienced cribbage players takes on a jargon reminiscent of a tobacco auction, which is another of its fascinating features. This business of adding up the values has two purposes: it enables a player to score two points if he hits fifteen; and it also keeps track of the count as it approaches thirty-one, which is the ultimate goal in the play of the hand and also allows the player to score two points.

These various features are nicely illustrated in the following play:

Opponent:	♢**3**	♣**3**	♢**J**
Dealer:	♡**3**	♠**6**	♡**6**

The opponent plays the ♢**3** and says "Three." The dealer plays the ♡**3**, stating "Six and a pair," giving himself two points for the pair. The opponent lays down the ♣**3**, announcing "Nine and a pair royal," scoring six points for the pair royal (or three threes). The dealer then plays the ♠**6** and announces "Fifteen–two." This means he has hit fifteen in the value count and is scoring two points.

Now the opponent lays down the ♢**J** and says "Twenty-five," adding the value of the face card, namely, ten. This enables the dealer to play the ♡**6** and announce "Thirty-one–and two." This means he has hit the target of thirty-one in the value count and is scoring two points as his reward.

The cards played so far are turned face down and the play starts over with the remaining cards in the hands. In our example there are only two cards left, the opponent holding one, the dealer the other. Suppose the opponent has the ♡**Q** and the dealer the ♢**K**.

The opponent simply lays down the ♡**Q**, saying "Ten"–the value of a face card–and the dealer lays down the ♢**K**, announcing "Twenty." No points are scored for a pair, because two face cards must be of the same denomination to be rated as such; say, two queens or two kings. But the dealer does add, "And one for the last card." With that he scores himself one point, which goes to whoever plays the last card.

Another situation often arises during the play of a cribbage hand. A player may find himself unable to lay down a card without raising the count value to more than thirty-one, which is not allowable.

In that case he says, "Go." This means that the other player must lay down whatever cards he can without going over thirty-one. For this, he scores one point, unless he makes exactly thirty-one, in which case he scores two points.

A player often is unable to lay down a card when told to go. He still scores one point for the privilege. In any case the procedure is the same. The cards on the table are turned face down and the play reverts to the opposite player, who begins a new count toward thirty-one.

The same applies if a player runs out of cards during the process. The other player takes over and makes a fresh start, if he has any cards in his own hand. In any event one player or the other is sure to score one point for last card, which means the *last playable card* left in either hand.

A sample round will illustrate some of these features. Suppose the cards are dealt thus:

Opponent:	♡**K**	♡**J**	◇**J**	♣**10**	♠**9**	♡**4**
Dealer:	♣**K**	♠**K**	♡**9**	◇**9**	♣**7**	♠**4**

Each player studies his hand, and the opponent lays away the ♡**K** and the ♡**4** in the crib; these are of least value to his own hand or to the dealer, who will have a chance to pick up points from the crib after it is shown.

By holding the two jacks, the opponent keeps a pair in hand and may match one jack with the starter's suit when it is turned up. Also, each jack heads a three-card sequence consisting of **J 10 9**.

The dealer lays away the ♣**K** and ♠**K** in the crib, giving himself a future pair, as the crib will become his property. It's a good discard, for the opponent is likely to lay away a king–as in fact he has!–which will benefit the dealer still more. The dealer also keeps a pair–the nines–in his hand.

The starter is now turned up, and it proves to be the ◇**8**, which is a good card for the opponent but even better for the dealer, as will be seen. But that comes later. For the present we are concerned with the play.

The holdings now stand:

Opponent:	♡**J**	◇**J**	♣**10**	♠**9**
Dealer:	♡**9**	◇**9**	♣**7**	♠**4**

The play proceeds as follows:

The opponent plays the ♡**J**, announcing "Ten." The dealer plays the ♣**7** and adds "Seventeen." The opponent plays the ◇**J**, saying "Twenty-seven," and the dealer promptly tacks on the ♠4, declaring "Thirty-one–and two!" With that he scores two points for having built the count to thirty-one.

The cards on the table are turned down and the opponent leads the ♣10, saying "Ten." The dealer plays the ♡9, stating "Nineteen." The opponent promptly plays the ♠9, saying "Twenty-eight–and a pair," giving himself two points for the pair of nines.

Now the dealer is in a dilemma. He would like to play the ♢9 and credit himself with pairs royal (or three nines), but he can't, because the count would go over thirty-one. In fact, he can't play at all, having only the ♢9 left in his hand, so he is forced to say "Go."

The opponent announces "One for go" and scores one point. He doesn't need to have a card in his hand. On the last card he played, he announced the count at twenty-eight and the dealer is unable to bring it closer to thirty-one. So, as the player who brought it closest, the opponent scores the "go" point.

The cards on the table are turned down and it is again the dealer's turn to play. He starts at scratch again and plays his only card, the ♢9, but now he has no opportunity to match it with anything. However, it is the last card, so the dealer announces that fact and scores one point for it.

During the play, the following points have been scored:

Opponent		*Dealer*	
A pair of nines	2	For making thirty-one	2
For go	1	For last card	1
	3		3

Now comes the reckoning of the hands, which, with the crib as a separate hand, are composed of the following cards, including the wild starter:

Opponent:	♢8	♢J	♡J	♣10	♠9
Dealer:	♢8	♡9	♢9	♣7	♠4
The Crib:	♢8	♣K	♠K	♡K	♡4

The opponent scores a "double run of four," for ten points. This consists of two four-card sequences, ♢J ♣10 ♠9 ♢8 and ♡J ♣10 ♠9 ♢8, worth four points each plus two points for the pair of jacks. He also scores one point for holding His Nobs, the ♢**J**, which is of the same suit as the starter (♢**8**).

So the opponent has eleven points from the showing of the hand, which, added to three points from the play, gives him a total of fourteen points.

The dealer scores a "double run of three" for eight points, consisting of ♡**9** ♢**8** ♣**7** and ♢**9** ♢**8** ♣**7** at three points each, plus two points for the pair of nines. He also picks up two points for a fifteen formed by the ♢**8** and ♣**7**.

This gives the dealer ten points from the showing of the hand in addition to three points from the play, making thirteen points with more to come, from the crib, which gives the dealer six points for pairs royal formed by the three kings. Added to the points already scored, the dealer's total is nineteen points.

The hands just described were quite simple as cribbage hands go. A hand consisting of four fives and a "Tenth" card (the name applied to a face card or a ten) would rack up a total of twenty-eight points, consisting of double pairs royal (four fives) for twelve points; four fifteens, each composed of the Tenth card and a different five, making eight points; and four fifteens, each formed from three different fives, making eight points more.

If one of the fives happened to be the Starter, and the Tenth was a jack of the same suit, the hand would show an additional point for His Nobs, making a total of twenty-nine.

To facilitate the scoring in a cribbage game, a special board is generally used. The simplest form is a long, narrow board with two rows of thirty holes along each side and a game hole at each end. This is placed broadside between the players, and each marks up his points by inserting pegs in the holes whenever scores are made.

Each player has two pegs, so that he can jump one ahead of the other as he pegs his points along the board and back, a hole for each point. In playing for sixty-one points, the winner goes once around the board and "pegs out" when he reaches the hole at the end. Many players prefer to go twice around, making 121 points the total for game.

In either case, if the winner attains game before the other player has passed the halfway mark, the loser is left in the lurch and the winner is credited with two wins, or double stakes. This does not ordinarily apply when the participants are playing strictly for points rather than for game, as the margin of points then determines the difference between the winner and the loser.

Two types of strategy figure in cribbage. One form is "playing on," which means inviting an opponent to score, in order to go him better. If you are holding two jacks, for instance, you may lead one in the hope that he will pair it for two points, giving you the chance to add your other jack and garner six points for pairs royal.

If you lead a Tenth card (**K**, **Q**, **J**, or **10**), there is always the chance that the other player will lay down a five, pegging two points for a fifteen. But if you, too, happen to have a five in your hand, you can play it and make two points for a pair, thus balancing your opponent's score.

That is a case of playing on, even though you do not increase your point margin. This is to your advantage when you are ahead, as it brings you closer to game. But when the score tightens and particularly when your opponent is approaching game, it is better to "play off."

Keep your cards well spaced in value, making it hard for your opponent to form a sequence. Don't risk forming a pair if you think he is lying back with a third card that will give him pairs royal. Don't play a card that will bring the count to twenty-one if you can avoid it, as the other player is apt to have a Tenth card which he can lay down and hit thirty-one for two points on the button.

Such factors must be borne in mind before you even come to the play. They help to determine what cards you should keep or discard when you lay away two for the crib. That, of course, is the first thing to think about when you look at your hand. What you lay away hinges primarily on whether you are the opponent or the dealer.

If you are the opponent or nondealer, it is smart to give cards to the crib that will balk the dealer's chances of forming fifteens or sequences. A king or an ace is a good balker because it comes at the end of a sequence and is therefore of very little help.

A king or any other Tenth card won't help the dealer toward making a fifteen in the crib unless he can lay away a five or its equivalent. Similarly, anything under a five may balk the dealer where fifteen is concerned. As the opponent, you should not lay away a five if you can help it, nor two cards adding up to five, as a four and an ace.

Cards well apart in value are termed "wide cards" and are good to lay away because they cannot be used in a sequence. As the opponent, you may do well to discard a king-four, as the king is a natural balker and the four is too low to be used in a fifteen, unless the dealer discards an ace, which is unlikely, as it is a card he can use in play.

A king-nine is a wide-card example, as the crib would need a queen-jack-ten to fill the run, and one of those would have to be the starter. So the opponent is likely to discard a king and nine when he can.

Roughly, the cards fall into three distinctive brackets: Tenth cards **(K Q J 10)**, middle cards **(9 8 7 6 5)**, low cards **(4 3 2 A)**. For the opponent, it is preferable to discard from the high group or the low rather than the middle. But, obviously, a jack-ten discard would be bad, as it forms two parts of a sequence. So would a four-ace discard, which adds up to five, the key to a fifteen.

In theory it is simple to name the proper discards, but in practice the player is limited to a mere six cards, which may shatter all his preconceived notions. However, these frequently work out their own solution.

Take this random hand picked up by an opponent:

♣Q ♣10 ♠10 ◇6 ◇3 ♣3

It would be unwise for the opponent to put a pair in the crib as a two-point gift to the dealer. So his discard is practically automatic. He keeps the two pair in his hand, where they are a sure score, and discards the queen and six as wide cards that should not help the dealer very much.

From the dealer's standpoint this hand would be treated quite differently. He can put away a pair in the crib and add it to his score later. It's a tossup which to discard, the tens or the threes. By keeping the tens the dealer has a chance of making a sequence with the queen during the play–if the opponent should happen to lay down a jack.

Otherwise, the threes are the pair to keep, as they offer certain advantages in the play, particularly when working toward a count of thirty-one. So it is largely a matter of choice on the part of the individual player.

As the nondealer or opponent, you are sure to encounter many heartbreakers where the discard is concerned, but that's cribbage. You also have some compensation in the fact that the other player may go through similar throes when you are the dealer.

Frequently, the six cards dealt you will show more points than you can possibly keep, so some sacrifice is necessary.

As the opponent, suppose you hold:

♡K ♠Q ◇J ♣5 ♡4 ♠3

Here are two three-card sequences worth three points each. A discard of the wide king and three would break up both. So it's better to break up one of the runs and keep the other. Here again you have some pointers to guide you.

The hand contains three fifteens at two points each. Each depends on a different Tenth card. By discarding the ♡**4** and ♠**3** you keep the upper run and the three fifteens as well, a total of nine points for the showing of the hand.

Discarding a four and a three is not good policy, as they constitute two parts of a sequence, which may help the crib. But in this case, that is the chance you have to take.

In the play of the hand, the count of fifteen is a key value. If the opponent opens with a lead of a low card (under a five), he will prevent the dealer from hitting fifteen on the return play, as the most he can add is ten with a Tenth card.

Low cards are handy, however, in approaching thirty-one, and it is a doubtful policy to lead one, particularly if your own hand is heavy with high cards. However, if you hold a combination of ace-four or two-three, it is good to lead one of them. If the other player responds with a Tenth card, you can then hit fifteen with your second low card; together they total five.

A three is a good lead if you also hold a nine, because if the other player pairs your three, you can lay down the nine and hit fifteen for two points. But if you hold a three and a six, lead the six; if the other player pairs the six, you can hit fifteen with the three.

Similarly, when holding a four and a seven, the four is a good lead. If the other player pairs it, you can lay down the seven for a fifteen. In all these cases you equalize the two points scored by the other player.

It is generally bad policy to lead a seven or an eight, as the other player may be holding middle cards and can make a fifteen by playing an eight on your seven, or vice versa. But if you also hold a six or a nine (along with your original seven or eight) you can invite the other player's fifteen, using your six or nine to form a sequence, which gives you three points to his two points.

Smart cribbage players watch for a chance to add another card to an opponent's run, thus topping his score by one point more. Suppose two players are holding:

Opponent:	♡**J**	♣**8**	◇**8**	♠**6**
Dealer:	♡**10**	♡**7**	♡**6**	♡**5**

The opponent leads the ♣**8**, figuring thus: if the dealer can pair it, the opponent can add the ◇**8** for pairs royal, gaining six points as against two points. If the dealer has a seven–which is more likely–and plays it to pick up two points for fifteen, the opponent can lay down his ♠**6** and score three points for a sequence.

That is exactly what does happen, but the dealer is primed for it, with both a ♡**10** and a ♡**5** in his hand. So the play proceeds:

Opponent:	♣**8**	♠**6**
Dealer:	♡**7**	♡**5**

The dealer scores two points when he plays the ♡**7** for fifteen, and the opponent tops it with three points by playing the ♠**6** for a three-card sequence. But the dealer adds the ♡**5** and scores four points for a four-card sequence. What's more, the opponent is forced to say "Go," so the dealer racks up one point more.

If the opponent had been holding a four instead of the jack, he could have played it for a five-card sequence, scoring five points and forcing the dealer into saying "Go," giving the opponent one point more.

In this instance, both the opponent and the dealer are playing on—a common practice in the early stage of the game and a desperation move by a player who is far behind. When a player has passed the halfway mark in a sixty-one-point game, he is "at home," and if he leads by seven points or more, he is regarded as "safe at home."

From then on he should play off by keeping and playing wide cards to prevent the other player from making a sequence; he should use other measures, too, to balk or block the other player's scoring chances. Also, he shouldn't regard himself as safe at home even with a seven-point margin at the halfway mark, unless it is his turn to deal.

The dealer's score (with crib) averages about five points more than the opponent's, and if the other player is the dealer, he may catch up. Another thing: a player will need a seven-point margin if he deals the final hand, for whoever pegs out first wins the game. After the hand is played, the opponent shows his hand and scores it ahead of the dealer, giving the opponent an advantage in a photo finish.

Old-time cribbage players claim that a four is the best opening lead, being the highest of the low cards yet not high enough for the other player to add a card and make a fifteen. By the same token, a five is the worst opener, as any Tenth card can be added for fifteen.

There is a tendency to avoid opening with a Tenth card on the assumption that the other player may be sitting back with a five, ready to make his fifteen. But that assumption is not necessarily correct. The dealer is very apt to stow a five in the crib, hoping that the opponent has parked a Tenth card there.

So the opponent may do well to keep a Tenth card and lead it, particularly if he has kept a five of his own. Then, if the dealer hits fifteen with his five and scores two points, the opponent can come right back with his own five and score two points for a pair.

These and other factors show up in every cribbage game, making experience and judgment the deciding elements. Perhaps the biggest complication is the adding up of the score when showing a hand or the crib. Some of the combinations are apt to be overlooked, particularly by beginners.

This complication is a feature in the variant of cribbage known as muggins. In that game, if a player fails to announce and peg any points during the play or the showing of the hand, his adversary can call "Muggins" and claim the points for his own score. He must wait until after the score has been incorrectly pegged or the hand turned down before making the claim.

Another rule is recommended in muggins, namely, that if a player overcalls his score, his adversary may demand that he move his peg back to the proper hole, and the adversary may then peg the extra points for himself. Unless the muggins feature is included, there is no penalty for pegging a wrong count, except that an overlooked count may be lost and an overcount must be moved back if detected.

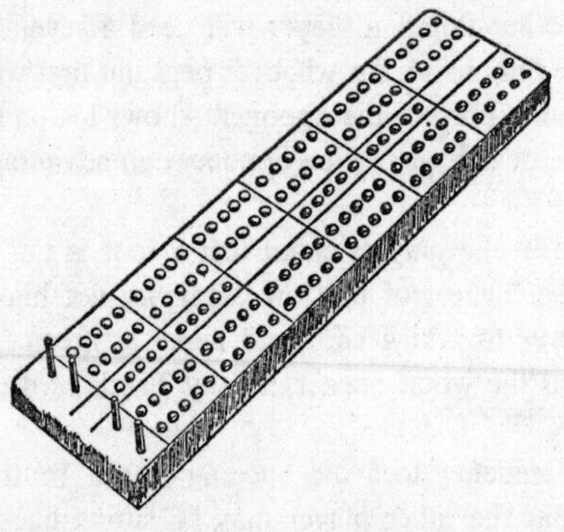

The cribbage board described on page 79. One player uses the two rows at the left; the other, the two rows at the right. Each player pegs along his entire outside row away from him, and back along the inside row toward himself. After going out and back twice, he places the peg in the hole at the near end of the inner row to mark the final point of 121. For a sixty-one-point game, a player goes out and back once.

The extra holes in the center section of the board are for keeping count of games won, each player using a row of ten holes. If one player is "lurched" (that is, his opponent has attained game before he, the player mentioned, has passed the halfway mark), the winner moves a peg two holes ahead in his game row.

Hearts

Here we have an exciting, sometimes hilarious game, suitable for young and old and therefore a great favorite around the family circle. But it should not be belittled because of its comparative simplicity. Actually, hearts offers opportunity for a surprising amount of skill, which accounts for its continued popularity.

In the four-handed game the entire pack of fifty-two cards is dealt equally among the players, each of whom operates on his own. After the players look at their hands, the player on the dealer's left places one of his cards face up in the center of the table. This is called leading a card.

Each succeeding player lays down a card in the same fashion and must follow suit, if possible, by playing a card of the suit led. The high card of that suit takes the rest, and this group constitutes a trick, which the winner turns face down in front of him. It is his turn, then, to make another lead.

The term "winner" often carries an ironical touch, because, in hearts, tricks have no value in themselves. The purpose of the game is to avoid taking hearts, so tricks are generally unwanted. Each time a player captures a heart, or in popular parlance is stuck with one, it counts a point against him.

In playing value the cards run ace, king, queen, and so on down to deuce. If a player is unable to follow suit, he must throw off a card from another suit. Very often, he throws off a heart, to the discomfort of the unfortunate winner of the trick. When a heart is led, the taker of the trick fares still worse.

The simplest form of scoring is to play for fifty or one hundred points, the person first reaching that total being pronounced the loser, not the winner. The actual winner is the lowest scorer, and so on up the scale.

Such is hearts, in rudimentary form, but there are added features that give the game a peculiar piquancy and are therefore recommended as accepted rules of play.

First, there is a special valuation given to certain cards, as follows:

The queen of spades, known as the Black Lady, is counted as thirteen hearts and adds that many points to the score of anyone taking that particular card.

The jack of diamonds is rated as a bonus card and as such subtracts ten points from a player's score. Taking less than ten hearts and the jack puts him below zero, a minus score being all the more to his advantage. Five hearts and the jack, for example, give a score of minus five.

These special cards do more than step up the scoring opportunities. They give significance to spades and diamonds as well as to hearts, and clubs are the only neutral or unimportant suit.

A second feature unique to hearts and therefore an integral portion of the game is the preliminary passing of three cards by each player to the person on his left, which operates thus:

After each player studies his hand, he chooses the three cards that he thinks will be least helpful to his play. He places these face down on the table at his left. After he has done this, he picks up the three cards laid down by the player on his right and adds them to his hand.

Whether his hand goes from bad to worse, or vice versa, depends on a combination of luck and judgment on the player's part. In any event it adds a surprise element that frequently forces a player to revise his calculations in relation to the play that follows.

The fun in hearts lies in its comparative ease of play. The game has been called a reverse of whist or bridge, but that is an erroneous concept. Instead of each trick becoming more and more vital as the play of the hand proceeds, it may become meaningless.

Early unloading of hearts and the spade queen may upset the most carefully laid plans; conversely, a player may find himself "boxed" toward the end of a hand and thereby confronted with a load of losing points that he thought he could easily avoid.

When one is playing against keen competition, some hands demand a close study of the cards and of those that have been played; but in many instances the play will follow a pattern not only obvious but almost automatic.

If a hand contains an average quota of low cards, it is possible to lead them or keep playing just under the top cards in tricks you do not want to take, so that you can keep clear of hearts or the spade queen. As fourth hand, you can get rid of high cards by taking harmless tricks.

If you have too many high cards, it may be worth the risk to lead a few early in the round, thus taking tricks before the other players are out of suit and thereby able to throw hearts. The ♣**A**, ♣**K**, or ♣**Q** is a typical lead of this sort, and it is even worth wasting the ♢**A**, ♢**K**, or ♢**Q**–rather than hold them in the hope of catching the ♢**J**–if they threaten to become troublesome.

Judicious combining of these two patterns of play may bring surprisingly good results with seemingly bad hands. Always remember that you never need the lowest card to avoid taking a trick; the second highest card is good enough to get by. In theory you could hold the **4**, **8**, **Q** of a suit and drop them in successive rounds of a four-handed hearts game, always to a card only one unit higher than another person would be forced to play.

Though in actuality this hardly could happen so fortunately, at least it should wean fainthearted players from the notion that they need a plethora of twos and threes when playing hearts, as they would aces and kings in games where taking tricks is the sole mission.

Naturally, the ♠**A** or ♠**K** would be a suicidal lead in hearts if the ♠**Q** were out against you. But the ♠**J** or ♠**10** is an excellent lead when it is your highest card in that suit. Through such spade leads you can force out the ♠**Q** to keep it from being unloaded on you later, if you have to play high in some other suit.

The motto "Take high–lead low" holds good even if you are forced to take a few hearts with a high card rather than sacrifice a low card that you need for an ensuing lead. Otherwise, you may be deluged with hearts later.

When you are out of a suit, it is better to throw off dangerous high cards than simply to soak a foe with a heart that you can dispose of during normal play. Thus, if you are out of diamonds and are holding ♠**K** and ♡**3**, it is best to throw the ♠**K**–which might take the ♠**Q**–rather than the ♡**3**, which can duck under any heart lead.

This principle applies to the early stages of the game, but more subtle situations can develop that will prove similar when analyzed. You won't have to unload the ♠**K** in a hurry if you hold a lot of lower spades; even the ♡**3** can be dangerous when there is a chance that only one other player is holding hearts, the ♡**2** among them. But even an ordinarily innocuous ♣**A** may be dangerous if not unloaded early.

In hearts, skulduggery commences with the preliminary passing of the three cards to your left, or to your right if players prefer, the direction being optional. While there are some fairly obvious passing procedures, much depends upon the type of competition you are up against, particularly the mood of the player who passes you the three cards he doesn't want and which you may like even less.

You may become so upset at the mere sight of the Black Lady that you will pass her along, with any high hearts you have as well. This is often poor policy if you have four or more cards in these suits (♠ or ♡), including some low ones, that give you a chance to unload the high ones. That's better than having "chickens come home to roost," the Black Lady being "some chicken."

This raises the question of the ♠**A** and ♠**K**, the two most dangerous cards in the pack. Should you pass them along rather than risk being forced to take the ♠**Q** with one of them?

If you hold ♠ **A K Q**, you can pass along the whole kit and caboodle. But if you hold a couple of low spades as well, your suit is long enough to warrant keeping the lot. The ♠**A** and ♠**K** can't hurt you, and you can toss the ♠**Q** on somebody's lead when you have run out of their suit. If you have three, or preferably four, small spades to go with the queen, you can pass along the ace, king, or both–if you have them–putting the man on your left in a difficult situation indeed.

The danger in retaining the ace, king, or queen of spades is almost entirely that of being caught short with a suit of three cards or fewer. But if you shorten your suit still more by passing one of them to the man on your left, you may get stuck with one of the terrible trio (♠ **A K Q**) by the player who passes you three cards from your right.

This takes us to the matter of that player's mood. If he habitually hands you the ace, king, or queen of spades, you may be smart to hold on to such a card and lengthen the suit with any cards that come from him. However, if he never gives you high spades, you are safe in getting rid of yours.

As for the players generally, if they are of the type who open with spade leads and keep repeating them, you will be in trouble if you are short-suited with the ♠**Q** or a higher card without the queen. But some players like to get rid of cards in their own short suits, and others prefer to lead low hearts. In such company you can take longer risks when short on spades.

This brings up two optional rules of play:

One is that no hearts can be led until the second, or even the third, round. Though more or less obsolete, this rule is worthy of consideration, particularly on a third-round basis. It prevents a lucky holder of low hearts from punching away at his less fortunate opponents before they can get rid of other suits.

The other rule concerns the play of the Black Lady. Seasoned players follow the principle that the ♠**Q** must be thrown at the first available chance. This prevents one player from favoring another at the expense of a third player, the sort of thing that might make a shambles out of serious play.

But unrestricted play of the ♠**Q** adds zest to a casual game. It can be used to prevent the high scorer from going out by unloading it on another player instead. It allows one player a chance to get back at another for soaking him in a previous hand.

There is also the problem of penalizing the player who forgets to play the queen. Such oversight is termed a revoke, so that the ♠**Q** counts against the player who inadvertently holds the card too long. It is better, then, to forget the rule and let the players gang up if they choose. As a matter of fact, they are forced to combine their efforts if they include the feature called:

Take All Hearts: Here, the player's purpose is to capture all the hearts and the Black Lady as well, on the basis of a special rule granting him a *deduction* of twenty-six points for taking all, instead of the customary addition. If he falls even one point short, all the hearts he takes are added to his score.

This feature should be agreed upon before the game, but once the take-all rule is incorporated, the player does not have to announce his intention. If he can slip by, so much the better; but the moment the other players notice what is up, they try to grab a heart trick for themselves or toss an odd heart to another player, thus thwarting the effort to take all.

The take-all rule adds interest and intensity to the game and is now generally accepted. But if you want to put still more zing into the game, you can introduce the almost-forgotten variant of:

Pink Lady: The Pink Lady is the queen of hearts. Like the Black Lady, or queen of spades, the queen of hearts also counts thirteen points against the player unfortunate enough to take it. Thus there are thirty-eight adverse points in each hand: thirteen for the ♠**Q**, thirteen for the ♡**Q**, twelve for the remaining hearts. The ◇**J** still deducts ten points from its captor's score.

The introduction of the Pink Lady serves two purposes. It makes the ♡**A** and ♡**K** just as dangerous as the ♠**A** and ♠**K**–in fact, a trifle more so. It also provides a counter to the queen of spades, sometimes giving a player caught with one queen a chance to retaliate by unloading the other.

Far from turning hearts into a wild game, it makes the high hearts all the deadlier and gives the low leads in hearts a poignancy rivaling the low spades. Since the score mounts more rapidly, it is better to play for one hundred than for fifty.

Inclusion of the take-all rule means that the player capturing all hearts and the queen of spades deducts thirty-eight points from his score, registering thirteen minus for the Pink Lady as well as for the Black Lady.

The Widow: When there are four players in a hearts game, the deal comes out even. But with three, five, or six players, odd cards are left over. With three players there is one extra card; with five players, two extras; with six players, four extras. The pack may be equalized by first removing one low club or diamond, or more, but it is preferable to deal the extra card, or cards, face down in the center of the table.

This face-down deal becomes a widow, which goes to the player who takes the first trick. Naturally, he risks getting hearts or the queen of spades, though he also has a chance of picking up the diamond jack. In any case he alone looks at the widow before adding it to the trick that he took. This may give him a slight advantage if he decides to try and take all the hearts.

The widow feature can be incorporated into the four-handed hearts game by dealing twelve cards to each player and four into the widow. In this form the game was originally known as heartsette.

Russian Bank

Originally a form of double solitaire, Russian bank has been developed into a highly popular two-person game demanding sound play and keen observation. Play can best be followed by a step-by-step description introducing the fine points and pitfalls of the game in a somewhat chronological order.

Two packs are used, with contrasting backs so that they can be separated easily after each game. Each player shuffles a pack, and the packs are then exchanged and dealt as follows:

First, a player counts off twelve cards one by one and places them in a face-down pile at his right. This is known as the misery pile, because it can cause exactly that. More technically, it is referred to as the stock.

Next, the player deals off four more cards, laying them face up so that they form a column extending from just beyond the stock toward the opposing player. These two columns–each on a player's right–form a mutual "layout" or "tableau" with a wide space in between.

Each player then puts the remainder of his pack–thirty-six cards in all–face down at his left. While actually the pack, this is more generally styled the hand, because it is played from, like a hand of cards.

First play may go to the player dealing the lowest card in the layout. Assuming that player *X* deals ♡**J**, ♠**4**, ♡**A**, ◇**Q**, and that player *Y* deals ♡**9**, ◇**10**, ♣**A**, ♣**10**, both have dealt aces, which are low in this game, but *X*'s next low card (a four) gives him precedence over *Y* (with nine low).

The layout and the face-down piles appear as follows:

	Y
Stock	*Hand*
♡**9**	◇**Q**
◇**10**	♡**A**
♣**A**	♠**4**
♣**10**	♡**J**
Hand	*Stock*
	X

The central area between the two columns is for the placement of "bases," which are to be built upward, ace, two, three, and so on to king. All cards built upon a base must be of one suit, regardless of which pack they come from, making eight possible bases.

Play to those bases takes priority over all other plays. So player *X* begins by moving the ♡**A** and the ♣**A** into the center. He is then free to make another type of move, the formation of sequences among the layout cards. These are made in descending value and with alternating colors, namely:

Player *X* places the ♣**10** so it overlaps the ♡**J**. He then places the ♡**9** so it overlaps the ♣**10**. The result is the formation of four "spaces" in the layout, which must be filled by fresh cards. Player *X* takes care of this by turning cards face upward on his stock, at the same time remembering the rule that a play upon a base comes first.

Player *X* turns up the ♡**K** and places it in the first space at the left.

He turns up the ♡**3** and places it in sequence with the ♠**4**.

He turns up the ♠**5** and places it in the second space on the right.

He turns up the ♡**8** and places it in the third space on the left.

He turns up the ♣**2**, which belongs on a base (the ♣**A**), so he puts it there.

He turns up the ◇**9** and places it in the fourth space on the left.

He turns up the ♠**6**, which cannot be placed anywhere, so he leaves it on the stock.

The layout, bases, and other piles of cards now appear thus:

	Y	
Stock		*Hand*
♡K	**(♣A) ♡A**	**◇Q**
	♣2	
◇10		**♠5**
♡8		**♠4 ♡3**
◇9		**♡J ♣10 ♡9**
Hand		*Stock*
		♠6
	X	

Since he cannot move the **♠6** from the stock, player *X* has only one remaining play; that is, to turn up the top card of the hand, allowable as a last resort. It proves to be the ♡**2**, so in keeping with the rule of "bases first," he builds it on the ♡**A.** Now he checks the stock to see if this has opened a play from there.

There is none, so he checks the layout and sees that he can build the ♡**3** on the ♡**2,** so he does so. There are no more plays from the layout or from the stock, so *X* must turn up another card from the hand.

X turns up the **♣J.** He puts it on the ◇**Q** and then puts the ◇**10** on the **♣J,** leaving a space. He returns to the stock and moves the **♠6** from there into the space. He turns up the next card of the stock. It is the ♡**7,** offering no play.

Again player *X* turns up the top card of the hand. It is the ◇**10,** with no possible play. So he puts it face up between the hand and the stock, to start a discard or trash pile, from which no plays may be made. That ends *X*'s turn.

The board now stands:

		Y			
Stock			*Hand*		
♡**K**	(♣**A**)	(♡**A**)	◇**Q**	♣**J**	◇**10**
	♣**2**	(♡**2**)			
♠**6**		♡**3**	♠**5**		
♡**8**			♠**4**		
◇**9**			♡**J**	♣**10**	♡**9**
Hand		*Discard*			*Stock*
		◇**10**			♡**7**
		X			

Some important points should be noted here:

If *X* had overlooked his chance to build on a base, as with the ♣**2**, ♡**2**, or ♡**3**, his opponent, *Y*, could have called "Stop," and *X*'s turn would have ended. Any other move would have been illegal and therefore a last move for *X*.

If *X* had failed to notice that the ♣**J** could go from the hand to one of the layout heaps (namely, onto the ◇**Q**) and had laid down the ♣**J** as a discard, *Y* could have called "Stop" and ended *X*'s turn, as discarding is a player's final move. But if *X* had corrected any of those illegal moves before *Y*'s call, *X* could have proceeded with his turn.

If *X* had refused to fill spaces from his stock—say, the ◇**9** or the ♠**6** later on—he would have stopped automatically and it would have been *Y*'s turn to play. However, if he had wanted to keep the ♠**6** on his stock, he could have done so by leaving the ◇**10** in a layout heap of its own, instead of putting the ◇**10** onto the ♣**J**. Then there would have been no space for the ♠**6** to fill.

In short, the shifting of cards from one layout heap to another is optional. It is also confined to the top card of each heap—the one that is lowest in sequence—so that spaces come in useful when transferring cards one by one. This will become more apparent as the game proceeds.

It is now *Y*'s turn to play. First, he exercises a special privilege which is allowable from this point on. He takes the ♡**8** from the layout and puts it on the ♡**7** that is showing on *X*'s stock. *Y* then takes the available ♡**9** from its layout heap and puts that on the ♡**8.** Next, he takes the ◇**9** from the layout and puts it on the ◇**10** that shows on *X*'s discard. He then takes the ◇**10** from its layout heap and puts it on the ◇**9.**

This is called feeding or loading, and a player may feed cards onto his opponent's stock or discard, provided they are in sequence and of the same suit as the card showing there. Such sequences can run either up or down and can reverse direction whenever desired (as with ◇**9** on ◇**10**, then another ◇**10** on ◇**9**).

Y now turns up the top card of his stock. It is the ♡**5**, and he puts it on the ♠**6** in the layout. He moves the ♠**4** onto the ♡**5**, leaving a space. This gives him three spaces in all.

Next, *Y* turns up the ◇**7** on his stock. He puts it in a space. He then moves the ♠**4** to a space and the ♡**5** to a space. This enables him to put the ♠**6** on the ◇**7**, the ♡**5** on the ♠**6**, and the ♠**4** on the ♡**5**.

Another turn up of *Y*'s stock produces the ♣**Q**, *Y* puts the ♣**Q** on the ♡**K**, then moves the ♣**10** to a space, puts the ♡**J** on the ♣**Q** and the ♣**10** on the ♡**J**. There are now four spaces in the layout. But they do not remain long.

In succession *Y* turns up the following cards on his stock: ♣**2**, ♣**4**, ♠**K**, ♡**7**, each going into a space. He turns up the ♣**K** and leaves it on his stock. He then turns up the top card of his hand, which proves to be the ♠**A**, so he places it in the center as a base. *Y* turns up the ◇**4** on his hand and moves it onto the ♠**5**. He then turns up the ♡**8** on his hand and is forced to lay it between the hand and stock as a discard. That ends *Y*'s turn and the board now shows:

Y

Stock	*Discard*		*Hand*
♣K	♡8		
♡K ♣Q ♡J ♣10	(♣A)	(♡A)	♢Q ♣J
	♣2	(♡2)	
		♡3	
♣2	♠A		♠5 ♢4
♣4			♢7 ♠6 ♡5 ♠4
♠K			♡7
Hand	*Discard*		*Stock*
	♢10		♡9
	(♢9)		(♡8)
			(♡7)

X

In his turn *X* retaliates swiftly. Since the ♡**9** is the top card of his stock, he plays it right back where it came from, on the ♣**10** in the layout. He puts the ♡**7** from the layout on *Y*'s discard, which shows the ♡**8**. He then puts the ♡**8** from his stock on the ♡**7** of *Y*'s discard and puts the ♡**7** from his stock on the ♡**8**.

Unfortunately, *X* cannot play the ♢**10** because no play is allowed from the discard. But he has loaded *Y*'s discard very solidly with cards that are sure to stay there. *X* is now ready to turn up the top card of his stock and proceed with his turn.

The play up to this point gives a good idea of Russian bank, and its intricacies increase as the game progresses, often confronting a player with deep problems or neat choices that make it all the more intriguing. For that reason, Russian bank is sometimes played as a four-person game, the two active players (*X* and *Y*) each having a consultant sitting by.

After a player uses up his stock, he turns up cards as required from the hand, until all have been played or put into the discard. He then turns the discard face down and continues to play it as the hand. When a player has disposed of all such cards, he wins the game.

Score for such a win is thirty points, plus two points for each card that an opponent still is holding in his stock, and one point for each card still in the opponent's hand or discard. If neither player is able to dispose of all his holdings, the game is a draw, regardless of how far ahead one player may be.

Russian bank has provided many variations in its course of evolution, but one rule has remained constant; namely, that a card must be built on a base immediately, when so available, and that a card once placed upon a base cannot be brought back to the layout.

In modern practice, however, a card is *not* available for play upon a base if it is in either player's discard. In fact, no play whatever is allowed from a discard pile, until after it has been turned over and converted into a new hand, when it is treated only in that capacity.

Nor can a player use a card from an opponent's stock, even to build on a base. The opportunity must be ignored, though the opponent may be able to use it to advantage when his turn comes up. Such plays were formerly allowable, but have been generally abandoned as detracting from the game.

While the forming of sequences in layout heaps is normally an optional procedure, there are modern rulings that make this compulsory, when circumstances warrant it.

For example, an opponent may demand that a player add to sequences (by putting a lone ♢**5** on a ♣**6**, etc.) in order to provide a space that the player must then fill from his stock.

Also, an opponent may demand that a player shift cards in a layout in order to free a card that may be played upon a base. For example, a base has been built up to ♣**6**. A layout sequence shows ♡**10** ♠**9** ♡**8** ♣**7** ♡**6** ♠**5**. There is another sequence ♠**7** ♢**6**, and also a space. By moving the ♠**5** to the ♢**6** and then moving the ♡**6** into the space, the ♣**7** is freed to be played upon the base represented by the ♣**6**.

It may be asked, why should an opponent want to see a player profit by such a build?

The answer is quite simple: the opponent may be in a position to profit more. Face up on his stock may be the ♣ **8 9 10 J**–the ♣**8** being the card in sight–that were fed there, not long ago, by the player who now does not want to release the ♣**7**, because on his next turn the opponent may unload them.

Such rulings are therefore justifiable, if only because they add to the sportsmanlike quality of the game, which seems to have inspired Russian bank from the outset. Generally, any "demand" ruling that is in keeping with the accepted play and the spirit of the game may be incorporated by common consent.

Minor misplays may be corrected without penalty. This applies to mistakes in the transfer of layout cards, such as putting a ♢**5** on a ♡**6**. A play from the discard can also be called back, or a play from the hand instead of the stock, provided that the player does not put a card upon a base, or overlook such a vital play.

However, if a player should glance at two cards in his turned-down stock, instead of only one, or should turn up a card from the hand before the proper time, his opponent can call a stop then and there.

Certain exceptions are made to this; namely, after a player has once turned up the top card of his stock and has played it, he may turn up the next card of the stock before moving a layout card, even if the layout card must be built upon a base. The reason for this is that the stock card takes precedence over the layout card when the play is compulsory (as onto a base), and where the play is optional the player is entitled to know what is coming up in the stock, before making a layout play.

The other privilege is that of looking through the discard to see what cards it already contains. A player may check his trash pile at any time, provided he lets his opponent have a look at it. But he can't go through his opponent's discard, unless he asks and is granted permission!

Continuation of *X*'s second turn:

Turn up ♢**2** on stock; move into space. Turn up ♢**4** on stock; it remains there, unplayable. Turn up ♠**3** from hand; put on ♢**4** in layout. Move ♢**2** onto ♠**3**. Put ♢**4** from stock into space. Turn up ♣**9** on stock; it remains there, unplayable. Turn up ♢**6** on hand. Put in discard, ending turn.

Y

Stock			*Discard*		*Hand*			
♣**K**			♡**7**					
			(♡**8**)					
			(♡**7**)					
			(♡**8**)					
♡**K**	♣**Q**	♡**J**	(♣**A**)	(♡**A**)	♢**Q**	♣**J**		
♣**10**	♡**9**		♣**2**	(♡**2**)				
				♡**3**				
♣**2**			♠**A**		♠**5**	♢**4**	♠**3**	♢**2**
♣**4**					♢**7**	♠**6**	♡**5**	♠**4**
♣**K**					♢**4**			
Hand			*Discard*		*Stock*			
			♢**6**		♣**9**			
			(♢**10**)					
			(♢**9**)					

X

Y's second turn:

♣**K** unplayable from stock. Turn up ♣**8** from hand and put on ♡**9** in layout. Turn up ♢**3** from hand and put on ♣**4** in layout; then put ♣**2** on ♢**3**, making space.

Put ♣**J** in space; put ♢**Q** on ♠**K**, then ♣**J** on ♢**Q**, making two spaces.

Move ♠**4** and ♡**5** into spaces. Put ♠**4** on ♡**5**; move ♠**6** into space. Put ♢**7** on ♣**8**, then ♠**6** on ♢**7**; again, two spaces. Put ♠**4** in space, ♡**5** on ♠**6**, ♠**4** on ♡**5**, making three spaces.

Move ♣**K** from stock into space. Turn up ♢**2** on stock; move into second space. Turn up ♢**6** on stock; move into third space. Turn up ♡**K** on stock; unplayable, so leave it there. Turn up ♢**9** on hand and put into discard. End of *Y*'s turn.

The board now stands:

				Y					
Stock				*Discard*		*Hand*			
♡K				◊9					
				(♡7)					
				(♡8)					
				(♡7)					
				(♡8)					
♡K	♣Q	♡J	♣10	(♣A)	(♡A)	◊6			
♡9	♣8	◊7	♠6	♣2	(♡2)				
♡5	♠4				♡3				
♣K				♠A		♠5	◊4	♠3	◊2
♣4	◊3	♣2				◊2			
♠K	◊Q	♣J				◊4			
Hand				*Discard*		*Stock*			
				◊6		♣9			
				(◊10)					
				(◊9)					
				X					

Spite and Malice

As a two-person game with elements of solitaire, this comparative newcomer ranks with such stand-bys as multiple Klondike and Russian bank. Two packs of cards are used: One, known as the "pay-off pack," is a standard pack of fifty-two cards, and is divided equally between the two players; while the other pack contains fifty-six cards, being a standard pack plus four jokers, and serves as a mutual pack from which each player draws in turn. This pack is termed the "stock."

The purpose of the game is to dispose of cards by building them into center piles. In building, the cards run in ascending sequence from ace up to king (**A, 2, 3, 4, 5, 6, 7, 8, 9, 10, J, Q, K**). Other cards can be temporarily placed in discard piles; these run in descending sequence from king down. Suits play no part whatever in this game, and jokers are regarded as "wild cards," representing any value that the player chooses.

As preliminary, the pay-off pack is shuffled, and twenty-six cards are dealt to each player, forming two individual pay-off piles. Each player places his pay-off pile to his right and turns its top card face up. Whoever has the higher card plays first, becoming player "A," while his opponent is designated as player "B." If both cards are the same in value, they are turned down, the pay-off piles are shuffled separately, and another card is turned up on each to designate "A" and "B."

The mutual pack (of fifty-six cards) is then shuffled and placed face down near the center of the table to serve as a stock. Player A then draws five cards from the top of the stock, holding their faces toward him as a playing hand. Player B does the same, so that each has a concealed hand of five cards. Play then proceeds as follows:

If an ace is showing on A's pay-off pile, he must place it face up in the center of the table to start a build. He then turns up the next card of his pay-off pile. If he is holding any aces in his hand, he can play them as well, using each to start a center pile; but that is not compulsory except under special circumstances that will be detailed later. If an ace has been played and a two is the top card of A's pay-off pile, he must build it on the ace. Similarly, if he has a two in his hand, he can build it on an ace, though that is not compulsory as yet.

Beyond that, all builds are optional, all the way up to king. Generally speaking, the more builds the better, but there are times when it is profitable to block a build, which is an intriguing feature of the game. If player A is able to play all the cards in his hand—as occasionally happens—he draws five more from the stock and continues as long as he can, or as long as he wants. In any case, he completes his turn by laying an odd card from his hand face up in front of him, to begin a discard pile. He then draws enough cards from the stock to replenish his hand to its original five, so he will be ready for his next turn.

Player B proceeds in exactly the same fashion, either making new builds or adding cards to builds begun by A. He also makes a discard to complete his turn and draws enough cards from the stock to restore his original quota of five. Play then reverts to player A.

However, as the play proceeds, new factors enter. In discarding at the end of his turn, a player has two privileges: he can start a new discard pile, with a limit of four in all; or he can discard a card of the same value on one already discarded—as a nine on a nine—or a card in descending sequence on one already discarded, as an eight on a nine.

He also can build from any discard pile directly on a center pile, just as from his hand or from his pay-off pile. Thus, as a discard pile increases in size, a player may often extend his turn by that many cards. Example: After several turns, a player has discarded on one pile in the following order: **9**, **8**, **7**, **6**, **5**. He happens to draw a four, and on his coming turn he plays it on a three that is showing on a center pile. He can then build **5**, **6**, **7**, **8**, **9** in order from his discard pile.

Often, however, a player may prefer to interrupt such a sequence by building from his hand, since that enables him to draw another card from the stock. (Example: Having built a five and a six from the discard pile, the player might build a seven from his hand, letting the eight and nine wait until later.) Even better is a build from the player's pay-off pile, as his ultimate objective is to play out his entire pay-off pile and thereby become the winner.

When the stock has been reduced through continued drawing so that it contains only a few cards, play is suspended, and any center heaps that have been built up to kings are gathered and thoroughly shuffled along with the stock, which again becomes the mutual pile from which the players draw. Occasionally, the stock may run out before any center piles reach the king state. In that case, all center piles are gathered and shuffled to form a stock. Once the stock has been replenished, it will usually contain cards that originally came from the pay-off piles, but that does not matter.

Since jokers are wild, they can be used in both building and discarding. In building, assuming that a player needs a four but has none, he can play a joker instead, calling it a four and continuing the build from there. In discarding, he simply places a joker on any discard pile he wants and specifies its value later. For example, if he placed the joker on a nine and later decided to discard another nine, he could call the joker a nine in order to place the nine upon it. Or he could call it either a nine or an eight in order to discard an eight on it. Or by calling it simply an eight, he could discard a seven on it. A joker can also be discarded on a joker. Thus, in the example just given, three cards, running nine, joker, joker, could be regarded as **9 9 9**, **9 9 8**, **9 8 8**, or **9 8 7**.

When a joker is uppermost on a discard pile, it can be built on a center pile just as if it came directly from the player's hand. Being no longer functioning as a discard, it becomes wild again and can be valued as anything from ace up to king. But once used in a build, a joker's status cannot be changed until after it has been shuffled back into the stock, when it becomes a wild card for whichever player draws it later.

If a player is unable to make a build or a discard, his hand becomes "frozen" and play reverts to his opponent, who sometimes may take turn after turn while the player with the frozen hand remains idle. It is often an advantage for a hand to be frozen, as an opponent may then play certain cards that he might otherwise withhold. Hence a player is allowed to freeze his hand purposely by simply refusing to build or discard, unless he has an ace showing on his pay-off pile; or a playable two on either his pay-off pile or one of his discard piles. He does not have to build an ace or a two from his concealed hand, unless both he and his opponent are frozen. In that case, each, in proper turn, can demand that the other build an ace or a two from his hand, if he can.

Summarized: Each player, in turn, can build any available cards from his hand, his pay-off pile, or a discard pile, making all such builds in the center; and a player can end his turn by making a single discard from his hand. No other plays or transfers of cards are allowable. At no time is a player forced to build or discard a joker.

A player's ultimate object is to dispose of his pay-off pile by utilizing all of its twenty-six cards in center builds. His opponent's pay-off pile is then counted, and the winner is scored one point for each card remaining there. In case both hands become frozen so that no further play is possible, whether purposely or not, the pay-off piles are left exactly as they are, while all other cards—hands, discards, center piles, and stock—are gathered together, thoroughly shuffled, and placed face down as a mutual pack. From this new stock, each player, according to his turn, draws five cards, and play proceeds exactly as when the game started, the only difference being that the stock is larger and the pay-off piles are smaller than originally.

Poker: The Hands

The Great American Game of poker once required a standard pack of cards, some chips or similar tokens, a stout table, sturdy chairs, and slightly optional equipment in the form of green eye-shades and a smoke-filled room. But this long-familiar setting has been going into oblivion while the new poker has emerged as a social pastime and a form of family fun. Yet, despite many innovations and casual ways of play, the game has maintained its basic structure.

The idea still is to outbluff or outguess your opponents, unless you prefer simply to outstay them by coming up with a better hand than any of them can produce.

The customary poker hand consists of five cards from a standard fifty-two-card pack. Each hand is valued according to certain groups or combinations of cards that it contains. Through the years certain hands have gained recognition and have stood the test of time and countless games.

In order of importance, these are the hands:

THE ROYAL FLUSH

♠ A K Q J 10

This is formed from the five highest cards in one suit, a sequence headed by the ace; it is a straight flush, the highest of its kind. The chance of getting such a hand in a five-card deal is 1 in 649,740.

If two players held a royal flush, neither suit would rate higher, as there is no suit precedence in poker. Actually, it has never been known to happen. Following the royal flush comes

THE STRAIGHT FLUSH

♡ **K Q J 10 9** ♣ **10 9 8 7 6**

The king-high straight flush shown at the left is one step below a royal flush. It outranks the ten-high straight flush shown on the right. Because the chance of being dealt a straight flush is 1 in 64,974, there is seldom any competition between them.

Next in order of rarity is

FOUR OF A KIND

J J J J 3 7 7 7 7 10

The higher group of four of a kind wins over the lower if two players hold these hands at the same time. It isn't likely, however, as the chance of being dealt four of a kind is 1 in 4165.

Next in line is

THE FULL HOUSE

A A A 3 3 5 5 5 K K

This hand, sometimes called a full hand, contains two combinations, three of a kind and a pair. The triplets are more important than the pairs, and a full house with "aces up" is therefore top in its category. The accompanying pair (of threes) is important only because it fills the hand.

The other full house is simply fives up, and the pair of kings that supplies the "fill" might just as well be a pair of fours. Although full houses are fairly rare, they occasionally encounter competition, and sharp players are prepared for it. Chances of being dealt a full house are 1 in 694.

And now, in order of scarcity, comes

THE FLUSH

♣ A 7 5 3 2 ♠ K Q 10 9 7

Here, the emphasis is on suits again. A flush is a fairly rare hand and a strong one. When two come into conflict, the one with the highest card wins.

◇ 10 8 7 4 3 ♡ 10 8 7 4 2

Here, the hands match card by card until the fifth or lowest, which enables the diamond flush to win over the heart flush. Chances of being dealt a flush are 1 in 509.

Next in value is

THE STRAIGHT

♠A ♡K ♡Q ♠J ♣10 ♠5 ♡4 ♡3 ♣2 ♡A

This is a sequence of cards in mixed suits. The highest card determines the winner of two straights. An ace-high straight, shown at the left, takes precedence over a king-high. The five-high shown at the right is possible because an ace may be classed as low to complete a straight.

There is 1 chance in 255 of receiving a straight in a deal of five cards.

Next in order is

THREE OF A KIND

♠A ♡A ◇A ♡9 ♣7 ♠3 ♡3 ◇3 ♣K ◇10

This is a hand containing three cards of the same rank, with two extra cards. Three aces win over any other combination in this group, such as the three threes shown here.

Chances of being dealt triplets are 1 in 47, so there is more competition between two hands of this variety than between those of higher value.

TWO PAIR

♡A ◇A ♠5 ◇5 ♣7

◇K ♣K ♡J ♣J ♠3 ♠K ♡K ♠9 ◇9 ♣Q

♣10 ♠10 ♡6 ♠6 ◇4 ◇10 ♡10 ♣6 ◇6 ♣3

This type of hand contains two separate pairs, with an odd card as the fifth. Competition is sharp in this bracket as a player has a 1-in-21 chance of being dealt such a hand.

The top pair determines the winning hand, one with aces up rating higher than kings up. In competitive hands topped by identical pairs, as those with kings up shown here, the lower pair decides the winner, kings over jacks beating kings over nines.

If both pairs are alike, as shown in the hands with tens over sixes, the odd card is the deciding factor, the ◇**4** bringing a win over the ♣**3**.

The lowest regular combination is

ONE PAIR

♠A ♡A ♠6 ◇5 ♣3 ♡J ◇J ♣A ◇K ♡Q

♠9 ◇9 ♠10 ♡8 ♠6 ♣9 ◇9 ♣10 ◇8 ♠3

These hands each contain a matched pair of cards, nothing else. A pair of aces wins over a hand containing a lower pair, for example, the jacks shown. A pair of jacks is significant, however, as in some games "jacks or better" are required as "openers."

In two hands containing equal pairs the highest odd card decides the winner; then the next, and finally the last. This is shown in the two hands containing a pair of nines. The ♠**6** puts its hand above the one with the ♠**3**.

Chances of being dealt a single pair run about 1 in every 2½ hands.

HIGH CARD

♣A ♠K ♡Q ♠J ♢9 ♡7 ♡5 ♣4 ♢3 ♠2

Approximately 50 per cent of the hands dealt in a regular poker game are lacking in any combination, even the smallest pair.

The hands above are rated according to their highest cards. The hand shown at the left is the best possible ace-high hand, and any hand headed by an ace tops a hand headed by a king or lower. A king-high takes precedence over a queen-high and so on, down the line.

The lowest possible poker hand is shown at the right, a seven-high hand with its next best card a five.

Draw Poker

In straight poker, the great-great-granddaddy of the modern game, players were dealt five cards each, and after looking at their hands they proceeded to bet and bluff it out to the limit of their capacity. Later, the "draw" was introduced, each player being allowed to discard unwanted cards and draw other cards from the top of the pack as replacements.

This added a double zest to the game. It gave a weak hand a chance to become a strong one. It also gave players a general idea of one another's holdings as well as their possibilities of improvement from the draw. These factors, in turn, furnished new bluffing prospects, and draw poker soon became the standard version of the game. It is still generally regarded as such, and many variations have stemmed directly from it.

Draw poker is played as follows:

Each player contributes a chip as an "ante" to a pool that is termed the "pot." Or, if preferred, the dealer may ante for everybody, as the deal changes after each hand, and it amounts to the same thing in the long run.

Cards are now dealt singly to each player in rotation until each player has five cards, all face down. The players look at their hands and the player at the dealer's left has the privilege of "opening" the pot for betting by putting in one or more chips. If he prefers he may pass, and the privilege of opening then goes to the next player on the left. If all pass, the hands are thrown in. A new ante is made and the deal moves to the next player.

When a pot is opened, each player in turn has the following options:

1. He may "drop out" or "fold" simply by tossing in his hand, face down.

2. He may "call" or "stay" by putting up an equal number of chips.

3. He may "raise" or "bump" the pot by putting up the required chips plus an additional number of his own.

After a raise, each successive player must put up the additional number of chips in order to stay. Otherwise he must drop out, unless he has already done so. If a player wishes, he can make a further raise of his own, forcing the others to put up that much more if they want to stay in the pot.

For example, suppose that in a five-handed game player *A* passes; *B* opens for two chips; *C* drops out; *D* raises, by putting in two chips to match *B*'s and adding two more of his own; and *E* raises two more by putting in four chips to match *B* and *D* and adding two more, making six in all.

To stay in the hand, *A* must then put up six chips, in order to call the initial bet and the two raises; *B* would have to put up four chips to call, bringing his total to six; *D* would have to put up two to call, making six.

Note that *A* is allowed to stay, because he passed before the pot was opened, whereas *C* dropped out and therefore could not come back into the betting. Any of the three players who stayed, *A, B,* or *D,* could have raised *E*'s bet instead of just calling it; then the betting would have continued around again.

A player may raise as often as he wants, until all the players have called, following his raise. This means that any raise must be raised again by another player before the first player can raise again.

The players who stayed are now entitled to draw. The first such player on the dealer's left states how many cards he wants, laying that many face down from his hand. He does not actually draw cards; the required number is dealt to him face down by the dealer. The next eligible player is then served, and so on, until all have drawn. If a player wishes, he can "stand pat" by retaining his original cards and doing without replacements.

The betting is then resumed, starting with the player who opened the pot. He has the same original privileges, but in a slightly different form. He may start the betting by putting some chips into the pot, just as when he opened, or he may "check" the bet by leaving it up to the next player.

Once a player bets, the succeeding players must fold, call, or raise until finally, when all bets have been called, the surviving players lay their hands face up on the table. This is called the "showdown" and the highest hand wins the pot. In the case of two equal hands, the pot is split, each player taking half.

If all players simply check, the showdown follows in the usual fashion; but if all drop out except the biggest better, he automatically wins the pot and does not have to show his hand. This is an advantage after winning a pot by a bluff, as the other players do not learn how easily the winner took it.

BETTING METHODS AND LIMITS

When poker is played as a social game, three factors enter into the betting: the ante, the minimum bet, and, most important, the limit.

In perhaps the most rudimentary form of penny ante, these can all be one and the same. Each player makes an ante of one chip; an opening bet must be one chip and no more, and a raise is limited to a single chip.

It is more usual, however, to operate on a "one-two" basis, with one chip the lowest bet allowed, but with two chips as the limit for a bet or raise.

This is the essence of the "five-ten" game, perhaps the most popular form of poker. Assuming each chip to be worth five units, the ante could be set at five and the bets would necessarily be either five or ten.

But with each chip valued as a unit, the ante could be set as low as one or placed at any variable figure; and the bets could run anywhere from five to ten.

This would apply whether the units were mills, cents, dimes, dollars, or eagles. Similarly, a game with a five-ten limit can be jumped to ten-twenty or twenty-forty, and so on, without losing its basic characteristics.

Some players prefer to set a high ante but a low betting minimum, as this encourages more players to stay in the hand and take longer chances on the draw. The pot is large to begin with and coming in may be cheap, but they may regret it when others begin to bump the pot!

Sometimes, in a five-ten game, the *lower* figure signifies the betting limit *before* the draw, while the *higher* figure applies *after* the draw. But usually three figures are named in such a game. For example, five–ten–twenty-five would mean that a player would have to bet at least five units, but could not go more than ten, *before* the draw. *After* the draw his minimum bet would be ten units, and he could go as high as twenty-five if he preferred.

In low-limit games it is often wise to restrict the number of raises in a single betting round, before or after the draw. Each player, for example, can be allowed only three raises until there are only two players left in the hand. Then, it does not matter, as either can call the other without having someone else raise again.

This prevents players from raising wildly, just to increase the pots and bring more "action," as they term it. With two such players constantly raising each other, conservative players are forced to overbet their hands, which defeats the very purpose of the limit. Restriction of raises prevents this.

JACK POTS

Today, most games of draw poker include a jack-pot ruling: the player who opens must hold a pair of jacks or something better. This livens the game by forcing it to a higher level, and it increases the pot whenever a hand is dropped because no one can open, as a new ante then follows.

However, a player does not have to open even if he holds the required cards. Thus a player who is "under the guns," directly at the dealer's left, may pass with a strong hand and let someone else open. This gives the player who "laid back" a good opportunity to make an immediate raise, which is something like a bluff in reverse.

Upon opening a pot, a player should keep his discards separate from those of the other players, either by placing them under his own chips or beneath those in the pot. This enables him to "split" his openers if he so desires. Suppose, for example, he holds

♣J ♢J ♣10 ♡9 ♡8

The two jacks give him the privilege of opening, but if he discards one, he may draw a queen or a seven to complete an "open-end" straight. Later, however, he may be asked to show his openers, which a player must always do at the end of a hand. Hence he would need the discarded jack to show that he opened legitimately. By having it handy, he does not need to announce at the start that he has split his openers. By keeping that fact to himself, he may cause other players to suppose that he opened with two pair and is drawing one card in hope of filling a full house. They are then unlikely to suspect that he is actually going after a straight.

In progressive jack pots, after a hand is passed, a pair of queens becomes the minimum opener; after another pass, kings; then aces, and finally two pair if the participants decide to carry it that far. After a pot is opened, the next deal goes back to a pair of jacks as the opening requirement.

TYPES OF DRAW

If a player should hold a hand with no prospects whatever, he would be apt to make a five-card draw, calling for an all-new hand. Or he might hold a high card and make a four-card draw. In some circles, draws of more than three cards are outlawed; and in any circle, a four- or five-card draw gives away the fact that the hand does not even contain a pair.

Working from low hands up, the customary draws are as follows:

High Card: Typical hand: **♣A ♢10 ♣9 ♡7 ♠3**

A four-card draw is commonest, when allowable, on the chance of matching the high card to form a pair, which should happen in about 1 out of 4 times. There is, of course, a long-shot possibility of getting something better. But, except in certain games or circumstances, this is an unwise draw.

A three-card draw made when one does not have a pair reduces chances of improving the high card to about 1 out of 5; this also may be unwise, but it does have some bluffing value, as other players may think the hand holds a pair.

With two high cards, as in ♡**A** ◇**K** ♣**9** ♠**5** ♠**4**, the chances of making one pair or the other are about 1 in 2½ times, with the same bluffing potential; but neither is a good draw, normally.

One Pair: Preferably high, as ♠**Q** ◇**Q** ♡**8** ♣**7** ♠**3** A three-card draw gives about 1 out of 3½ chances of improvement, making this a standard draw. Two pair will occur in about 1 out of 6 times; three of a kind, in about 1 out of 9. Long-shot possibilities are a full house or four of a kind. This draw has no bluffing value. It is tagged the moment it is made.

A two-card draw may be used with ♣**9** ◇**9** ♠**A** ♣**10** ◇**4**. Here, the player keeps his pair and the high card–an ace in this case–as a third card, or "kicker." He has slightly less chance of improvement–about 1 out of 4–but if he makes his two pair, it will probably be big enough to beat any opposing hand of that type.

Chances for making three of a kind are lessened; so are the long-shot prospects of a full house or four of a kind. But this two-card draw gives the hand a strong bluffing value, as opponents might think the player holds three of a kind. If he makes two pair, the hand is strong enough to bet; and if he gets triplets, so much the better.

Two Pair: ♣**A** ♡**A** ♡**Q** ◇**Q** ♠**5** or ♡**6** ◇**6** ♡**3** ♣**3** ♠**4** A one-card draw is the only solidly established procedure with hands like those shown here. Though there is only about 1 chance out of 12 that two pair can be improved, the result, when it does come through, brings the player a full house, which is a next-to-sure winner in practically any standard game of draw poker.

Standing pat, or drawing no cards at all, is a device employed occasionally by players holding two pair, particularly with aces up, like the hand shown at the left. Assuming that two or three players have each drawn three cards, the man with the high two pair reasons thus:

If he stands pat, his hand will still be strong enough to beat a "small" two pair, like the sample shown at the right, with its sixes over threes. But if one of the players happens to get a low three of a kind (as ♡**7** ♣**7** ◇**7**) he may be afraid to bet it against the pat hand.

This provides a strong bluff angle, which would be lost if the holder of the high two pair had made a one-card draw on the unlikely prospect of filling a full house.

A three-card draw is a desperation move by a player who has started with a low two pair, like the example on the right, and suddenly feels certain that another player is holding a higher two pair, like those in the hand on the left.

So he discards his lower pair (♡**3** and ♣**3**) and the odd card with them, drawing to the higher pair (♡6 ◇6) in the hope of getting three of a kind. This kind of draw should be avoided. Chances of triplets are 1 out of 9, which isn't much better than the 1 out of 12 possibility for a full house if the player draws to his small two pair.

Three of a Kind: ♡**K** ◇**K** ♣**K** ♡**5** ♠**3**

A two-card draw is the best for improving a hand of this type; it offers about 1 chance out of 16 of getting a full house and about 1 out of 24 of making four of a kind. However, because it affords no bluffing angle, many players prefer a one-card draw, holding the higher of the two odd cards (♡**5**) as kicker. This offers a slightly better chance of filling a full house; the chance of getting four of a kind is cut in half, but that doesn't matter if the one-card draw fools other players into thinking that you hold two pair instead of triplets. They may try to beat you with a big two pair or smaller triplets than yours. Or they may call you, thinking that you are bluffing on a straight or flush that you didn't fill.

In any case the high triplets are apt to be the "sleeper" that turns out winner. "Filling" the full house is, of course, an almost certain clincher.

Four Straight: ♣**10** ♠**9** ◇**8** ♣**7** ♡**3**
or ♡**K** ♣**Q** ♡**10** ◇**9** ♣**4**

A one-card draw is the only answer here. It's simply a case of discarding the odd card (♡**3** or ♣**4**) on the chance of picking up a card that will turn an otherwise worthless hand into a solid straight. That is, provided it is worth going after at all.

In the first example, the sequence **10 9 8 7** represents what is commonly styled an "open-end straight," because it can be formed into a straight by adding a card at either end (jack or six). The chance of doing that is about 1 out of 6. In certain low-limit games it is a worthwhile chance.

The second example shows an "inside straight" where the fill requires a jack and nothing else. That's about 1 out of 12 chances and the proper poker procedure is to pass it up as too great a risk.

Four Flush: **♣K ♣J ♣8 ♣5 ♡Q**

A one-card draw–as replacement for the ♡**Q**–is the one opportunity. It offers nearly 1 chance out of 5 of filling the flush, which is better than the chances for a straight. This may seem odd, considering that a flush rates above a straight; but that is because a flush is harder to acquire in the first place. Again, it's a question whether such a draw is worth the risk. That depends upon the size and type of the game.

Straight: **♣J ♡10 ♡9 ♠8 ♣7**

Standing pat is the only thing for a player to do in a case like this. He has the hand, so he lets the opponents worry about whether or not he holds it and how good it may be. The same applies to a

Flush: **♡J ♡10 ♡6 ♡4 ♡3**

Standing pat–with no draw–is the only policy here. An identical situation exists with a

Full House: **♢5 ♡5 ♣5 ♠3 ♢3**

Stand pat. You can't do better. As with the previous two hands, there is no chance to bluff, unless you can kid the opposition into thinking that you are betting on nothing. However, a rift in the clouds occurs with

Four of a Kind: **♡7 ♢7 ♣7 ♠7 ♡3**

A one-card draw is usual with such a hand. It is a case of throwing away the ♡**3** and picking up something else. Why? The something else can't possibly make any difference. But that is just the difference it can make.

It gives the impression that this may be a two-pair hand, which in a sense it is: "two pair–both sevens." It could also be assumed to be a frustrated straight or flush. In short, it might be a lot less than what it really is, a practically sure hand. So you should bluff with the one-card draw unless you have good reason to stand pat, without a draw. Standing pat is an open announcement of a good hand, such as a straight, a flush, or even a full house. If you think another player is holding one of these, particularly a full house, you should stand pat with four of a kind, hoping he will convince himself that his pat hand is better than yours.

Possible Straight Flush: **♡6 ♡5 ♡4 ♡3 ♠A**

A one-card draw is the right thing here, with 1 chance out of 3 of making *one* of these hands: a straight, a flush, or, more seldom, a straight flush. Discard the **♠A** and hope for a seven or a two, particularly in hearts—or for a heart, particularly a seven or a two.

The chance is only 1 out of 4 with holdings like these:

♣9 ♣8 ♣6 ♣5 ♡K or **◇A ◇K ◇Q ◇J ♠7**

But these are still good hands for a one-card draw after discarding the odd card. The hand on the right has four parts toward a royal flush, even though the chances are nearly 50 to 1 against making it. But the straight and flush possibilities make it a good draw in most circumstances.

Straight Flush: **♠ J 10 9 8 7**

Standing pat is the procedure with this hand; it is complete, without need of a draw. The same applies to a royal flush, the top hand in this category.

A HAND OF DRAW POKER

Here is a game of poker with five players, illustrating how they might bet their respective hands:

First Player: **♣K ♡K ♠8 ♡8 ◇9**

Assuming that a pair of jacks or better is the opening requirement, the first player opens on the strength of his two pair. In a game with a five-ten limit he could wager up to five chips or units, prior to the draw. He opens with five.

Second Player: ♡J ♡9 ♡8 ♡3 ♣5

Holding a four flush that might be filled with a one-card draw, this player decides to stay and puts up five chips for the privilege.

Third Player: ♣J ♢J ♠J ♡10 ♠3

With three jacks this player definitely stays. Though he feels he has the best hand, he does not raise–as yet. He prefers to encourage competition.

Fourth Player: ♡7 ♢7 ♡6 ♣6 ♠A

With his small two pair this player wants to drive out others. He figures that the first player opened on a high pair, such as aces or kings, and that the second and third may each hold a low pair or be banking on the chance of filling a straight or flush. If they drop out, the fourth player may make his two pair good; if they stay, one of them might beat him with a lucky draw. So he raises by putting in ten chips.

Fifth Player: ♡Q ♣9 ♡5 ♣4 ♢2

This hand has nothing, so the player simply folds and tosses in his hand, face down.

That brings the betting back to the first player, who announces that he will bump the fourth player's raise by raising it again. He puts in five to match the raise and then five more, making fifteen, including his opening bet.

The second player still decides to stay. He has already contributed five chips; now he adds ten more, to match the two raises. The third player decides to stay and puts up the same number.

The fourth player is worried now, because even the double raise didn't drive out the competition. He wonders if the first player raised on a pair of aces, as some players do. He wants to know what possibilities the second and third players are banking on, so he simply stays by putting in five chips to meet the first player's raise.

Now comes the draw:

The first player takes one card. Since he opened, he must have a pair of jacks or better, so the fact that he bumped a raise would indicate that he probably has a high two pair (which is the case). But if he opened on three of a kind, he would be very smart to hold an odd card with them, making his hand look weaker than it is; that prospect should not be discounted by the other players.

There is a very slight possibility that he holds four of a kind or that he is splitting an opening pair, such as jacks or queens, to go after a possible straight or flush. More likely he would have bumped on a pair of aces, hoping to catch a small pair or a third ace to beat the fourth player's probable two pair.

The second player draws one card, signifying a possible two pair, but with such a holding he might have raised the first player immediately after he opened. The same could apply even more strongly if the second player is holding three of a kind, with an odd card. So it seems pretty sure that he must be going after a straight or a flush (actually, he is going after the latter).

The third player draws one card, creating exactly the same impression as the second player, which is what he wants to do. Under many circumstances a two-card draw would be preferable, but here, where everybody else appears to have two pair, or to be hoping to fill a straight or a flush, he might as well get in the act, thus hiding his real colors.

The fourth player is in a quandary. He is sure the first player has a higher two pair than his. Either the second or the third player may also have him beaten, or may fill a straight or flush. He discards his ace and draws one card, hoping for a full house.

Assuming that none of the hands was improved, the betting might proceed thus:

First Player: Bets the limit of ten chips–allowable after the draw–hoping his two pair with kings up will be strong enough to win.

Second Player: Folds his hand, as he failed to fill his flush.

Third Player: Raises the first player ten, by putting in twenty chips. He correctly figures that the first and fourth players each hold two pair, which his triplets can beat.

Fourth Player: Correctly figures first player for a higher two pair than his own. So he folds his hand, without worrying about what the third player holds.

Now it is back to the first player: though he is now almost sure the third player holds a better hand than his, the first player calls by putting ten chips in the pot. The hands are shown and the three jacks held by the third player take the pot, defeating the two pair held by the first player.

In theory it is sound policy either to raise or drop but not to call. Often, chips are simply wasted by players who insist upon "seeing" an opponent's hand when common sense indicates that they are beaten. But in games with a low limit, a call may be advisable just as a safeguard against a cheap bluff.

With a higher limit the situation changes. Suppose that this had been a five–twenty-five game and the fifth player had decided to stay with his entirely worthless hand. Then, suppose that after the others had drawn one card each, the fifth player had announced that he was standing pat and drawing none. To give it authority, he would then have bet the limit of twenty-five units.

The fifth player would have been taking a chance that all the others, figuring that he held a pat straight or better, would drop out. If their hands had been weaker than they were, they might have done just that rather than throw away chips when faced by such a strong hand.

If that had happened, the fifth player would have taken the pot with a hand that had nothing. Bluff would have succeeded where cards failed. The higher the limit, the better the chances of bluffing, a fact that accounts for the many stories of fantastic bluffs in the no-limit days of yore.

Today, bluffing is more a matter of psychology than nerve. They say it's easier to bluff a skilled poker player than a tyro, which is true, as long as the beginner knows nothing about the odds. But let the beginner gain the right smattering of ignorance, and he becomes a sitting duck who can be bluffed over and over by the same stratagem.

As an example, take a player who never bets if he doesn't improve a pair of openers (as ♡**K** ◇**K**) but always checks by leaving it up to the next player, which is allowable in some games. If such a player has shown a proclivity for dropping when raised by someone who made a one-card draw, he will be mousetrapped every time. A shrewd opponent who drew to a "bobtail" straight (♡**9** ♠**8** ♡**7** ◇**6**) and missed will simply bet the limit, as if he had made it. The timid player will then fold with his pair.

In a casual low-limit game many players will stay with a small pair–tens or lower–which is helpful in a way to the man who opened. Statistics support an old poker adage that "whoever goes in best is most likely to come out best." The times that your pair of jacks loses to someone who began with less are outweighed by the times your jacks come through.

Provided, of course, that your pair *is* the best going in. That is why many players won't open on a pair of jacks except when practically everyone ahead of them has passed. If you are dealer in a five- or six-handed game, you are generally safe when opening on jacks.

By that same rule, however, some players won't open on less than a pair of aces when sitting just to the dealer's left. They want kings if seated second or third, and queens a place or two beyond that. So, as dealer, you might open a six-handed game on a pair of jacks and find yourself chagrined as well as beaten by the first player with kings and the second player with queens.

Similarly, if you rigidly require a pair of aces to open as first player, everybody with a pair of kings, queens, or jacks will fold, knowing you have them beaten. It will bring you a cheap pot, but it may be smarter to coax them in, at the cost of extra chips on their part. That can be done by passing with a pair of aces, on the chance that another player will open.

Much depends on your analysis of the ways and idiosyncrasies of the opposing players and on their analysis of yours. That's poker, and in carefree company it plays a bigger part than the law of probabilities.

For instance, in a serious, high-limit game a player may throw away an open-end straight or a four flush, rather than try to fill it. He figures thus: it will cost him one chip to win three if three other players stay and he fills his straight or flush and wins the pot. But his chance of filling is only 1 out of 6 for a straight and about 1 out of 5 for a flush. So it is not worth the risk, where big money is concerned.

But in a loose, low-limit game, played chiefly for fun, most players will stay on a bobtail straight or a four flush, because the cost is low. This not only makes it a cheap investment, but causes other players to stay on equally doubtful hands. So the filling of a straight or flush is generally profitable. However, there is more chance of someone else filling a similar—and perhaps higher—hand of this type, since more are going after such long-shot prospects.

In a tight, high-limit game even a low straight is a likely winner against other one-card draws, which are usually two pairs or triplets with a kicker. But in a loose, low-limit game, a high flush is often required to beat other players who drew one card and filled their straights or flushes.

Paradoxically, a tight game can become too tight for comfort; a loose game, too loose for safety. So look for the middle course and then avoid it. Find the trend and follow it.

Various measures have been introduced to loosen or liven up a friendly poker game. When the session is undermanned—say with only three or four players instead of five or six—the best policy is to strip the pack of its lower cards—twos, threes, and fours.

With a forty-card deck the initial hands run better and the chances of improving them are also increased, except with flushes, where the draw remains proportionately the same. In the case of a low straight the ace comes directly below the lowest card remaining in the pack: **♣8 ♢7 ♣6 ♠5 ♠A**

The more popular procedure, however, regardless of the number of players, is to switch to the game of draw poker with deuces wild.

Draw Poker with Deuces Wild

Here, the full fifty-two-card pack is customarily used, but each deuce is given the status of a wild card, which means that it may represent any card that the player desires. Yet, far from being a freakish game, deuces wild falls into established patterns that are reasonably predictable, although they upset the more common probabilities.

Most important is the fact that the winning prospects of a hand depend primarily upon the number of deuces that it contains. As the top example:

♣2 ♢2 ♡2 ♠2 ♢6

This hand contains four deuces and therefore rates as five of a kind, which in deuces wild is a special category, ranking higher than a royal flush. In this instance it stands for five sixes, one deuce representing a six in an unnamed or imaginary suit, while the other three deuces are regarded as the ♡**6** ♣**6** ♠**6** or their equivalent.

Chances of being dealt such a hand are 1 in 54,145, and if it ever does occur, it can be played as is, or the odd card can be discarded and a one-card draw made to the four deuces. Either way the hand is unbeatable, because it contains all the deuces and therefore no other player can possibly hold five of a kind.

If a player should be lucky enough to gain all four deuces as the result of a draw, he should back the hand to the limit, as it is a sure winner.

On an average of 1 in 624 hands a player will receive three deuces in the deal, giving him a hand such as:

♡2 ♣2 ♢2 ♣K ♠7

Such a hand is automatically rated as four of a kind, in this case four kings. The usual procedure is to discard the odd card (♠**7**) and draw one, in the hope of improving the hand to the status of a straight flush (by drawing ♣**A**, ♣**Q**, ♣**J**, ♣**10**, or

♣9) or, better still, five of a kind (by drawing **♠2**, **♢K**, **♡K**, or **♠K**).

Some players prefer to discard the two odd cards (particularly if both are low in value (as **♣8** and **♠4**) and then draw to the three deuces. This gives a double chance of catching the fourth or "case" deuce, and the hand is sure to be four of a kind or better, no matter what comes in the draw.

A hand containing three deuces can usually be played as a sure winner following the draw, as chances are slight that an opponent will hold four of a kind or better with only one available deuce.

Be sure to study each hand carefully before the draw, in order to rate it at full value, as with

♣2 ♡2 ♠2 ♡9 ♡5

This hand is actually a straight flush (**♡ 9 8 7 6 5**), with the deuces representing the in-between cards. No draw is necessary, as the hand is already better than any four of a kind.

With a hand containing two deuces, competition becomes keener, but the odds are still strongly in your favor. You know for a certainty that no other player can hold more deuces than you do, and probably they hold fewer or none. With two deuces you are sure of three of a kind; for example

♡2 ♢2 ♢A ♣9 ♡5

Here, the hand already rates three aces, so the best plan is to discard the **♣9** and **♡5** and draw two cards, hoping to hit four or five aces or whatever long-shot combinations the draw may bring. If the hand contains nothing as high as an ace or king, some players prefer to draw three cards to the pair of deuces, as this gives them more chance to catch a third deuce.

There are also hands that offer special opportunities, and should be played accordingly, such as

♡2 ♣2 ♡9 ♡7 ♣4

By simply discarding the **♣4**, a one-card draw provides the following prospects:

Any of seven cards (**♣2 ♠2 ♡ J 10 8 6 5**) will bring a

straight flush. Six cards (**♣9 ♠9 ◇9 ♣7 ♠7 ◇7**) will make four of a kind. Five cards (♡ **A K Q 4 3**) will fill a flush. Any of fifteen cards (**♠ ♣ ◇ J 10 8 6 5**) will produce a straight.

Added up, there are 33 chances in 47–about 2 out of 3–that the hand will bring something better than three of a kind. When you hold two deuces, there often are such possibilities, so it is wise to be on the watch for them.

After the draw a hand with two deuces has a good chance of winning if it rates as three aces or better, but be wary of opponents who make a one-card draw. The reason for this becomes apparent when we study the possibilities of hands containing a single deuce, as:

◇2 ♠Q ◇10 ♣8 ♠4

Here, one player might hold the deuce and the high card (**♠Q**) and draw three to see what it would bring. But another might simply discard the **♠4** and try to fill a queen-high straight. In ordinary draw poker there is little chance of filling an inside straight, but in this case the **◇2** may be termed either a jack or a nine. Hence there are eleven cards (four jacks, four nines, three deuces) that can make this hand into a straight.

Even better chances occur with

♣2 ♡J ♠10 ♣9 ◇6

Discard the **◇6** and the deuce will fit either end of the bobtail straight. There will then be nineteen cards (four kings, queens, eights, sevens, plus three deuces) that will produce a straight, a 1 in 2½ chance.

The following is a frequent type of lone-deuce hand:

♡2 ♣10 ◇10 ♡8 ♣4

Here, the play is to hold the deuce and pair of tens; with a two-card draw you have 10 chances out of 47 of catching a deuce or ten to make four of a kind. A draw of an odd pair (as **♣J ◇J**) will produce a full house, and there is a long-shot prospect of making five of a kind.

A hand with only one deuce may win when rated at three aces, but generally only by default; namely, because opposing players failed to connect and simply folded. Otherwise, a high straight or even a flush is needed to meet the competition, as more players go after straights and flushes in deuces wild than in regulation draw poker, since the chance of making them is so much greater.

This also applies to natural hands, the term given to those that contain no deuces. With such hands the draws may run as follows:

One Pair: Not worth keeping, except in a game where it costs practically nothing to stay. In that case, draw three cards, in the hope of making four of a kind.

Two Pair: Even worse than one pair, as the best you can hope for is a full house, unless you split them and draw to the higher pair.

Three of a Kind: A two-card draw is the thing here, as there are five cards that can give you four of a kind–the fourth card that matches your three of a kind, or any one of the four deuces. Your chance of making four of a kind is better than that of getting a full house in ordinary draw poker.

Inside Straight: Many players draw to this (as **J 10 9 7**), as there are eight cards that will fill the gap, in this case four deuces or four eights, which is as good as an open-end straight in regular draw.

Open-End or *Bobtail Straight:* In a hand containing **Q J 10 9** there are twelve cards (four kings, four eights, four deuces) that will complete the straight. Many players consider this a "must" draw.

Four Flush: The chance of filling four cards of a given suit (as ♡ **J 9 6 3**) jumps to 1 out of 4 in deuces wild, as a deuce may represent any suit. A good one-card draw.

Straight Flush: With four parts toward a straight flush (♣ **10 9 8 7**) there are six chances for a straight flush, six more for a flush, six more for a straight, making 18 out of 47, or better than 1 out of 3. The best draw of all.

In deuces wild almost every hand can be opened with jacks or better, but it is preferable to pass up the opportunity unless you hold a potentially strong hand, such as:

Any hand containing two or more deuces.

A straight or better, with or without a deuce.

Three of a kind, with or without a deuce.

A pair consisting of a jack, or higher, and a deuce.

After the pot has been opened you can stay with any of the above; also with an inside straight, bobtail straight, or four flush, as the chances of filling those are strong in deuces wild. If you wish, you can raise with a pat straight or anything higher, and also with two deuces. A full house or better practically demands a raise.

In the showdown, if there have been few or no raises, a two-deuce hand may win with a high three of a kind, particularly three aces. A one-deuce hand may get by with three of a kind but will be safer with a straight or better. A natural hand of three aces seldom is strong enough to win, as all the deuces are out against it. It may take a natural flush or full house to insure a winner.

Certain rules in deuces wild differ from those of standard poker and should be noted.

For one, the cards are what the player declares them to be in the showdown. In standard poker if he miscalls three aces they are still three aces, and the error, if noted, can be corrected. But in deuces wild, a hand can actually be two things, as

♡A ♠2 ♣2 ♡9 ♡5

A player can lay down those cards and declare them as three aces, with the deuces representing aces. But he would do better to class the deuces as hearts and declare the hand to be a heart flush. Whichever he names is the one that stands.

Since deuces are wild and may represent anything, the lowest card in the pack is a three, except when a player declares an ace to be low. Thus it is possible to form a straight as follows:

♣6 ♡2 ♣4 ◊3 ♠A

The ♡**2** in this case represents a five, and the ace is next below the three in value.

While in standard poker two hands of equal value split the pot, in deuces wild a natural card takes precedence over a deuce, thus:

♠K ♡Q ◊2 ♣10 ◊9 ◊K ♡2 ♣J ◊10 ♣9

Both hands are king-high straights, but the hand on the left wins because it has a natural queen, whereas a deuce serves as queen in the hand on the right.

This rule cuts down on the number of ties but does not eliminate them all. It is a good plan to have this rule understood and agreed upon before playing deuces wild.

Since a deuce often duplicates a card in another player's hand, the question arises, why not let it duplicate one in the player's own hand? Thus, with five aces, the deuce in the hand could be classed as an existing ace–say the ♡**A**–instead of some mythical suit.

Such sound logic leads to odd situations, as

♢A ♣2 ♢Q ♢8 ♢5   ♣A ♣K ♣Q ♣8 ♣5

Each of these hands can be rated as an ace-high flush, with the **♣2** standing for the ♢**K**; the hand on the right would be the winner, since it is composed entirely of natural cards, thus breaking the tie.

But if the **♣2** in the hand on the left is promoted to the status of a duplicate ♢**A**, it becomes an ace-ace-high flush and is the winning hand.

This ruling is strictly optional and should be definitely specified beforehand, otherwise it should not apply.

DEUCES WILDER

There are many variations of deuces wild, some approaching the fantastic. One of the first to become popular was

Deuces and One-eyed Jacks Wild

In this game there are six wild cards; four deuces and two jacks –spades and hearts–which show the jacks in profile and are therefore "one-eyed" jacks. With six wild cards in play it is possible to hold a hand of five wild cards (as **♠2 ♡2 ♢2 ♠J ♡J**) and still be beaten by a hand with one wild card and four natural aces (as **♣2 ♠A ♢A ♣A ♡A**).

Though that is quite unlikely, it goes to show that you can't depend on four wild cards as a winner; with three wild cards, you're really vulnerable unless you're holding five of a kind. This makes the game too wild for sound play.

Even more freakish are such versions as

Deuces and Threes Wild

With eight wild cards there is no chance to analyze hands intelligently even if you hold four wild cards yourself. Players sometimes arbitrarily name the cards that are to be wild, as "sevens and eights" or "fives and red nines," the last-named being the same as deuces and one-eyed jacks.

In any case, you add up the wild cards and play accordingly. The number of wild cards makes–or breaks!–the game.

Threes (or **Sevens**) **Wild**

Some games are played with threes or sevens wild, or any other denominations that meet the company's whim. When only one value is involved, the game is practically deuces wild. Adding new values simply makes it wilder.

Deuces and Joker Wild

Sometimes the joker is added to the pack and is declared wild along with the deuces, putting five wild cards into the game instead of only four. If the extra joker is also added as a wild card, the game becomes similar to deuces and one-eyed jacks.

Joker Wild

With a single joker as the only wild card, a game of draw poker can be livened to the point where it becomes deadly. If you are dealt the joker, you have a sharp advantage. A pair plus the joker means three of a kind, which is often good enough to win. If a two-card draw brings you another pair, you have a full house; while a third card to go with your original pair means four of a kind. It is possible to make five of a kind, but that is extremely rare.

If you hold the joker, a one-card draw to an inside straight is as good as drawing to a bobtail in standard poker and offers three additional possibilities of making three of a kind, which is a likely winner; and the same applies to a draw to a four flush.

However, if you do not receive the joker in the deal, you must allow for someone else's holding it. In a five-handed game, where twenty-five cards are dealt, there is about an even chance that someone will have it. This causes many wary players to drop out more quickly than in ordinary draw poker.

One remedy is to use two wild jokers, providing possible competition between two players and encouraging others to stay even if they do not hold a joker, on the assumption that although one may have been dealt, there is a chance of drawing the other.

Anyone holding both jokers has an automatic three of a kind; this should be bet to the limit before the draw. Even if it does not improve, such a hand is normally a winner.

Optional wild-card rules apply in all forms of joker wild.

Poker with the Bug

This game keeps joker poker within bounds by limiting the joker's scope and is therefore quite popular with skilled players. The joker is termed the "bug" and is rated as a fifth or extra ace, but not as any other denomination where pairs, triplets, and four or five of a kind are concerned.

However, the bug may be *any* card that is needed to fill a straight, flush, or straight flush. This considerably increases the chances of such hands without greatly altering the proportions in the lower brackets (pairs, two pair, and three of a kind).

Again, options are allowable, and anything goes in a wild game, provided the players agree to it beforehand.

OTHER SUGGESTED WILD HANDS

Among the many possible types of wild-card hands, the following have gained recognition in many poker circles:

One Wild Card. At the conclusion of play, each player is

allowed to declare one of his cards wild, for his hand only. Example: Holding **♣A ♣9 ♣7 ♡7 ♣3**, making **♡7** wild would give him a club flush. **(♣ A K 9 7 3)**

Any Value Wild. At the showdown, each player declares all cards of a specific value to be wild in his hand only. Example: With **♣Q ◇Q ♡10 ♠8** ◇8, making eights wild would produce four queens. **(Q Q Q Q 10)**

Low Card Wild. The lowest card in a player's hand becomes wild automatically, with any others of that value that he holds. Example: **♠K ♡Q ◇9 ◇6 ♣6** would become a king-high straight. **(K Q J 10 9)**

One Suit Wild. This rates among the "wildest." All cards of a specified suit–say clubs–are declared wild in all hands.

Five-Card Stud Poker

This game, in the opinion of many experienced players, represents the peak of poker perfection. It is a good game for a large group, as each player is dealt five cards at most, since in stud there is no draw. While the hands are generally ranked the same as in draw poker, they are appraised quite differently, as will be seen.

In stud the dealer starts by dealing a single card face down to each player; then he continues to deal each a single card face up. That constitutes the first round of dealing, each player then having two cards. One, the face-down card, is styled the "hole card," and the player can look at it before the betting begins.

Whoever has the highest face-up card bets first. The other players may then stay, raise, or drop out as their turns arrive. If two players have face-up cards of identical value—such as aces—the one nearest the dealer is the first to bet, counting from the dealer's left.

After all bets have been called, a second round is dealt, consisting of one face-up card to each player remaining in the hand. Again, bets are made on the strength of the cards that are showing, but now each participant has *two* face-up cards, and a pair takes precedence over a mere high card.

The deal is resumed with another round, so that bets are made on *three* face-up cards. Following that comes a final round, with a *fourth* face-up card. After bets are completed, the players show their face-down cards and the highest hand wins.

Take it from there, with this sample hand:

First Player:	♡**6** as hole card; ♢**8** up.
Second Player:	♡**A** as hole card; ♠**J** up.
Third Player:	♢**10** as hole card; ♣**K** up.
Fourth Player:	♣**4** as hole card; ♢**4** up.
Fifth Player:	♢**K** as hole card; ♢**9** up.

The first bet is made by the third player, who has the highest card showing (♣K). The fourth player raises, as his two fours represent a "back-to-back" pair, which is very strong. The fifth player stays, on the theory that it's worth while if one's hole card is as good as any that shows. (His ◇**K** is as good as the ♣**K**.) The first player drops, folding his hand by turning the ◇**8** face down. The second player stays on the strength of his ace in the hole.

New cards are dealt face up, resulting in:

Second Player:	♡**A** (hole) ♠**J** ♣**7**
Third Player:	◇**10** (hole) ♣**K** ♡**3**
Fourth Player:	♣**4** (hole) ◇**4** ♣**A**
Fifth Player:	◇**K** (hole) ◇**9** ♡**K**

The bet is up to the fourth player, whose hand now shows an ace as the highest card on the table. The fifth player has caught a pair of kings, giving him what is probably the strongest hand. The second player stays; but the third player folds for two reasons: he just drew a small card (♡**3**), which doesn't help his hand; and his chance of getting a king is lessened because the fifth player received one.

The next deal brings:

Second Player:	(♡**A**) ♠**J** ♣**7** ♠**7**
Fourth Player:	(♣**4**) ◇**4** ♣**A** ♣**J**
Fifth Player:	(◇**K**) ◇**9** ♡**K** ◇**J**

The bet is made by the second player, who is showing a pair of sevens. The fourth player stays, hoping to improve his pair of fours; the fifth player stays on his pair of kings. In both these hands, the existence of a pair is concealed.

Until now, the fourth and fifth players have been thinking that the second player might have jacks back to back, but with three jacks now in sight, that is regarded as much less likely.

The final deal produces:

Second Player:	(♡**A**) ♠**J** ♣**7** ♠**7** ♡**10**
Fourth Player:	(♣**4**) ◇**4** ♣**A** ♣**J** ♣**9**
Fifth Player:	(◇**K**) ◇**9** ♡**K** ◇**J** ◇**Q**

Again, it's up to the second player, who may either check or bet, according to his likes. He has the fourth hand nicely pegged for what it is—a pair of "wired" fours. His own ace in the hole causes the second player to doubt that the fourth player is similarly equipped. But the second player is worried about the fifth player, who shows a lot of high cards, any of which might represent a winning pair. It also represents a possible straight, which would be filled or completed by a ten in the hole.

The fourth player drops because the second player has him "beaten in sight" with a pair of sevens. However, the fourth player alone knows this, and in some high-limit games he might raise, hoping that the second player would be skittish enough to be scared out. But with the fifth player also a problem, the fourth player folds.

That is a great relief to the fifth player. He is almost certain that the second player does not have a jack in the hole and is positive that he lacks a third seven. In fact, the second player's hole card is very likely to be exactly what it is: an ace.

The fourth player's hole card was what worried the fifth player. Although he figured it for a four, it could have been an ace, giving the fourth player a winning pair. However, when the fourth player dropped, the way became clear. The fifth player, confident in his pair of kings, raises the second player's bet.

In most cases the second player will call. He may think that the fifth player stayed along, hoping to catch a high card for a pair, and that now the fifth player is trying to bluff on his possible straight. If the fifth player holds a pair of nines back to back, he should have raised early. His chance of having a pair of kings seems quite slim, as the third player turned down a king.

So the second player calls with his pair of sevens. The fifth player turns up his hole card, shows a pair of kings, and takes the pot.

This game illustrates the keen competition and close margins that exist in five-card stud, but unfortunately such hands may be few and far between. It is stud tradition to fold unless your hand is as good as anything showing on the board.

Thus, if an ace should crop up all alone in the first round of a six-handed game, any player who stayed would automatically imply that he had an ace in the hole or a pair back to back. In many tight games, all would turn down promising high cards.

As a result, straights and flushes occur only by accident, as the mere appearance of a visible pair in another hand will cause a cautious player to fold when he has three parts toward a straight flush. Deuces wild don't help a stud game, for when a deuce shows up, other players have all the more reason to drop out. The best way to loosen the game and encourage competition is to play

FIVE-CARD STUD WITH THE FOUR FLUSH

This simply means that a four flush is given an accepted rating, being placed higher than a pair but lower than two pair. The effect upon the game is electric. Two fairly high cards in the same suit automatically cause a player to stay.

If he gets a third, he can stay even in the face of a pair that is showing on the board, as his chances of a four flush are good indeed, with two more cards still to come. He figures he will hit on one, if not on the other.

Often, too, there is the chance of catching a high pair while going after a four flush. Sometimes, a player may already hold a pair and still have four-flush prospects on the final card, with the chance of making two pair or three of a kind as well. In brief, it liberalizes the game of five-card stud, which is all very well for those who are liberal-minded, except that they may prefer seven-card stud poker.

Seven-Card Stud Poker

This game apparently developed as a hopeful effort to "square the circle" and produce something that would combine the zest of draw poker with the nicety of stud. The two themselves were difficult to mix, having the relative consistencies of oil and water.

The simple plan was to deal an extra card face down and another extra card face up, making seven in all, thus giving stud some of the secrecy of draw along with a draw itself. But that still left too little to the imagination.

So an eighth card was dealt, face down. That allowed too much to chance. Maybe the player already had what he needed and found the extra card superfluous. However, "peek poker," as they then called it, hovered between these two schools of thought until some unsung genius struck upon the compromise of keeping it to seven cards, but turning the seventh down.

That is seven-card stud as known today: two hole cards and one up on the first round. Then, three rounds of single cards, each face up. Finally, a round of face-down cards, one to each player still in the hand. Bets are made after each round, and whoever comes up with the best hand is the winner.

Each hand must consist of five cards from the seven dealt, the other two being disregarded. Thus, a hand of three pairs has no status, as it requires six cards. It would simply rate as two pair with an odd card. In short, seven-card stud is like five-card stud and draw poker combined, except that every player must take two extra cards whether he wants them or not; and those two are the only additional cards that he is allowed.

In seven-card stud it is worthwhile to stay if your first three cards are all of one suit, promising a flush; or if they form three parts toward a straight, as king, queen, jack. If your fourth card fits with such a holding, giving you four parts toward a straight or a flush, you will have three more chances to fill what is very likely to be a winning hand.

But if the fourth card does not help, it is wise to fold unless no one has a pair showing and you can stay on a check or a small bet with no raise. Sometimes the fourth card may give you a high pair, making it worthwhile to stay, particularly if it beats anything else on display after the fourth card has been dealt.

Don't let another player's pair scare you, as he may have nothing to go with it. On the contrary, don't bank too heavily on an unsupported pair of your own. Your chance of catching a third card and making three of a kind is about the same as in draw poker with a three-card draw.

However, you have one advantage, namely, you can see cards belonging to other players. If one you need is not among them, you have that much more chance of getting it, and vice versa. Thus, in a six-handed game, if everyone stays through the fourth card and you hold a pair of jacks, there will be ten cards on display in other hands; if none happens to be a jack, you should keep going for your triplets.

But if there is a jack among those other cards, you might as well fold and end the agony. More chips are lost by players who let themselves be lured by long-shot hopes in seven-card stud than in any other way. Don't count on two pair to win a pot in seven-card stud. Often such a hand will be the winner, but only because the other players failed to get what they were after.

So the rule is to shoot for three of a kind or better, and if two pair are all you get, play them if they then look good. Opposing players will be showing four face-up cards at the finish, and by studying them and the manner of betting you can often judge whether your two pair will stand up.

But be wary! Never discount the likelihood of a small three of a kind or a low straight or lucky flush turning up as winner. In seven-card stud the four cards that show can prove to be deceiving. One seven-card veteran once said: "Any four cards that show can mean anything from a straight to four of a kind, unless each card is a different suit. Then you can be sure it isn't a flush, but it still could be almost anything else."

That very factor furnishes unusual bluffing possibilities in seven-card stud. With two pair showing as face-up cards, it is often smart to bet them with the authority of a full house, even though you don't have it. Similarly, four parts of a straight or flush may scare off opposition if you bet it to the limit, even with nothing in the hole.

Other players study each other's upcards too, and the display may be very much to your advantage, making it look as though your downcards were solid indeed. As a result, seven-card stud has taken its place among the standard brands of poker, like regulation draw and five-card stud.

In fact, seven-card stud has gained itself such a conservative status that players with a craving for excitement frequently go for

SEVEN-CARD STUD WITH DEUCES WILD

The nickname "Down the River," commonly applied to seven-card stud in general, is particularly appropriate for the deuces-wild version of the game, for you can really go down, down, down if you overbet your hand in this game.

Oddly, many hands are won with comparatively low combinations, as three of a kind or a straight, despite the power packed by the elusive deuces. The hope of catching a deuce causes many players to "stay on nothing" when no deuce shows among the up-cards, as chances of a player having a pair of deuces in the hole are very slim.

Take this series of hands as an example:

Player One:	**(♡10**	**♡6)**	**◇5**	**♡3**	**♣10**	**♡J**	**(♠2)**
Player Two:	**(♣7**	**♠K)**	**◇7**	**♣8**	**◇8**	**◇4**	**(♡K)**
Player Three:	**(♣A**	**♣K)**	**♣2**	**♠A**	**♠5**	**◇3**	**(♠8)**
Player Four:	**(♠7**	**♠Q)**	**♣J**	**◇10**	**◇J**	**◇Q**	**(◇K)**
Player Five:	**(♡9**	**◇J)**	**♡8**	**♠3**	**♣Q**	**♣9**	**(♡2)**

In regular seven-card stud only players two, three, and five would normally have stayed after the first round, with three cards dealt. Player two has a pair of sevens at that point. Player three has three clubs toward a flush. Player five has three parts toward a straight. But with deuces wild, everybody is apt to stay. So it is assumed that in this game everybody did.

Note that one deuce is showing as an upcard, in the hand of

player three. With deuces wild, player one and player four would be wise to drop, with one deuce showing against them, but in a low-limit game they might decide to stay in hope of catching a deuce themselves.

The fourth card, which is often the heartbreaker in regular seven-card stud, does not change the scene very much. Player one gets encouragement from the ♡**3**, as it gives him three parts toward a flush and three parts toward a straight.

Player two is still nursing a mere pair, but player three—thanks to his wild deuce—is sitting back quite smugly with three parts toward a royal flush (which he had at the start) and three aces already in the bag. If the other players could see his hole cards, they would probably fold. But they can't see them, so they stay.

Player four has three parts toward a straight, working either up or down, and now is actually better off than player five, who still has only his original prospect of a straight, but with one less card coming to him. All stay, however, as no new deuce has turned up.

With the fifth card, player one gets a pair of tens, which he doesn't want, but he stays on his existing prospects. Player two gets an eight, giving him two pair, and he is now aiming for a full house. Player three is disappointed by the ♠**5**, but still has a strong hand, oddly with a chance for a flush in either clubs or spades, as his deuce can go with either suit. Player four has a pair of jacks, while player five is gladdened by the ♣**Q**, giving him four parts toward a straight.

Still, no more deuces have turned up, and everybody stays. With the sixth card, player one becomes flush conscious, thanks to the ♡**J**. Player two rides along on his two pair. Player three is now hoping for four aces or a full house, though he might catch a low straight. Player four now has two pair—queens over jacks—and is eager for a full house. Player five is stuck with a pair of nines, but still hopes for a straight. Since no deuces have popped up, everybody stays.

The final card tells the story.

Player one picks up a deuce for a heart flush. He had good chances of hitting, with seven hearts and three deuces available out of thirty possible cards, or 1 out of 3. This proves to be the winning hand, though player one would have been wise to drop out at the start, especially in a tight game.

Player two missed his full house. He wound up with three pairs —kings, eights, and sevens—which are the bane of seven-card stud, as a player can count only his five best cards, in this case two pair —kings over eights.

Player three received the unwanted eight of spades and lost, with three aces. Out of thirty possible cards, five (three deuces and two aces) would have given him four aces. Six cards (three kings, two fives, one three) would have given him a full house, also good enough to win. But he missed on his better than 1 out of 3 chance.

Player four hoped for a deuce to make a full house, as his chance for a natural full house was slim, though he might have caught a case queen or jack. As it was, he received the ♢**K**, which didn't improve his existing two pair.

Player five stayed on a 1 in 6 chance of catching any of five cards (three deuces, two tens) to fill his straight. He picked up a deuce, but would have been better off if he had gone "bust," because his straight was beaten by player one's flush.

Study the last round that was dealt, and you will see how close some of the other players came to having the winning hand. If player two had caught the ♠**2**, ♡**2**, or ♠**8**, he would have had a full house. If player three had caught the ♠**2**, ♡**2**, ♡**K**, or ♢**K**, he would have been the winner. The ♠**2** or ♡**2** would have given player four a full house; instead, player five drew the ♡**2**—and lost.

That is seven-card stud with deuces wild, and it explains why some people like it. Almost anything can happen, and incongruous things often do occur. For instance, player one might have thoughtlessly declared his hand to be three tens, and would have lost to player five's straight.

In the old, old days of poker the game followed the rule that "the cards speak for themselves." That is still true, in draw and five-card stud. But in seven-card stud—plain or wild—and in certain other games, you speak for the cards. Whatever you say, stands, provided the cards come up to it. Be careful not to understate the hand's real value.

In addition to deuces, other cards may be declared wild in

seven-card stud. Jokers, one-eyed jacks, threes, or what have you, all add to the uncertainty of the game. But, at that point, more players prefer other types of wild games.

Games of that sort will be found under Poker Today, beginning on page 150, which covers all the latest developments in modern poker and contains an individual section (page 170) devoted exclusively to special forms of seven-card stud.

Poker Variations

SPIT IN THE OCEAN

This is a form of draw poker in which only four cards are dealt to each player, after which an odd card is dealt face up on the center of the table to represent a wild fifth card in every player's hand. Not only that; any card of the same denomination automatically becomes wild.

Suppose that these hands are dealt:

Second
♣K ♣J ♠9 ♢3

First
♣A ♢A ♡9 ♠2

Third
♣Q ♡10 ♡8 ♠8

Center
♣5

Fifth
♠A ♠K ♢Q ♡Q

Fourth
♡J ♡7 ♡5 ♠4

The first player holds three aces (counting the wild ♣5) and will draw two cards.

The second player would do best to work on a pair of kings, holding only the ♣K and drawing three cards.

The third player has three parts toward a straight flush, and also three eights. Best bet is to hold the two eights and draw three cards.

The fourth player is sitting nicely with a wild card (♡5) and might as well draw three cards, fooling the others into thinking that he holds a weak hand.

The fifth player has three parts toward a royal flush, and also three queens. Drawing to three queens is preferable.

Here is what they drew:

First Player:	♣7 ♢7	Full House: **A A A 7 7**
Second Player:	♡K ♢5 ♠3	Four of a Kind: **K K K K**
Third Player:	♢8 ♢4	Four of a Kind: **8 8 8 8**
Fourth Player:	♣4 ♡3 ♠2	Straight: **6 5 4 3 2**
Fifth Player:	♢10 ♣10	Full House: **Q Q Q 10 10**

The second player is the winner with four kings. As you see, you can get some high hands in "Spit," as the game is sometimes inelegantly called. Often they don't come that good, but you can generally bank on a full house or four of a kind to show up as the winner, unless a straight flush or five of a kind appears as the topper. Don't depend on ordinary straights or simple flushes. They just won't stand up.

AROUND THE WORLD

This is a combination of Down the River and Spit in the Ocean, resembling stud rather than draw. Each player is dealt four cards, which he holds as he would an ordinary hand in draw poker, though actually they represent his down cards in a game of stud.

A single card is dealt face up in the center of the table, and each player regards it as belonging to his hand. More cards are dealt face up in the same fashion and with the same proviso, a round of bets following the deal of each card, as in seven-card stud.

Originally, there were three of these center cards, and the game could be calculated on the same basis as seven-card stud; but because this allowed only three betting rounds, four cards are usually dealt face up, making the game a form of eight-card stud, four down, four up, with four betting rounds.

From that developed the game of

CINCINNATI

Sometimes styled, appropriately, "Lame Brains," this version requires very little headwork, as five cards are dealt to each player face down, followed by five cards face up in the center. The upcards are mutual and are bet round by round, as in stud. With ten cards in all, flushes are very common in this game and it is unwise to stay on anything less; even then, a full house is liable to be the winner.

All these games can be played with wild cards and are stepped up accordingly. In Cincinnati it often takes five of a kind to win such a mix-up. What gives the game its punch is the manner of choosing the wild card. Instead of an arbitrary value being named, it is usually specified that the lowest center card will be wild.

Here, the turnup of a lower card may switch the hands completely, as in the following example:

First Player:	♢**A**	♠**A**	♠**9**	♣**7**	♣**5**
Center Cards:	♢**K**	♡**5**	♣**8**	♣**9**	♡**3**
Second Player:	♣**K**	♡**8**	♡**6**	♠**3**	♢**3**

The second card dealt up in the center (♡**5**) gave the first player a potential hand of four aces, provided the card remained low and therefore wild, since the first player held a wild card (♣**5**) in his hand. But the final card (♡**3**) killed the first player's chances. His holding was reduced to a full house (**A A A 9 9**), with the new wild card as his third ace.

The second player, who had been stringing along on a full house (**K K K 3 3**), with the earlier wild card as his third king, suddenly came into a bonanza on that last turnup. His hand became five kings, three of them wild ones, formed by the three of hearts in the center and the two wild threes in his hand.

The correct procedure in Cincinnati–if anything is correct in such a game!–is to deal the five center cards in a face-down row and then turn them up, one by one, rather than deal them from the deck as in stud. Actually, it makes very little difference, but the row of five is helpful in one version that might be titled

Last Card Wild. In this case the "last" card is the center card of the row on the table, and it is turned up last. That card and all others of its value are wild. This holds people in suspense until the bitter end. From it has derived a still wilder game called

Crossover. In this each player is dealt five cards; then nine cards are dealt face down on the table to form two crossing rows, vertical and horizontal, with a common card in the center. A card is turned up at the end of each row and betting begins in stud style, but with each player choosing the row (vertical or horizontal) that offers the most help to his hand.

Two more cards are turned up, one in each row; then two more; again two more; and finally the middle card, which belongs to both rows. This card is wild and so are all others of the same value, whether in one of the rows or in a player's hand.

Each player then chooses the row he prefers to go with his hand. The showdown follows the final bet, and the highest hand wins. Often, players switch from one row to another when the wild card appears, particularly if there is another like it in one of the rows —vertical or horizontal.

Fiery Cross. High-low crossover, with each player choosing one row for "high," the other for "low." No wild cards.

Criss-Cross. This is played like fiery cross, but with five cards in the cross instead of nine, so that each row has only three, making a faster and tighter "high-low" game.

Cross Widow. This uses the five-card cross, like criss-cross, but play is for "high," with center card wild as in crossover.

Poker Today

Poker, as played today, has so many ramifications that there really is no way to keep up with it. So the proper answer is to keep ahead of it, which is not so difficult as it might seem. Actually, players have been keeping ahead of it for years, under the name of "dealer's choice," which means that you can call the shots as you like them. For example:

Someone, away back when, became tired of hearing "Let's make deuces and one-eyed jacks wild" (see page 133), and suggested, "Why not deuces and mustached kings wild?" So they played it that way, with seven wild cards instead of only six, as there are three kings with mustaches (♢**K** ♣**K** ♠**K**). Many other games evolved in much the same way, until it became a common practice for a dealer to specify just how the coming hand should be played. No matter how crazy the rules, the other players had to go along with them or drop out.

Other players often did drop out, hence dealer's choice narrowed itself to games that were generally acceptable and were given titles of their own; these varied in different localities, as did the rules. Some of the most popular are described in brief under the headings that follow. Any of the games described earlier may also be stipulated, including all standard types. Finally, you can still make up a game, name it after yourself or your home town, and announce it as "dealer's choice," provided that you adhere to the rules once you have stated them.

High-Low Poker

Though dating from the early 1920s, this game has only recently come into its own, largely because of some intriguing variations that have added greatly to the action. They all follow the pattern of the basic game, which is simply this: When hands are compared at the "showdown," instead of the high hand taking the entire pot the *highest* and the *lowest* hands divide it equally.

While this tends to cut a player's potential profit in half, it doubles his chances of winning; and the betting is often very spirited, because more players are apt to "stay." When three or even four players stay, a player with only a fairly high hand is sure to win half the pot if all the others are going for "low."

Since high-low is a direct development of standard poker, all hands are ranked in their usual order, the lowest hand being **7 5 4 3 2** of mixed suits (as specified on page 111 unless certain lower combinations are agreed upon, as will be discussed later. But first, let us study the play of high-low in its basic form.

HIGH-LOW DRAW POKER

The deal and betting are the same as in draw poker (pages 112–115), the only difference being the objectives of the players, as illustrated in the following game with six players:

First Player: **♣K ◊K ◊J ♣9 ♣7**

Opens exactly as in ordinary draw poker or jack pots, going for "high" on the strength of a pair of kings. Discards **◊J, ♣9, ♣7.**

Second Player: **♣8 ♡8 ♡6 ♡3 ♡2**

Raises on chance of a heart flush for "high" or an eight-high hand for "low." Discards **♣8**, hoping to draw a heart; or a **7, 5,** or **4.**

Third Player: **♣J ♠J ♡4 ♠4 ◊A**

Stays on two pair for "high." Might have raised (as in ordinary draw), but is justifiably suspicious of second player's raise. Discards ♢**A**.

Fourth Player: ♡**Q** ♠**8** ♢**7** ♣**6** ♣**4**

Stays, meeting the raise, as hand offers an "inside straight" (**8 7 6 4**) for "high," with possible eight-high hand for "low." Discards ♡**Q**.

Fifth Player: ♡**K** ♢**8** ♠**6** ♡**5** ♢**2**

Strictly a "low" prospect, but with a possibility of an "eight-six" hand instead of just eight-high. Stays, meeting raise. Discards ♡**K**.

Sixth Player: ♡**10** ♡**7** ♢**6** ♠**5** ♠**2**

Stays, plus raise, with an almost "pat hand" for "low," but a ten-high is shaky. Better to go for **9**, **7**, **4**, or **3**. Discards ♡**10**.

That was the way it was. Now, let's see what developed, remembering, of course, that the "draws" were at the whim of each player and that the results depended totally on luck:

First Player: ♣**K** ♢**K** ♠**A** ♣**Q** ♢**9**

No improvement for "high." He checked.

Second Player: ♡**8** ♡**6** ♡**3** ♡**2** ♢**3**

He dropped, because he drew the ♢**3**, giving him a pair of threes, which ruined him for "low" and was no good for "high."

Third Player: ♣**J** ♠**J** ♡**4** ♠**4** ♢**Q**

Still only two pair (**J J 4 4**) for "high." But the dangerous second player "folded," so the third player bet the limit.

Fourth Player: ♠**8** ♢**7** ♣**6** ♣**4** ♠**7**

Pairing up those sevens is murder. Good-bye "inside straight" (**8 7 6 5 4**) or "low hand" (**8 7 6 4 3** or **8 7 6 4 2**). Fold and that's it.

Fifth Player: ♣**9** ♢**8** ♠**6** ♡**5** ♢**2**

Drawing ♣**9** isn't good enough for "low." He folded.

Sixth Player: ♡**7** ♢**6** ♠**5** ♢**4** ♠**2**

What a hit! A "seventy-six," as they call a **7 6 5 4 2**, which can only be beaten by a **7 6 4 3 2**, or a "seventy-five" (**7 5 4 3 2**). So the sixth player raised, as he rightfully should.

The first player calls. Having drawn three cards, he is obviously going for "high." If he had improved his pair, he might have raised. So the third player raises, considering his two pair as a good "high." The sixth player raises with his almost sure "low." More such raises follow, with the first player continually calling on the chance that both opponents are going for "low." The sixth player finally calls and wins "low" in the showdown, with the third player winning "high." They split the pot equally unless it contains an odd chip, which goes to the player who won "high."

Note that in this case the first player was "caught between" two stronger hands, which often happens in the high-low game. So in many circles it is customary to limit each adversary to three successive raises, rather than victimize the "in-betweener," though in some cases he may come out a winner.

HIGH-LOW FIVE-CARD STUD

Originally, this was simply five-card stud, played on a high-low basis. However, with only one hole card, a hand is apt to be an obvious loser for "low." So the game is usually played as a form of "English stud," which allows the option of drawing cards after the deal. Hence the name "option" has been used to designate the game itself.

After a round of betting on the fifth card, the player showing the highest hand can make a single discard and call for a replacement. Others may exercise the same option in turn, a card being dealt face down to replace a hole card and face up for an upcard. A final betting round follows.

Here is a sample showing the advantage of the option:

♣**2** ♣**4** ♡**4** ♣**7**

If the player's hole card should be a club, he would discard the ♡**4**, hoping to draw a club and make a flush for "high." With a low club in the hole, as ♣**3**, ♣**5**, ♣**6**, or even ♣**8**, he could be going for "low" as well. Indeed, with any **3**, **5**, **6**, or **8**, he could go for "low." But if his hole card happened to be a **7** or a **2** (giving him two pair) or a **4** (giving him three of a kind), he would be wise to keep his pair of fours and make a suitable draw toward "high."

Additional options, or "twists" as they are also called, may be exercised, if agreed upon beforehand. Two is a good number, and such a game is sometimes termed "bank night"; but three or even more replacements may be allowed. Another type of option is a "double twist," in which a player can discard and replace two cards at once. Always, of course, a player can stand pat instead.

HIGH-LOW SEVEN-CARD STUD

This is high-low poker at its best. The basic play is exactly as in seven-card stud poker (pages 140 to 142), giving a player a choice of five cards out of seven when he declares his hand; but here, he can call either "high" or "low." For example:

(♣7) (♡5) ◇2 ♠8 ◇6 ♣K (♠9)

In regular seven-card stud, where only "high" counts, the player would fold on the two hole cards and the first upcard, as being hopeless. They are too low and too widely spaced for a straight **(7–2)**, and the mixed suits (♣ ♡ ◇) injure flush chances. But the **7 5 2** combination is fine toward "low" in high-low, and by the fifth card, the hand showed an open-end straight **(8 7 6 5)** toward "high." With the final card, it makes it **(9 8 7 6 5)**, and meanwhile the hand has been riding along quite nicely with an **8 7 6 5 2** toward "low."

So if this player should find his straight beaten by a higher straight or a flush, he could switch to his "low" hope, which might win, unless someone else showed a hand such as **8 6 4 3 2** or **7 6 5 3 2**. That was how the game was originally played, and still is in some areas. But to forestall such switches and to avoid freakish situations where a player may win "high" or "low" practically by default, the more modern form of high-low seven-card stud incorporates the following rule:

Declaring for High or Low

Immediately following the final round of betting, each player must state whether he decides to declare his hand as "high" or "low." Since each hand still in the game has four upcards showing, a player can judge what his opponents are after and change his course accordingly, but that will often prove deceptive. Declarations can be made progressively by one of two predetermined methods, namely:

The first active player on the dealer's left declares "high" or "low," and the rest follow in rotation to the dealer. Or, if so agreed, the last player who raised or bet must be the first to declare, with anyone who merely called being free of responsibility. This is preferable, as it gives each player the chance of forcing someone else to declare first. However:

A more equitable plan is to make declarations simultaneously. The dealer calls for all active players to respond "High" or "Low," which they do. Or, to make it clearer, each player can be told to hold a chip in his right hand, red for "high," blue for "low," so all can be shown at once. The hole cards are then turned up, and the hands are read accordingly.

Declaring for Both High and Low

A still more modern rule is to allow a player to declare "high-low" by holding both a red chip and a blue chip (or some other designated token). He first makes up a "high" hand from his cards—as a **9 8 7 6 5** straight—and then changes them around as needed to form a "low" hand (as **8 7 6 5 2**). But he must win in each category; otherwise, his hand is nullified and he loses both.

When a "high-low" declarer is thus eliminated, the usual rule is to give the portion of the pot that he might have won to the best hand held by a player who declared in that category alone. But in some circles, the whole pot goes to the player who defeated the "high-low" declarer, since he produced the outcome. Whichever rule is used should be specified beforehand. However, when a "high-low" declarer is merely tied in either category, he can still win; but he must split that portion of the pot with the player who tied him.

Optional Valuation of Cards in High-Low Poker

High-low innovations include optional valuations of certain cards or combinations. The most popular is the "swinging ace," which allows a player to declare an ace as "high" or "low" as he chooses. This makes a great difference in a "low" hand. Ordinarily, the lowest possible combination is **7 5 4 3 2**; but with the "swinging ace," the following are lower: **7 5 4 3 A**, **7 5 4 2 A**, **7 5 3 2 A**, **7 4 3 2 A**, **6 5 4 3 A**, **6 5 4 2 A**, **6 5 3 2 A**, and **6 4 3 2 A**, lowest of all.

This not only sharpens the play with "low" hands; it puts new emphasis on aces in "high" hands. Take this example:

(♢A) (♡3) ♣5 ♡A ♠7 ♡6 (♠A)

From the upcards, that looks like a good "low," since any hole card between an ace and a five will assure a good one. But with two aces in the hole, the hand is a powerful "high" that can beat anything up to three kings. This could be a dandy hand for a "high-low" declaration.

Many groups of players are content to stop at "swinging aces"; but others have carried the "high-low" principle further, making such combinations as straights and flushes either "high" or "low" as the declarer may decide. Thus, **5 4 3 2 A** becomes the lowest possible hand, if you want to call it such. Should it be ♡ **5 4 3 2 A**, it would still be the perfect "low," but it would also be "high" indeed, representing a five-card straight flush. To declare "high-low" with such a setup would be an almost certain win, with the *same five cards* representing both "high" and "low."

On a lesser scale, five cards such as ♡**6**, ♣**5**, ♢**4**, ♠**3**, ♣**2** could be shown as a straight for "high" and then as a **6 5 4 3 2** for "low." Similarly, ♢ **A 7 4 3 2** would be an ace-high diamond flush for "high" and also a **7 4 3 2 A** for "low." As with the "swinging ace," all rules applying to "swinging hands"–specifically flushes and straights–should be agreed upon beforehand.

OTHER FORMS OF HIGH-LOW POKER

The "high-low" feature can be injected into many types of poker. One of the most obvious is six-card stud, as an extension of the five-card high-low game, with or without one or more "twists." Similarly, eight-card stud can be played "high-low" as an extension of the seven-card game. Other forms of stud are adaptable to "high-low," but it is by no means limited to stud. Almost any type of poker can be played on a "high-low" basis, provided that all rules and limitations are fully stipulated.

Wild cards are frequently introduced into high-low poker, and here it is suggested that instead of the time-honored "deuces wild," some intermediate value be specified, as "eights wild," or perhaps "sevens wild" if the "swinging ace" rule is in effect. The reason is that deuces, or other values up to sixes, are natural "low" cards and therefore should be retained as such, as helps toward "low" hands.

Lowball: Low-Hand Poker

Following the introduction of high-low poker a half century or more ago, some astute devotees of the grand old game raised the query that if high-hand poker had needed low-hand poker to spice it up, why wasn't low-hand poker a good enough game in its own right? The answer was: It was, and is. Thus lowball was born.

The basic rules are the same as standard poker, but instead of the highest hand winning, the lowest hand does. In the original "low-hand" or "low poker," the lowest possible hand is **7 5 4 3 2**, as an ace is always high; and other hands range upward as in "high" or standard poker, with an ace high except in a **5 4 3 2 A** straight. That game is rarely played today, having been supplanted by lowball.

In lowball, an ace is always low, making **5 4 3 2 A** the lowest possible hand, since straights and flushes do not count. This rule was a matter of gradual evolution, hence in some circles straights and flushes–or just flushes–may still be classed as high hands. But the "all low" ruling is not only preferable, but justifiable, for this reason:

Originally, only pairs and three or four of a kind rated as higher combinations in poker, with straights, flushes, and finally straight flushes being introduced later, to increase high prospects. Conversely, in lowball, the aim should be to increase low prospects, hence the elimination of straights and flushes is a step in the right direction, as it may change otherwise useless hands into winners.

All types of poker–draw, stud, spit, and others–are adaptable to lowball. The prevalence of fairly low hands is an intriguing feature of the game, but that can be deceptive, as there are times when a hand containing a pair may be the winner. A "wheel" or "bicycle," as a **5 4 3 2 A** "low" is called, is the equivalent of a royal flush in high poker, where rank is concerned; but in frequency, it is only about the same as an ace-high straight, or **A K Q J 10** of mixed suits.

Lowball sprang to popularity in California, where it is now the most popular game in many legalized poker parlors. Those have their own "house rules," which of course do not apply to lowball as played elsewhere, particularly in social circles; but they have gone far to shape the game. One noteworthy feature stemming from that source is:

Lowball with the bug: Here the joker is added to the pack as a wild card or "bug," representing any value that the holder wants. Thus **7 5 4 2 Joker** would be the equivalent of **7 5 4 2 A**; while **7 4 Joker 2 A** would be **7 4 3 2 A**. This makes the "bug" the deciding factor in many close hands, as a **9 6 Joker 3 2** read as **9 6 4 3 2** would beat **9 6 5 3 2.**

Lowball with wild cards can be like any wild game where high hands are concerned, the players simply going for "low" instead. Thus with "nines wild," **8 6 9 2 A** would be **8 6 3 2 A,** beating **8 6 4 2 A**; while **6 9 3 2 9** would be **6 4 3 2 A**, beating **6 5 3 2 A**. With the "bug" also in the game, a player holding **9 9 9 9 Joker** would have the equivalent of **5 4 3 2 A**, but still could be tied by someone with a "wheel," or natural **5 4 3 2 A.**

That, however, is conservative compared to a newer innovation in which wild cards are rated as "zero" or one point below an ace in a hand of lowball. Here, with "nines wild," **8 6 4 A 9** would be **8 6 4 A 0**, or **8 6 4 9 9** would be **8 6 4 0 0**, as pairing zeros wouldn't matter, since they are automatically no pair. But either of those hands could be beaten by a natural **8 6 3 2 A**, since "**8 6 3**" is a better "low" than "**8 6 4**."

However, in this type of wild game, a **4 3 2 A 9** would stand as **4 3 2 A 0**, beating even a wheel (**5 4 3 2 A**); and even lower hands would be possible, such as **3 A 9 9 9** for **3 A 0 0 0**, or **A 9 9 9 9** for **A 0 0 0 0**, which is almost absolute "low," but not quite. For if the pack also includes the joker as "bug," which is common practice in many wild games, **Joker 9 9 9 9** would stand for **0 0 0 0 0**, and even nothing can't be lower than that!

Special Forms of Poker

As one delves into the intricacies of high-low poker and its country cousin, lowball, it becomes increasingly apparent that no matter how unorthodox a game may set out to be, it often tends to level off and develop its own technique. Indeed, both high-low and lowball have gained top rating in the most serious poker circles. However, the seeds of wild oats are also present, to be sown and reaped as grist for the wild player's mill. The same is true of other poker variants, for even those that seem innocent in themselves can prove wild indeed when blended with others of their ilk. Experiment with the games that follow should prove this to every poker player's satisfaction.

Special Forms of Draw Poker

Along with jack pots, about the only early change in draw poker was an occasional limiting of the draw to three cards. This discouraged players from staying with less than a pair, which lessened freakish wins; and it is a good rule to adopt with six or more players in a game. Otherwise the pack may be exhausted before all players have been served, which means taking time out to shuffle the discards so the remaining players can draw. However, special forms of draw poker gradually made their appearance, increasing in popularity when dealer's choice took over. Here are some, ranging from simple to complex; and remember, you can still add your own variations if you wish.

Cold Hands with Draw. Poker hands dealt face up are called "cold hands," and who gets what is therefore obvious. But when players put up equal chips and are dealt cold hands, it makes a good game when each player is allowed to discard and draw, as in regular poker, but with the "draw" face up. There is no chance to bluff, but each later player can gauge his draw by watching how the others fare and shifting from a standard draw to a riskier one, if need be. For example: Assume that three players are dealt these cold hands:

X:	♠**Q**	♢**Q**	♠**9**	♡**5**	♢**4**
Y:	♢**10**	♡**10**	♣**9**	♣**7**	♠**6**
Z:	♡**K**	♡**7**	♣**6**	♠**5**	♡**4**

Player X keeps his pair of queens, tossing the other cards from his hand and calling for a "draw" of three. He is dealt the ♠**2**, ♣**Q**, ♠**A**, face up, giving him three queens.

Player Y intended to keep his pair of tens and go for a third, but sees they would be beaten by X's three queens. So he discards the ♢**10** and makes a one-card draw, hoping to fill an "inside straight," his only hope here. Luckily, he is dealt the ♣**8**, giving him his straight: **10 9 8 7 6**.

Player Z planned to discard the ♡**K** and go for an open-end straight, ordinarily a good draw, but useless now, as Y has hooked a higher straight than any that Z might get (**10 9 8 7 6** against a possible **8 7 6 5 4**). So Z discards the ♣**6** and ♠**5**, making a desperation two-card draw, hoping to get two odd hearts and complete a flush. He is dealt the ♡**2** and ♣**J**, which leaves him one heart short.

A full round of this game should always be played, giving each player a chance as dealer, which is the best spot. The game can also be played as high-low poker.

Automatic Lowball. This speeds the action when jacks are required as openers. Instead of all players throwing in the hand when they are forced to pass, the game is automatically played as lowball poker. This is quite appropriate, as most of the players are apt to be headed in that direction. In this game, the first player with jacks or better must open.

Anything Opens. A game so obvious that it is often overlooked, because the so-called "jack pot" ruling is so customary. A player simply opens on anything, as in old-style poker, which allows for some bold bluffs and also is essential to high-low poker and other games.

High Spade Split. This is one of those "other games" where anything has to open, because even the poorest hands may produce action. It is played like regular draw, but the pot is split between the player holding the highest hand and the player holding the highest spade (♠**A** being high). One player can win the entire pot, but the game should be limited to five players, so that only forty cards will be dealt, at most. This means that the ♠**A** will be absent from nearly 25 per cent of the deals, so that a player holding the ♠**K** or even the ♠**Q** will be encouraged to "stay," on the chance that he is holding the highest spade in play. This game is also played as seven-card stud under the name of "Chicago," but it is much better suited to five-card stud, as the high spade becomes more elusive with fewer cards dealt.

Shotgun. Here is real action, as the name implies. Three cards are dealt to each player, as in regular draw; but there the players pause to study them and bet on possibilities, on the basis of "anything goes." Two more cards are then dealt to complete the five-card hands, and another betting round follows. After that, the game proceeds as in regular draw poker. If it is desired, a betting round can be held after the dealing of the fourth card; then another after the fifth.

Double-barreled Shotgun. This is "shotgun" without the "showdown." Instead, the game moves into another area, becoming a reversed form of stud poker. From his hand, each player lays down a single card, and a betting round follows in the same order; then the process is repeated, card by card, like five-card stud in reverse, until four are face up, with one more to show. That final card represents the showdown, since the hand is then complete. This game, which is usually played as "high-low," is also called "Texas Tech." From that derived another game, appropriately titled:

TNT. This game gets away from draw poker, but must be considered in that category because of its origin. Each player receives three face-down cards, followed by a betting round; then singles, each with a betting round, until there are seven in all. Then, instead of taking a draw, each player makes two discards, leaving him with a hand of five. Those, he lays face up, card by card, as he chooses, each being followed by a betting round, exactly as in double-barreled shotgun.

Pinochle Poker. Reverting to regular draw poker and all the efforts to enliven it—such as stripped decks and wild cards—the most unusual was an accidental discovery in which some happy-go-lucky poker players were amazed by the wonderfully high hands they drew until they discovered that they were mistakenly playing with a pinochle pack! (See page 231). But it wasn't such a bad mistake, after all.

With such a pack, running only from aces down to nines, with each card duplicated, all hands are sure to be amazingly high. The highest of all is five of a kind, with one card duplicated—for example ♡**A** ♡**A** ♠**A** ♣**A** ◊**A**—which doesn't matter. Next is a straight flush—which can be a "royal" such as ♡ **A K Q J 10**—and from there on down the combinations follow the usual order; but the worst possible hand that anyone can hold is **A Q J 10 9** of mixed suits. It's worth playing, just for the fun of it!

Special Forms of Stud Poker

In addition to five-card stud and seven-card stud, which are classed as standard games, the following are entitled to a similar rating when played in simple form:

Six-card Stud. Very popular with serious players. Like five-card stud, but with a sixth card dealt face down as an extra hole card. Each player chooses five cards for the showdown, as in seven-card stud. High-low and other variants may be introduced.

Eight-card Stud. Like seven-card stud, but with an eighth card dealt face down as a fourth hole card, followed by a betting round. Some prefer to deal the first three and the eighth face down. Any variants of seven-card stud may be included in this more liberal game.

Nine-card Stud. Similar to eight-card stud, with nine cards, first two and last two usually dealt as hole cards, though this is variable.

Ten-card Stud. Nine-card stud with an extra, either face down or face up as the dealer prefers. A loose, prolonged game, limited to five players.

Special Forms of Five-Card Stud

The simplest way of adding action to five-card stud is by raising a four flush one notch higher than a pair, as described on page 139. But that well-accepted variation, sometimes termed "New York stud," is a mere preliminary to other measures that have been introduced over the years. The next step upward is:

Canadian Stud. Similar to "New York stud," but with a four straight, of four cards in sequence (as **J 10 9 8**), ranking above a pair; and a four flush above that. This keeps still more players in the running up to the final card. This ranking can be applied to any of the games that follow.

Hole-card Stud, or "pistol," in which the hole card is dealt singly, face down, and followed by a round of betting, before dealing the first upcard. This encourages players to stay in the game to see what is coming next; and it adds the action of an extra betting round.

Mexican Stud, also known as "flip," is an excellent game in which the first two cards are dealt face down, allowing each player to turn up either that he wants, which can be a great help. Even better, each succeeding card is dealt *face down* instead of face up, giving the player the privilege of turning up his old hole card and retaining a new one, which may prove helpful indeed. All new upcards must be turned up simultaneously, which adds zest to the procedure. That leads to:

Mexican Wild. Here, each player can declare his hole card "wild," as well as any others of its value. Thus, if he retains the ♠**8** as his hole card, all other eights fulfill the same function. This can be devastating to the opposition, but it can boomerang on the average player if he makes a bad guess. This game is also called "shifting sands." Don't ask why. Just try it and find out.

Five-card Final is more on the conservative side, which may be more in its favor. The big question mark in five-card stud is the player's hole card. If everyone else wonders what it is, he is that far ahead of the game. But if he suddenly goes "bust" on his fifth, or final card, who cares about the hole card? They all will care if the final card is *also* dealt face down, giving the canny player *another* hole card. If he does go "bust," his opponents will have to pay to find out; and perhaps they would sooner drop. This game is a slightly abbreviated version of six-card stud.

No Low Cards really punches up the action in five-card stud. Twos, threes, and fours are the bane of every stud player's existence. So whenever he is dealt one—whether a hole card or an upcard—he is entitled to reject it and be dealt another. It's like stripping a pack of low cards, but better, because at times a player may want a low one, like a ♡**3** to complete a heart flush (as ♡ **J 10 9 7 3**). So, in that case, he keeps it; and what could be better?

Stud with a Spit is a good answer to that question, as it keeps many eager players in the game right up to the last card. It is standard five-card stud up to then, but the fifth card is dealt face up in the center of the table, as a common card for all surrounding hands; and not only that: whatever its denomination, it makes all the cards of that same value wild!

Low Card Wild is nicely adapted to five-card stud. After the turn-up of the hole cards, as in the standard game, each player counts his lowest card as wild, along with any others of the same value that his hand contains. Thus (♢**J**) ♠**9** ♡**5** ♢**K** ♣**10** would be a **K Q J 10 9** straight; while (♢**7**) ♡**7** ♣**Q** ♣**8** ♠**7** would represent ♣ **Q J 10 9 8** for a straight flush. This can be varied with:

Mexican Low Card, the same game, but played like Mexican stud, so a new low card can be kept in the hole to bluff opponents.

Example: With cards dealt in the following order (♡4) **♣9 ◇4 ♡10 ♠2**, a player's best possible hand would be three tens. But if he retained the **♠2** as a new hole card, turning up the **♡4** for his fifth card instead, it would be **(♠2) ♣9 ◇4 ♡10 ♡4**. With a four still showing as his "low," it would look like a sure straight, with a good chance of four tens or four nines. Such situations add zest to the game.

Take It or Leave It. Each player is dealt a hole card, face down, but when the player to the dealer's left receives his first upcard, he may keep it or reject it, as he pleases. If he rejects it, the card moves around the board, and if nobody takes it, including the dealer, it is put on the bottom of the pack. An upcard is then dealt to the first player who rejected it; and he must keep that card. This is repeated with each player in turn, skipping any who have taken a rejected card.

Once the hands have been thus equalized, a round of betting takes place. This is followed by another deal as described, and another betting round; and so on, completing the hand as in regular five-card stud. This game is particularly suited to high-low, as it encourages more players to stay in. If the dealer drops, the privilege of taking a rejected card ends with the last active player on his left.

Special Forms of Seven-Card Stud

The game that has probably done the most to popularize "dealer's choice" is seven-card stud with deuces wild, as described on pages 142 to 145. It has remained a stand-by with many dealers, because, as mentioned there, the adding of extra wild cards made the results so freakish that many players were more inclined to drop than stay if a wild card popped suddenly in an opponent's hand.

So it remained, until someone hit upon the happy notion of making the lucky player pay for it, or else drop out himself, which encourages the others either way. As a basic example, consider:

Five and Dime. The name makes it easy to remember that fives and tens are "wild" (instead of deuces) and that if a five is dealt to a player as an upcard, he must put five chips in the pot or fold his hand, the wild card along with it. If a wild ten is dealt, he must contribute ten chips or fold. This game was once appropriately styled "Woolworth," which probably inspired the title of a more drastic version:

Heinz. The wild cards in this game are fives and sevens, but instead of paying fixed amounts for drawing one, a player must contribute chips equal to the total already in the pot. This does two good things: it encourages early betting by players with strong hole cards, who feel they can afford to pay high for a "wild" card; and it increases the cost of wild cards as the play progresses. This, too, is a good game in its own right, but it leads to other developments, most notably:

Baseball. Again, seven-card stud with two wild values: nines and threes. Because a baseball game has nine innings, a player receives a wild *nine* as an upcard without paying for it. But three strikes are "out," and so is a player who gets a *three* as an upcard, unless he puts up enough chips to match the pot. Since four balls represent a "free trip" to first base, a *four* retains its normal value, as an upcard, but the player is dealt a free card face down, as an extra hole card.

All this is based on the absurd notion that baseball is America's national game, though everyone knows that America's national game is poker. The proof is that millions of poker players have never played baseball; but it is hard indeed to find a baseball player who has never played poker. So if you don't like baseball, you can take up:

Football. This is essentially the same game, except that sixes and fours are wild. In real football, a touchdown counts as six points, so a player receiving a *six* as an upcard does not have to pay for it. But as there are four periods in a football game, a *four* as upcard demands a penalty equal to the pot. In football, a safety counts two points, so a *two,* or *deuce,* as an upcard is an ordinary card, but the player is promptly dealt an extra hole card, face down.

In baseball and football, all other rules are identical, and if matching the pot becomes too steep a tax for some players, a limit can be set upon the amount; but it is best to keep it high, so that the cost becomes greater as the game gets hotter. High hands are prevalent in both games, with five of a kind outranking a straight flush.

Seven-card Flip. An extension of "Mexican stud" or Five-card Flip, with each player receiving four face-down cards and turning up any two as upcards, so the first round of betting involves four cards. From then on, the game proceeds like seven-card stud, two more cards being dealt face up and one face down, with a round of betting after each. Can be played high-low or with wild cards.

Seven-Five Reverse. Each player is dealt a hand of seven cards, which he holds as though playing draw poker. He chooses one card, which he lays face down; when all other players have done the same, the cards are turned up and a round of bets is made, beginning with the high card, as in stud poker. This is repeated, card by card until the fifth cards, which are bet around while still face down, then turned up to decide the winner. Ideal for simple high-low, in which the cards "speak for themselves," as the two extra cards are simply discarded. Thus, though seven cards are used, the hand is played like five-card stud in reverse.

Seven-card Mutual. The fastest, most practical form of seven-card stud when time and space are limited; yet the number of players can be almost unlimited! Each is dealt two face-down hole cards; then a single card is dealt face up in the center of the table to serve as a mutual upcard for each hand. A betting round follows; then three more mutual upcards are dealt, with bets as usual. Finally, each player is dealt an individual down card, giving him his quota of seven (counting the mutuals) for a last betting round. As many as sixteen players can participate in such a game, which is suited to any form of high-low. Variants of seven-card mutual are given in the next section.

Other Variations of Dealer's Choice

From seven-card mutual, it is a logical step to "around the world," as described on page 147, which is a very similar game, but played with eight cards. Other variants involving a center deal of mutual cards include:

Omaha, in which two cards are dealt face down to each player, followed by a betting round; then five cards singly to the center, face up, each followed by a betting round; and

Hold 'Em, which is the same thing, but faster, as three center cards are dealt face up for one betting round; then the next two singly, which reduces the total betting rounds. Both games may be played "high-low."

Twin Beds. This game is a doubled-up version of Cincinnati, described on page 148. Each player receives five face-down cards to form a hand, as in draw poker. Two cards are then dealt face up, each starting a separate row (instead of a single row, as in Cincinnati), and a round of betting follows. Four more such deals are made, with betting rounds, until two rows of five cards each are on display. In the showdown, a player can combine *either row* with his own hand, to form a winning–or losing!–combination.

The emphasis on "either row" is important, because the game is ideally suited to "high-low," which enables a player to pick one row for "high" and the other for "low," though he is not restricted on that score. He can use one for both, which makes it all the more sporting; or he may use either–or neither, if he wants to fold his hand, which he can do at any time, often for the best.

Double Twin Beds. To give "twin beds" a really modern touch, it can be carried further. After the two sets of cards representing the twin beds have been turned up, the players lay their cards face up on the table, one by one, with a betting round to follow. This makes four rounds of "stud in reverse," or nine betting rounds in all. When the rows are being dealt on the table, betting begins with the first active player on the dealer's left. But as the players "roll," or turn up their own cards, the highest card or highest combination bets first, as in stud. The game at this point actually becomes stud in reverse.

Pass the Garbage. Known in more polite circles as "pass the trash," this game literally lives up to either title. Each player is dealt a face-down hand, as in draw poker, but it consists of seven cards, not just five. After a betting round, he picks the three most worthless and passes them face down to the player on his left, who adds them to his hand after passing along his own three.

From his new total of seven cards, the player discards two, giving him a closed hand of five. These hands are bet around, beginning from the dealer's left, exactly as in draw poker; and when all have dropped or been called, the showdown follows. The game is almost invariably played as "high-low," giving players more choice of discards and adding to the uncertainty of what they may get instead. Also, it is impossible to start with a "pat" hand, such as a flush or a perfect "low," for if a player is dealt such a combination, he must break it up in order to pass along three cards.

Beat Your Neighbor. This is an automatic game that allows no chance to bluff, but still adheres to poker procedure and can produce some spirited betting. Each player is dealt five cards face down and keeps them in a packet, without looking at them. The first player at the dealer's left turns up his top card and bets it, with the others raising or calling as they choose. Since the game is for "high" only, they are apt to raise if he turns up a two or three, or call if he shows an ace or king.

The next player turns up cards one by one, until he shows something better than the first player–as topping a king with an ace, or a king and a side card, or coming up with a pair. The second player then starts another betting round; and following that, it is the third player's job to turn up cards until he beats the second player. Any time a player's hand runs out unsuccessfully, he drops out, and the next player takes over. This continues until a winning hand turns up and its owner takes the pot.

A sample round with five players will clarify this:

Player A turns up **♣9**. B turns up **♢5, ♡8, ♡K**. C turns up **♡Q, ♣4, ♢4** (pair of fours). D turns up **♡9, ♢2, ♢A, ♡J, ♣9** (pair of nines). E turns up **♡5, ♠6, ♠J, ♣5, ♠A**. Drops out. A turns up (**♣9**), **♣7, ♡10, ♢J, ♠8**, making a jack-high straight. When A bets, B folds, as he can't make better than three of a kind. C stays, hoping for a full house or four of a kind; but D drops, being already beaten. C turns up **♣Q**, getting two pair (**Q Q** over **4 4**), but his next and last card turns up as the **♢10**, so he misses his full house, and A wins the pot.

Poker with Fewer than Five-Card Hands

To speed up a poker session and accommodate more players, the following are recommended as forms of dealer's choice. Some circles also like them as a regular thing.

Four-card Poker. Four cards are dealt to each player, either face down with a "draw" to follow, or as a form of four-card stud with a hole card down and three upcards to follow. Hands rank as follows: four of a kind, straight flush, flush, straight, three of a kind, two pair, pair, high card. Can be played "high-low" or with "wild cards."

Three-card Poker. One round less in the deal, giving each player only three cards toward a hand in "draw" or "stud," with one down, two up. Hands rank: straight flush, three of a kind, flush, straight, pair, high card. Also suited to "high-low" and "wild card" games. Three-card poker has been nicknamed "three-card monte" after a game used by old-time card sharpers.

Two-card Poker. Two cards to each player, to be followed by a "draw"; or one down, one up, for a "stud" game. Highest pair wins; if there are no pairs, highest card. Can be played "high-low" or with "wild cards." This game is popularly known as "hurricane"; it moves that fast.

One-card Poker. One card to each player, face down. No draw unless specified by dealer. Bets follow, and high card wins; or the game can be "high-low," splitting the pot. Ace is always high and deuce low. This game is sometimes termed "Lazy Lucy."

Freak Poker Hands

Another way of turning poker into a "wild" game is by the introduction of "freak," or unorthodox, hands, giving players more chance to come up with surprise winners. One series of such hands that has won wide acceptance, particularly in the Midwest, is the following.

Big cat: king high, eight low, no pair, as **K Q 10 9 8**;
little cat: eight high, three low, no pair, as **8 7 6 4 3**;
big dog: ace high, nine low, no pair, as **A K Q 10 9**;
little dog: seven high, two low, no pair, as **7 6 5 4 2**.

These hands are rated below a flush, but above a straight, and are usually ranked in the order given. That, however, is arbitrary, as, in some circles, dogs are logically ranked above cats. So this should be specified beforehand. Often added to the list is

five and ten: ten high, five low, no pair, as **10 8 7 6 5**.

This, too, should rate above a straight, but because of some quirk it is frequently placed below. Hence, any of four schedules are allowable if five and ten is included with the group:

flush	flush	flush	flush
big cat	big cat	big dog	big dog
little cat	little cat	little dog	little dog
big dog	big dog	big cat	big cat
little dog	little dog	little cat	little cat
five and ten	straight	five and ten	straight
straight	five and ten	straight	five and ten

Such hands offer inviting prospects to standard draw poker, by making it worth while to draw to certain inside straights, or even to make a two-card draw, hoping to catch a "freak" that will be even better. All such hands must consist of *mixed suits,* because any composed of a *single suit* would automatically be a flush. In some circles, a cat flush (as ♡ **K Q 10 9 8**) or a dog flush (as ♠ **7 6 4 3 2**) is rated higher than a royal flush, which is fair enough but should be specified beforehand.

Another popular hand in some localities is the "blaze," which is formed entirely of face cards. As a result, there are four different types of blaze, which rank as follows:

blaze fours, containing four of a kind, as **Q Q Q Q K;**
blaze full, forming a full house, as **J J J K K;**
blaze threes, containing three of a kind, as **K K K Q J;**
simple blaze, containing only two pair, as **Q Q J J K.**

Because of its great rarity, blaze fours should be rated as the highest four of a kind, even outranking four aces. Similarly, a blaze full should outrank any other full house. But blaze threes and simple blazes are also so rare that they properly are rated higher than a full house. Hence, with the exception of blaze fours, *any* blaze is rated below four of a kind, but higher than a full house. Any lesser rating for a blaze is too ridiculous to be considered.

A very popular hand frequently allowed in modern poker is a *round-the-corner straight,* in which an ace serves as a connecting link between the lowest and highest cards, forming an artificial sequence, as **4 3 2 A K** or **2 A K Q J.** These are treated like any legitimate straight; hence, in the examples given, the four-high straight would beat the deuce high.

Many other freak hands are occasionally used. Here are a few that rate below a straight, but above three of a kind, in the order listed below:

Dutch straight, or *skip.* Formed by alternating values, as **A Q 10 8 6, K J 9 7 5,** down to **9 7 5 3 A.**

Skeet. A nine, five, deuce, with two other cards in between, as **9 8 6 5 2, 9 7 5 3 2,** or **9 5 4 3 2.**

Kilter, or *pelter.* Truly a "nothing" hand, so bad that it is good. No card above a nine, no pairs, not even a four flush or a bobtail straight; nor an ace, for it would be classed as "high." Examples: **9 7 6 5 3, 8 6 4 3 2.** Note that these resemble "low hands" in high-low poker, but in regular poker, if two players hold kilters, the higher wins. (Non-kilters: **7 6 4 4 2**; ♡ **9 4 3 2** ♠**6**)

Striped straight, or *zebra.* A hand without a pair or better, with cards alternating, red and black, in descending order. Examples: ♡**K** ♠**9** ♡**8** ♣**3** ◇**2** or ♣**J** ◇**10** ♠**6** ◇**4** ♠**3**.

Note that it is possible to hold a skip flush, such as ◇ **10 8 6 4 2** or a skeet flush, such as ♠ **9 8 7 5 2**. In some circles, such rare hands are rated higher than four of a kind, but below a straight flush.

Introduction to the Trump Games

In many of the most popular card games the procedure is as follows:

The pack is shuffled and is cut by the player on the dealer's right. An equal number of cards is dealt to each player, beginning with the dealer's left. These "hands," as they are called, are dealt face down, and each player then picks up his cards, holding the faces toward himself, so that the other players cannot see them.

Usually, each player arranges his cards fanwise, putting the cards of each suit in a separate group ranging from high card at the left to low card at the right. This arrangement is simply a convenience in appraising the hand and playing the cards.

One player starts the play by choosing a card and placing it face up in the center of the table. This is termed leading a card or leading to a trick. The next player to the left places one of his cards on the table, and so on until all have played.

Whatever the suit–hearts, diamonds, spades, or clubs–of the card led by the first player, the others must play cards of the same suit if they can. This is called following suit, and if all the players follow suit, the one who put down the highest card picks up the lot and turns them face down in a squared-up packet in front of him.

This is called a trick, and the player who wins it makes the next lead. The player who takes the second trick leads to the third trick, and so on, until all the cards have been played and the round is completed. The tricks are then counted and are scored according to the rules of the game. Another deal is made, and play follows as described until the game is completed.

If a player does not have a card of a suit that is led, he must play a card from another suit. Generally, such a card has no trick-taking power. It is termed a discard; in discarding, a player generally disposes of a card of little value or one that he is anxious to be rid of for some other reason.

In some of these games, however, *one* suit is declared to be the trump suit, and its cards, known as trump cards, are rated above those of the other suits. If an ordinary suit is led and a player does not have a card of that suit, he may play a trump card, thus trumping the trick and thereby winning it, unless another player, who is also out of cards of the suit led, plays a higher trump. This is called overtrumping.

Thus, if hearts are trumps and a player leads a high card in an ordinary suit, say the ace of spades, a player who is out of spades can take the trick with a trump card as low as the two of hearts.

The choice, or naming, of the trump suit varies in different games, some of which also have special rules applying to the play of trumps. These are detailed in the descriptions of the individual games, along with the scoring of tricks or cards taken in the course of play.

There are two special terms that should be clarified where these games are concerned. A round of play is seldom called a round but is more frequently referred to as a deal. That is, the term "deal," as applied to the actual dealing of the cards, is extended to include the play that follows.

Similarly, the term "hand" has come to mean exactly the same thing, namely, a round of play from the beginning of the deal through to the final counting of the tricks. This should not be confused with the "hands" of cards held by the players. The play of those hands constitutes a hand in itself.

In most trump games, with the exception of pinochle, which requires a special pack, the cards of each suit rank in value ace, king, queen, jack, ten, nine, and so on down. In some games, however, a special ranking is given to the trump-suit cards.

In euchre, the highest trump card is the jack. When hearts are trumps, the ♡**J** is the top card and is known as the "right bower." The trump next in value is the jack of the other suit of the same color, in this case the ◇**J**. Third in value is the ace of trumps (♡**A** in this instance).

Thus the ranking of the trump suit runs: right bower, left bower, ace, king, queen, ten, nine, and so on down.

In five hundred there are bowers, as in euchre, but the joker is also in the pack and ranks as a still higher trump. Thus, in a five-hundred game, if spades should be declared trumps, the rank of the cards in the trump suit would be: **Joker, ♠J, ♣J, ♠A, ♠K, ♠Q, ♠10, ♠9,** and so on down, to the lowest spade.

In all these games trump is chosen, or decided upon, after the cards have been dealt but before the hand is played. In whist and euchre the last card dealt is simply turned face up to represent the trump suit for that hand. The same method of designating trump is used in two-handed pinochle.

In more modern games the players bid for the privilege of declaring trump. In bridge and five hundred each bidder agrees to take a certain number of tricks if a specified suit becomes trump. The trump suit is determined by the highest bidder, who becomes the "declarer." A player can also bid no-trump; this means precisely what the name implies, that there is to be no trump suit in that hand.

Once a trump has been declared, the other, or ordinary, suits become known as side suits. In games of the whist family–which include bridge and five hundred–an ace is a sure winner when its suit is led, unless another player is out of that suit and therefore is allowed to trump the trick. In the case of no-trump, however, an ace is always a sure winner in its own suit.

After the ace has been played, the king becomes the dominant card of that suit, but there is often the danger that the king and ace may be played on the same trick; in this case the ace will capture the king. When a player holds a king and a smaller card of the same suit (as **♣K ♣7**), his king is said to be guarded, because the small card can be played on an opponent's ace, thus saving the king for a later trick.

Similar to a guarded king is a guarded queen, which must have two smaller cards along with it (as **♣Q ♣9 ♣2**). A guarded jack requires three cards of lower value in the same suit as companions (**♣J ♣8 ♣6 ♣5**).

Frequently it is possible to capture a guarded king by a type of play termed a "finesse." Assume that in a game of bridge the cards of a specific suit–say, diamonds–are distributed among the players thus:

North
◇ **A Q 9 7**

West ◇ **K 8** | *East* ◇ **J 4**

South
◇ **10 6 5 3 2**

South leads a low diamond to the ace and queen held by his partner, North. If West plays his low card (◇**8**), North takes it with the queen and still has his ace to take West's king later. This is called finessing the queen, and the purpose is to take the first trick with the queen, leaving the opposing king powerless to prevent it.

West has one alternative; that is to play the king and force the ace from North's hand. In that case no finesse is needed, as North's queen promptly becomes the highest card in the suit. So either play by West works to North's advantage.

However, if East had happened to be holding the guarded king (◇**K** ◇**8**) and West the other pair (◇**J** ◇**4**), the finesse would not work. West would play the low ◇**4** and North, hoping the king to be in West's hand, would play the ◇**Q**. East would then top the trick with the ◇**K**.

The finesse was originally used in whist and is also a valuable play in five hundred, but it has reached its highest development in the game of bridge, where it is used in rather surprising and ingenious variations. That is because in bridge, after trump has been declared, the declarer's partner lays his hand face up on the table. The declarer then proceeds to play both hands, the partner's hand being referred to as the "dummy."

By comparing the cards in his concealed hand with those showing openly in the dummy, the declarer frequently observes finessing opportunities and other possible plays that would never have been apparent in whist or the other games in which all hands are concealed from the other players.

In auction pitch and auction pinochle, players bid for the privilege of naming trump but do not have to specify what suit it will be until after the bidding is ended. In both pitch and pinochle, taking tricks is important, but score is determined not by the number of tricks but by the point value of certain cards, sometimes termed "counters," which are acquired with those tricks.

Rules as to trumping also vary with these games. In pitch a player may trump at any time, regardless of whether he is holding cards of the suit that someone else has led. In pinochle a player is forced to trump if he has no cards of the suit led, unless he is out of trump; then, of course, he can throw on a card from an odd suit.

Another pinochle peculiarity is that when a trump is led, the next player must top it with a higher trump, if he can, and the next must go still higher. These are all part and parcel of the games themselves, as will be explained under their individual heads.

In all trump games a shortage of cards in a side suit is often a great help to a player who has a fairly good holding in the trump suit. Once he has cleared himself of his short suit, he can use his trumps to take tricks led from that suit.

This is highly important in whist and bridge, where each player is dealt thirteen cards at the start; a shortage in one suit may mean abnormal length in another, often giving an inkling as to the probable holdings of the other players.

Whist and bridge players use a special nomenclature when referring to such suits, and the terms have been extended to other trump games:

When a player's original hand contains no cards whatever in a certain suit, it is termed a "blank suit" or a "void," for example, a "void in spades."

When a player is dealt only one card in a certain suit, that card is termed a "singleton." Thus, a hand containing only the ♡**8** would have a "singleton in hearts" or a "heart singleton."

When a player is dealt only two cards in a certain suit, the combination is termed a "doubleton." Thus, an original holding of ♣**J** ♣**9** would be a "doubleton in clubs."

A holding of three cards in a suit (as ◇**J** ◇**8** ◇**3**) is known as a "tripleton," but this term is seldom used.

Whist

Whist was one of the earliest card games to incorporate a trump suit that takes precedence over the other three suits. It is probably as old as the French game of *triomphe* (triumph), from which the word "trump" is derived, but its direct antecedent is the English game of Ruff and Honors, two terms still used in whist and its lineal descendant, bridge.

In whist the standard pack of fifty-two cards is used. There are four players, forming two teams: as *A*, the original dealer, and *B*, the person seated opposite him; the other team consisting of *X*, the player on the dealer's left, and *Y*, the player on the dealer's right. The pack is shuffled and the cards are dealt singly, beginning with *X*, the player on the left.

All the cards are dealt face down until the final one, which is turned face up but belongs to the dealer's hand. The suit of that card designates the trump. Thus, if the ♡**10** is turned up, hearts become trumps.

The player to the left (*X*) leads one of his cards, placing it face up on the table, and the other players follow suit if possible. Otherwise, a player may discard, or if an ordinary suit is led, and he is out of it, he may trump the trick, or "ruff" it, as they say in whist.

The winner of each trick leads to the next, and the tricks are gathered by one partner and laid in overlapping fashion, face down. Six tricks are called a book, and any additional tricks taken by a team are scored at one point each.

The first team to score seven points wins the game. This may be accomplished in a single hand by taking all the tricks, but that is not frequent in whist. The final hand is played through to the finish, enabling the winners to try for a higher score than seven. The losing score is subtracted from the winning score to determine the margin of victory.

Here is a hand that was chosen by Cavendish, the great whist authority of his day, as illustrating some of the imporant features of play:

B

♠ K Q J 4
♡ Q 5
♣ A 4 2
◊ K J 8 5

X

♠ 7 6 2
♡ K J 9 7 6 4
♣ J
◊ 10 7 6

Y

♠ A 9
♡ A 10
♣ 9 8 7 6 5 3
◊ Q 9 3

A

♠ 10 8 5 3
♡ 8 3 2
♣ K Q 10*
◊ A 4 2

*♣**10** was turned up as trump card

First Trick: *X*, ♡**7**; *B*, ♡**5**; *Y*, ♡**A**; *A*, ♡**2**.

Here, *X* led the fourth-best card of his longest or numerically strongest suit, in accordance with a well-accepted rule, thus informing his partner that he had three hearts higher than the ♡**7**.

B played the ♡**5**, conforming to a rule that the second hand should generally play his lowest card on the first round of a suit, since his partner has a later play.

Y played the ♡**A**, according to a rule that the third hand should generally play his highest card on the first round of a suit, to give his partner full support.

A, at this point, picked up the ♣**10** from the table and added it to his hand, a customary procedure, since the turned-up trump belongs to the dealer. *A* then played his lowest heart, the ♡**2**.

Y took the trick, gathering the four cards and turning them face down in a squared-up packet.

Second Trick: *Y*, ♣**6**; *A*, ♣**Q**; *X*, ♣**J**; *B*, ♣**2**.

Y led the fourth-best card of his longest suit, not just to inform his partner that this was his longest suit, but also to start forcing trumps from the opposing hands. By doing this he hoped to clear the way for *X* to take tricks with his long suit, hearts, without having them trumped.

A played the lower card of a high sequence (♣**Q**) rather than his lowest card (♣**10**). His partner had seen him pick up the ♣**10** and add it to his hand. So *A* was indicating that he could afford to throw away the ♣**Q** because he had the card above it (♣**K**) and possibly the ♣**A** as well.

X played his only trump, the ♣**J**; and *B* played his lowest trump, the ♣**2**, letting his partner's ♣**Q** take the trick.

At this point, *B*, holding the ♣**A**, knew that his partner, *A*, held the ♣**K** along with the ♣**10**. *X*'s play of his high trump (♣**J**) on a losing trick indicated that he had no more trumps. From this, *B* could correctly conclude that the remaining trumps–five cards in all–were in *Y*'s hand.

Third Trick: *A,* ♠**3**; *X,* ♠**2**; *B,* ♠**J**; *Y,* ♠**A.**

Here is complete conformity to the respective rules of "Lead the fourth highest of the longest suit," "Second hand low," "Third hand high," with the fourth hand taking the trick.

Fourth Trick: *Y,* ♣**5**; *A,* ♣**10**; *X,* ♠**6**; *B,* ♣**4.**

Here, *Y* continued his policy of forcing out the trumps, while *X* followed an accepted rule in discarding from his weakest suit, spades, informing his partner, *Y*, of that fact.

Fifth Trick: *A,* ♠**5**; *X,* ♠**7**; *B,* ♠**Q**; *Y,* ♠**9.**

A led again from his long suit (spades), and his partner, *B*, won the trick, with a play of "Third hand high."

Sixth Trick: *B,* ♠**K**; *Y,* ♣**9**; *A,* ♠**8**; *X,* ♢**6.**

This was criticized as a bad lead on *B*'s part; he should have known that his partner, *A*, held the only remaining spades, since he had led his fourth highest from that suit. Also, *B* should have recognized that *Y* would trump this trick and follow with a trump lead.

Seventh Trick: *Y,* ♣**3**; *A,* ♣**K**; *X,* ♡**4**; *B,* ♣**A.**

Y's lead of a low trump drew out the two highest trumps from *A* and *B*, leaving them without trumps.

Eighth Trick: *B,* ♠**4**; *Y,* ♣**7**; *A,* ♠**10**; *X,* ♡**6.**

B led the ♠**4**, forcing *Y* to trump with the ♣**7** or lose the trick.

Ninth Trick: *Y,* ♡**10**; *A,* ♡**3**; *X,* ♡**J**; *B,* ♡**Q.**

Here, *X* did not know who held the ♡**Q**, so he played the ♡**J**, hoping that the ♡**Q** was in *A*'s hand on the right. This is the play that is termed a finesse, and in this case *X* finessed the jack but lost the trick, as the queen was in *B*'s hand on *X*'s left.

X regarded the finesse as a good gamble, because if he had won the trick with the ♡**J**, he could have led the ♡**K** for another sure trick and possibly have taken still another with the ♡**9**.

Tenth Trick: B, ◇**K**; *Y,* ◇**3**; *A,* ◇**2**; *X,* ◇**7**.

B led the ◇**K** knowing that if his partner, *A,* held the ◇**A**, he would play a small card and let the ◇**K** win the trick. Since *A* actually held the ◇**A** and played the ◇**2**, this worked as *B* had hoped.

However, if *X* or *Y* (the opponents) had held the ◇**A**, it would have been forced by *B*'s lead of the ◇**K**. In that case the ◇**Q** would have become the top card in its suit and capable of taking a later trick. So *B* was depending on the strong chance that if *A* did not hold the ◇**A**, he would at least have the ◇**Q**.

Eleventh Trick: B, ◇**J**; *Y,* ◇**Q**; *A,* ◇**A**; *X,* ◇**10**.

Here, *B* tried a finesse in reverse. He knew that his partner, *A*, held the ◇**A** and that if the opposition held the ◇**Q**, it was probably in *Y*'s hand. So *B*'s finesse of the jack meant that if *Y* failed to play the queen, *A* could hold back the ◇**A** and play his low ◇**4**, letting *B*'s ◇**J** ride through as the trick taker.

However, *Y* played the ◇**Q** on the long chance that *B* held the ◇**A**. When *A* took the trick with the ◇**A**, *X* was forced to play his ◇**10** and, as a result, *Y*'s ◇**9** became high.

Twelfth Trick: A, ◇**4**; *X,* ♡**9**; *B,* ◇**8**; *Y,* ◇**9**.

A led the ◇**4** hoping that *B* held the ◇**9**, but *Y* had it and took the trick. However, it was *A*'s proper lead, as his only other card was the ♡**8**, which *X* was sure to take with the ♡**K**, as the other players were out of hearts.

Thirteenth Trick: Y, ♣**8**; *A,* ♡**8**; *X,* ♡**K**; *B,* ◇**5**.

Y took the final trick with his last trump, but *X*'s failure to make good the ♡**K** earlier gave the team of *A-B* one odd trick (seven out of thirteen) and they scored one point for the hand.

The term "ruff" was originally synonymous with "trump," and in modern usage a player is said to ruff a trick when he puts a trump card on a lead from a side suit. Ruffing is highly important in whist and bridge; often, a player makes a deliberate lead of a low card in a side suit, knowing that his partner, being out of that suit, can ruff the lead and win the trick.

When two partners are each out of a different suit, yet both hold trump cards, they can sometimes ruff back and forth from one hand to the other. This is called a cross-ruff, and it can prove devastating to the opposing team.

As an example, suppose that a hand has reached this stage, spades being trumps:

D
♠ K J
♡ Q J 7
◇ Q 5 2

W		*Z*
♠ 10 8 4		♠ 7 6 3
♡ 9 6 3		◇ 9 8 6
♣ 8 5		♣ 4 2

E
♡ 8
◇ K J 10 4
♣ J 9 3

It is *W*'s lead and his case is about hopeless, except that he knows–or guesses–that his partner, *Z*, happens to be out of one suit, hearts.

So *W* leads the ♡**3**, *D* plays the ♡**J** and *Z* ruffs with his ♠**3**, while *E* plays the ♡**8**. *Z* takes the trick.

Z, hoping or knowing that *W* is out of one suit, diamonds, but knowing that he has some trumps, spades, in hand, leads the ◇**6**. *E* plays the ◇**K**, and *W* ruffs with his ♠**4**, while *D* plays the ◇**2**. *W* takes the trick.

Now *W* leads another heart, *Z* ruffs it with a spade and leads back with a diamond that *W* ruffs. Again, *W* leads a heart for *Z* to ruff and *Z* leads back with a diamond that *W* ruffs.

Thanks to the cross-ruff, *W* and *Z* have taken six tricks between them, *D* being forced to throw high hearts on *W*'s low leads; and *E* having to throw high diamonds on *Z*'s low leads. *E*'s shortage of hearts is no help, as he has no trumps with which to overtrump *Z*'s ruffs.

Whist, in its heyday, became a highly developed game, combining stylized plays with good judgment, gaining a terminology of its own, and winning many keen minds to its cause. It became the progenitor of bridge, which wooed away many ardent whist enthusiasts while undergoing changes of its own; yet whist has retained a strong popularity, ranking it, according to some estimates, among the twelve most popular card games played today.

This is due largely to the fact that whist has one main aim, that is, simply and only to win tricks, many of its fine points being dedicated to that purpose. Comparative phases of whist and bridge are therefore in order, since whist is not only a good game in its own right; its fundamentals are good schooling for the prospective bridge player. Between them, the two games have enraptured card players for a few centuries, which puts them in a class with Edmund Hoyle himself.

In whist the four highest trump cards **(A K Q J)** are known as honors; in the English version of the game a team holding three honors was credited with two points, while a team holding all four honors gained four points. Honors are not counted in the American game of whist, as they introduce a freakish element of luck.

However, in bridge, honors are counted as part of a bonus score, and the top five trumps **(A K Q J 10)** all rate as honors. In auction bridge there are more than a dozen possible scoring combinations where honors are concerned, but in the modern game of contract bridge this has been winnowed down to the simple scoring of 100 points for four honors in one hand and 150 points for all five honors in one hand.

Since such scoring applies to trump holdings only, a special rating has been designed for no-trump, in which each ace, as the top card in its suit, counts as an honor. A player holding all four honors in no-trump gains 150 bonus points for his team score.

In contract bridge the element of luck is greatly tempered and sometimes nullified by the bidding factor, as a player may sometimes extend his bidding or allow it to be influenced by his potential honor holdings in one suit or in no-trump. If holding the four aces, for example, he might risk a bid in no-trump despite his partner's efforts to divert the bidding to some specific suit.

The term "honors," or "honor cards," has been extended to signify the highest cards in any suit. This is proper enough when evaluating a bridge hand, because all those cards are potential honors until a trump has actually been declared.

But the term should be avoided with other games; it is an affectation that bridge enthusiasts have carried into remote and unrelated fields of play. For example, there are no honors in the game of poker (and sometimes no honor, either, though that is another story).

Another confusing legacy of whist is the term "tenace," which is related to a French adjective meaning tenacious, or clinging together. A tenace, according to the original Hoyle, is the holding of the first- and third-best cards of any suit. This means specifically the ace and queen; but after the ace has been played, a holding of the king and jack attains that rating, and later, such combinations as queen-ten and jack-nine.

So, in the initial survey of a hand, practiced whist players made three distinctions: they rated any ace-queen as a major tenace and any king-jack as a minor tenace; if a player happened to hold the ace-queen-ten in any suit, he regarded it as a double tenace.

Modern bridge players have come to class any broken sequence of honors as a tenace. This has raised a new distinction between a perfect tenace, with a gap of only one card (as **A Q**, **K J**, and **Q 10**), and an imperfect tenace, where the gap is wider (as **A J** or **K 10**).

The widest possible gap between two honor cards is that of ace-ten, which also comes within the requirements of a tenace. As a result, many beginners in the game of bridge mistakenly suppose that the term "tenace" is derived from ace and ten. Such is not its origin, as whist players did not regard ace-ten as a tenace.

Oddly, however, the best way to define a tenace in its modern form is by means of its common misnomer. Any cards of the same suit from ten to ace in value, form a tenace, provided there is a gap somewhere in between. Every tenace holding may afford an opportunity for a finesse, a type of play already described in brief.

Factors already discussed in the sample whist hands (pages 187–190) will serve as steppingstones to the play of bridge hands as well, again emphasizing the affinity between those two great games. The line of demarcation comes with opening leads peculiar to bridge, because of its bidding feature, as well as later plays based on the presence of a face-up dummy, both of which are fully discussed in the chapter on contract bridge, which begins on page 259.

Euchre

This ever-popular, fast-moving game is played with a pack of thirty-two cards, aces down to sevens. In the two-handed game the pack is usually reduced to twenty-four cards by removing the eights and sevens. Since that is the simplest form of euchre, it will be described first.

Euchre is a trump game, in which one suit is declared trump for each new hand. In trumps the highest card is the jack, termed the right bower. Next highest is the jack of the suit of the same color (black or red), known as the left bower. This is followed by the ace of trump, and so on down. In ordinary suits ace is high and seven is low.

Thus, with spades as trumps, the suits would run:

Trumps:	♠J	♣J	♠A	♠K	♠Q	♠10	♠9	♠8 ♠7
Others:	♣A	♣K	♣Q	♣10	♣9	♣8	♣7	
	♡A	♡K	♡Q	♡J	♡10	♡9	♡8	♡7
	◇A	◇K	◇Q	◇J	◇10	◇9	◇8	◇7

Each player is dealt five cards, usually by threes and twos or vice versa. The next card is turned face up on the pack. Its suit represents the first choice for trump, though it is up to one player or the other to declare it as such.

The reason a player may hesitate is that if he declares the trump, he must take three of the five tricks in the play that follows. To clarify this situation, suppose that the following hands have been dealt in a two-handed euchre game:

Opponent:	♠J	♣K	♣Q	◇A	◇Q
Dealer:	♡K	♡J	◇J	◇10	♠10
Turned-up Card:	♠Q				

The opponent has two choices. One is to accept spades as trump and announce, "I order it up."

This means that the dealer can pick up the ♠Q and put it in his hand, discarding any odd card that he does not need. It also means that the opponent, who "ordered up" the trump card, must take three of the five tricks in the play that follows.

The other choice is for the opponent to say "Pass."

In this case the opponent would pass. He has the ♠J, which is the right bower, and the highest card in spades, good for one sure trick. He also has the ◇A as an almost sure trick. But what if the dealer has two or three spades and a few high cards of his own? That is the risk the opponent does not care to face.

When the opponent passes, it becomes the dealer's turn. He, too, has two choices where the acceptance of spades is concerned. He can say "I take it up," and therewith add the ♠Q to his hand, discarding any card in its stead; or he, too, may pass.

In this case the dealer passes. He has practically nothing in spades. His hope is to make a red suit trump, as he has both bowers in either hearts or diamonds. But he must wait until the opponent has another say. The opponent may pass; he might declare hearts or diamonds. Any of those choices would be good, from the dealer's standpoint.

Instead, the opponent states, "I make it clubs."

Why clubs?

Because the ♠J as left bower is a sure trick, with the protection of the ♣K and ♣Q, one of which should take a trick itself. With the ◇A for another, the opponent is sure that he can take three out of the five possible tricks–or more.

If he takes three or four tricks, he scores one point.

If he takes all five tricks, he is credited with a "march," which counts two points.

However, if he fails to take his required minimum of three tricks, he will be "euchred" and the other player will be credited with two points.

All such points count toward game, which is customarily five points.

In this hand the opponent has little trouble.

The opponent leads his left bower (♠J) and finding that the dealer has no clubs, he leads his ace of diamonds, then his two clubs, and finally the queen of diamonds, taking all five tricks and scoring two points toward game.

If the opponent had passed, as he might have if he had been holding some other spade than the jack, the dealer would have made diamonds trump and would have taken two tricks with the bowers, catching another with the ten of diamonds, then making good the king of hearts and possibly the ten of spades.

However, the opponent always leads the first card, regardless of whether he or the dealer named the trump. This gives him a definite advantage in the play of the hand. If he is strong in trump, he may be able to clear them by leading his high ones, following with high cards in other suits after there is no danger of the dealer trumping them.

Of course, if the lead changes because of the dealer's capturing an early trick, the advantage is reversed. But in euchre, taking tricks is like a hit-and-run play in baseball: you trust partly to luck that you will get the most while you have the opportunity. At that, if a lead strikes an unlucky snag, it still may not prove fatal.

If a player holds three trump cards, he generally has an edge. If he holds a king-high in a side suit, the ace is more likely to be in the pack than in an opposing hand. In the twenty-four-card pack recommended for two-handed play, there are fourteen cards out of circulation, compared to the mere five in an individual hand.

However, when your trump strength is doubtful or is likely to be challenged, a lead of a high card in a side suit may bring you a quick trick. If not, it will force a trump which would have taken a trick anyway. This improves your own trump holdings and gives you a chance for another force play with a smaller card of the suit you originally led, if you have one.

About the only bad lead is a small card in a side suit that can be taken by one a notch higher—say, a nine, which can be taken by a ten. Giving away a trick that cheaply is to be avoided whenever possible.

The game of euchre, simple in its two-handed form, takes on new stature, with added features, when played as a partnership in

FOUR-HANDED EUCHRE

Here, the thirty-two-card pack is used, and each player is dealt five cards—twenty in all, leaving only twelve in the pack. The top card, the twenty-first, is turned up as the prospective trump, and the players either pass or order it up into the dealer's hand, but with a slight difference.

If the dealer's partner, who sits opposite him, wants him to take the trump into his hand, the partner says "I assist," instead of "I order it up." It amounts to the same thing, but it puts the burden of taking three tricks onto the dealer and his partner, exactly as if everyone had passed around to the dealer, who then decided to take it up.

Should all the players pass, the trump is turned down and the privilege of making trump goes around the board. No one can make a trump that has been turned down, but once a trump is named, play is opened by the opponent on the dealer's left. He and the opponent on the dealer's right constitute a partnership.

Using bridge nomenclature, West and East (the opponents) combine their trick-taking efforts against South and North (the dealer and his partner), scoring points toward game exactly as described in two-handed euchre.

However, the partnership game offers a player a chance to "go for broke" that is not found in the two-handed game. If he feels he can win three tricks or more by playing a lone hand against the other team, he announces that fact. Let us assume that this occurs in the first round. An opponent wants to make such a try, and he states, "I order it up alone."

The dealer then takes the face-up card from the pack and adds it to his hand as a trump card. The opponent's partner lays his hand face down and takes no further part. If West is the opponent playing alone, he leads, and North and South follow. If East is the lone player, North leads.

Should the dealer (South) be playing alone, he simply takes up the trump card. His partner (North) then lays his hand face down, and West leads, followed by East and South. But if North plays the lone hand, the turned-up trump is simply turned down, along with South's hand, and West leads.

If the prospective trump is turned down and the bidding goes into the second round, a player naming a trump of his own choice may announce that he will "play it alone." The procedure is precisely as described above. The player's partner tosses in his hand, and the lead is made by the first player on the dealer's left.

The purpose of playing alone is simply this: in partnership euchre the scoring is ordinarily the same as in the two-handed game, but on a basis of teams instead of individuals. The team that names trump scores one point for taking three or four tricks; if it takes all five, it scores two points for a march. If it fails to take as many as three tricks, it is euchred and the opposing team scores two points.

However, when playing alone, a player gains four points for his team if he takes all five tricks; that is, his march–if he makes it!–counts double the usual two points. The other scores remain the same: one point for taking three or four tricks after naming trump; or two points for the opposing team if the lone player is euchred.

While the dealer (South) can sometimes help a lone hand by taking up trump, the player on his left (West) is in the most advantageous position to score a "double march" because he has the lead and might clear trumps so as to slip by with a dubious card in another suit for his fifth trick.

The big question is this: if you are *sure* of three tricks, but doubtful of the others, why not count on your partner to help gain the rest and be satisfied with an ordinary march and its two points?

There are three answers to that query: (1) you can't be sure that your partner has any help; (2) you may not need his help if you get the breaks you want; (3) the score may be the all-important factor.

Suppose the score stands four to one in the other side's favor. You and your partner make trump together and score two points on an easy march, where you take all the tricks. If you had played it alone, you would have bagged four points and game with it.

Instead, you and your partner still have to score a march, or win two ordinary hands in succession, to come out ahead. If you think that's easy, you just don't know your euchre. It's a case of getting points when you can, because you never know how good–or how bad!–the next hand may be.

In scoring euchre, low cards from the pack can be used to keep tab. One method is to place a black four face down across a face-up black three, so that only one spot shows, for one point. For two points, the cards are turned over to show two end spots of the four. For three points, place the three face up on the four; for four points, place the four face up on the three. For five points, turn the four crosswise to reveal one spot of the three, and move it to show another spot for six points. In this way the game can be carried up to seven points, which some players prefer as a total for game.

THREE-HANDED EUCHRE

This game is often termed cutthroat euchre, because one player must play each hand alone against the other two, who in turn may be fighting each other. It is played much like the two-handed game, but always with the thirty-two-card pack, and each player decides independently whether he should order up trump or pass. The dealer can take it up or pass as he prefers; in the latter case the players go into the second round of making trump.

If the first and second players have scored one point each and are combined against the third player, who has already scored four, obviously they will be eager to defeat him when he has named trump. If he wins the hand, he will gain one point and will win game at five points. But if the third player fails to take three tricks and is euchred, the first and second players, scoring two each, will still be even at three points each, the third player's score remaining at four points.

Suppose, however, that the first player already has three points and that the second and third players are tied at two each. Now, if the third player names trump, the situation is radically changed. If the first and second players combine and euchre the third player, they will score two points each. The first player would thereby make game, with five points, while the second player would fall short, with only a four-point total.

So although the first and second players are nominally partners for that hand, the second player would have to play it both ways in order to stay in the game. By throwing a trick or two to the third player, the second player would enable the third player to win the hand and gain one point, so the score would then stand: first, three; second, two; third, three.

But the second player should be careful not to throw too many tricks to the third player, or the third player might take all five and thereby literally steal a march, gaining three points and game with it. So the second player must see to it that he or the first player snags at least one trick.

Note: In all forms of euchre, if all players pass twice around, the cards are gathered for a new deal by the player next to the left. The same applies to five hundred, the game that follows.

Scoring in three-handed euchre: 1 point for naming trump and taking three or four tricks; 3 for all five. Failure to take three tricks (being euchred), 2 points to each opponent.

Five Hundred

This fast, intriguing game is adaptable to play by three, four, five, and even six players. During its heyday it became so popular that special five-hundred packs were designed and manufactured with the extra cards needed in the six-handed game. These have been obtainable ever since.

In its basic three-handed form, five hundred is known as bid euchre, as it stems directly from euchre. It also incorporates features of whist and auction bridge, particularly in the four-handed game, which is played in partnership, two players to a team.

Since the three-handed game is the simplest, it will be described first; the same general rules as to play and scoring apply to the later developments.

THREE-HANDED FIVE HUNDRED

The euchre pack of thirty-two cards (**A K Q J 10 9 8 7** of each suit) is used, plus the joker, which becomes the highest card in the pack, making thirty-three cards in all.

Ten cards are dealt to each player, usually by threes, with one card on the last round. In the course of this deal, however, an odd group of three cards is laid aside, face down, and becomes known as the widow. Usually, the widow is dealt after the first round of threes.

The players look at their hands and bid for the privilege of making trump, beginning with the player on the dealer's left. Each player either passes or states that he will try to take six or more tricks in the play that follows, provided that a specified suit is trumps, or if there is no trump.

The privilege goes to the highest bidder, in keeping with the following schedule:

Trumps	6 Tricks	7 Tricks	8 Tricks	9 Tricks	10 Tricks
Spades	40	140	240	340	440
Clubs	60	160	260	360	460
Diamonds	80	180	280	380	480
Hearts	100	200	300	400	500
No-trump	120	220	320	420	520

Thus, a bid of six hearts at 100 could be topped by a bid of seven spades at 140, which in turn could be topped by a bid of seven no-trump at 220. With a strong hand an early bidder will often bid at a level of eight or nine to discourage others from outbidding him.

This is often necessary when only one bid is allowed each player, as was originally the rule in five hundred, though later, unrestricted bidding was introduced into the game, as will be described.

The highest bidder gains these four privileges:

1. The hand is played with the trump suit, or no-trump, according to his declaration.

2. Before the play the bidder picks up the widow and adds its three cards to his hand. He then discards any three cards that he chooses, laying them aside and face down. This discarded group replaces the original widow and remains out of play. Often, the bidder's hand is improved by cards taken from the widow.

3. The bidder makes the lead to the first trick, using any card in his hand.

4. If he takes the required number of tricks, or more, during the play of the hand, he scores the amount of his bid.

Thus, a bid of eight diamonds would give the successful bidder a score of 280 toward a total of 500, which is the amount necessary to win the game.

Against these advantages, the bidder runs one big risk; namely, if he fails to take the number of tricks required by his bid, that amount is deducted from his score. This may result in a minus score, putting the player "in the hole." Thus, with a bid of eight diamonds in the opening deal, a bidder taking only seven tricks, or less, would be charged with a score of minus 280.

Opposing players, meanwhile, score ten points for each trick that they take individually, whether the bidder makes his bid or not.

In the play of the hand, the highest trump is the joker. Next is the jack of the trump suit, or right bower; then the jack of the other suit of the same color, or left bower. The remaining trumps follow in order, **A, K, Q, 10, 9, 8, 7,** making ten trumps in all. This is exactly as in euchre, except for the addition of the joker; but in five hundred all the cards are dealt out, so that all ten trumps are in play during every deal. Ordinary suits run from ace down to seven.

The play proceeds. After discarding three extra cards in the widow, the bidder leads from any suit he chooses. The other players follow suit, if possible. If out of a suit, a player may throw off a card of another suit.

The trick is taken by the highest card of the suit led, except when an ordinary suit is led and a player who is out of the suit plays a trump card upon it. In that case the trump takes the trick, unless the next player overtrumps it. In any event the winner of a trick leads to the next trick.

In no-trump the joker is regarded as a lone trump card, which may be played upon a trick only when the player is out of the suit led. The joker then takes the trick. However, a player may lead the joker, calling it the top in any suit he chooses, and the other players must follow suit if they can.

This makes the joker essential to many no-trump bids, as it can be used to draw out a high card from an opponent's hand, enabling the bidder to win tricks with lesser cards of that suit. In no-trump all suits are valued from ace down to seven.

The following hands illustrate the bidding and play in a deal of three-handed five hundred:

Player C (Bidder)	*Opponent A*	*Opponent B*
Trump **Joker ♢J ♡J ♢Q ♢8**	♢ **A K 10**	♢ **9 7**
♠ **A Q 10**	♠ **K J**	♠ **9 8 7**
♣ **J 7**	♣ **Q 10 8**	♣ **A 9**
	♡ **K Q**	♡ **A 8 7**

Widow: **♣K ♡10 ♡9**

Assume that the bidder went as high as eight diamonds in the hope of getting something better in the widow. Adding the widow cards to his hand, he keeps the ♣**K** and discards the ♣**7** along with the ♡**10** and ♡**9**.

Play then proceeds:

First Trick: *C* leads **Joker**; *A* plays ◊**10**; *B* plays ◊**7**.

Second Trick: *C* leads ◊**J**; *A* plays ◊**K**; *B* plays ◊**9**.

Third Trick: *C* leads ♡**J**; *A* plays ◊**A**; *B* plays ♠**7**.

The bidder has now cleared trumps from the other hands. *B* played the ♠**7** to show *A* that he (*B*) is weak in spades and would prefer a lead in another suit, if *A* gets the opportunity, as *A* and *B* are temporarily in partnership, hoping to prevent the bidder from making eight diamonds. However, the bidder uses this information to his own advantage:

Fourth Trick: *C* leads ♠**A**; *A* plays ♠**J**; *B* plays ♠**8**.

Fifth Trick: *C* leads ♠**Q**; *A* plays ♠**K**; *B* plays ♠**9**.

Here, the bidder forced *A* to take the trick with ♠**K**, and since the ♠**J** was already played, the ♠**10** will be good to take a trick later.

Sixth Trick: *A* leads ♡**K**; *B* plays ♡**7**; *C* trumps with ◊**8**.

Seventh Trick: *C* leads ♠**10**; *A* plays ♣**8**; *B* plays ♡**8**.

Eighth Trick: *C* leads ♣**J**; *A* plays ♣**Q**; *B* plays ♣**9**.

The bidder hoped that either *A* or *B* was holding a lone ♣**A**, which would be played on the ♣**J**, making the bidder's ♣**K** good. But *B* (holding the ♣**A**) was able to duck under *A*'s winning ♣**Q**.

Ninth Trick: *A* leads ♡**Q**; *B* plays ♡**A**; *C* trumps with ◊**Q**.

Tenth Trick: *C* leads ♣**K**; *A* plays ♣**10**; *B* plays ♣**A**.

Since the bidder won only seven of the ten tricks, he lost his bid of eight diamonds and went 280 points in the hole. Player *A* won two tricks, scoring 20 points; player *B* won one trick, scoring 10 points. Continuing with further deals, this game worked out as follows, with *A, B,* and *C* (the bidder in the first hand) as the participants:

	SCORE		
First Deal: *C* bid eight diamonds.	*A*	*B*	*C*
C took 7 tricks; *A* took 2; *B* took 1.	20	10	−280
Second Deal: *A* bid seven hearts.			
A took 8 tricks; *B* took 1; *C* took 1.	220	20	−270
Third Deal: *C* bid seven no-trump.			

C took 9 tricks; *A* took 1; *B* took 0.	230	20	−50
Fourth Deal: *B* bid seven spades.			
B took 5 tricks; *C* took 2; *A* took 3.	260	−120	−30
Fifth Deal: *C* bid six no-trump.			
C took 7 tricks; *A* took 2; *B* took 1.	280	−110	90
Sixth Deal: *A* bid nine spades.			
A took 9 tricks; *B* took 0; *C* took 1.	620	−110	100

Player *A* became the winner, since his score went over 500. Note that the scores are added to the existing scores after each hand, showing the totals as they then stand.

Also note that each winner receives credit *only for the amount bid,* not for any extra tricks that he made. This encourages high bidding, in order to get the full worth from the hand. Often, however, it is smarter to bid conservatively, but a bidder may be forced to go the limit to top a desperation bid on the part of an opponent.

For example, in the sixth and final deal, *A* could have gone out on a bid of eight spades, which would have given him 240 points for a total score of 520. Obviously, he was forced to a bid of nine spades to prevent the other players from overbidding him, which they would naturally do to keep him from going out.

To put a curb on wild overbids, there is a rule that a player going minus 500–or 500 in the hole–is declared the loser, whereupon the player with the highest score automatically becomes the winner. Thus, in the sample game just given, if *B* had overbid *A*'s nine spades with nine no-trump and *B* had lost, *B*'s score would have dropped to –530 and *A* would have won the game.

This rule is sometimes modified to make minus 1000 the losing score.

Other special rulings are as follows:

Any player taking all ten tricks is credited with 250 points, provided his bid was less than that amount. Thus, a bid of seven diamonds would jump from 180 to 250 as a score, if the bidder took all the tricks; but a bid of eight diamonds would still rate only 280 points.

A special bid termed "nullo" may be introduced if desired. This gives the bidder 250 points if he can play a hand in no-trump without taking any tricks. If he holds the joker, he will have to discard it in the widow, as it constitutes an individual trump and must therefore take a trick if played.

Nullo rates as a bid of 250 and if the bidder takes any tricks at all, that amount is subtracted from his score. Both opponents score ten points for each trick that the nullo bidder may be forced to take in play.

Any bid of higher than 250 outbids a nullo.

In bidding a five-hundred hand a player can count: (*a*) positive tricks, in the form of high trump cards that are sure winners or can be turned into such; (*b*) probable tricks, in side suits, as aces, ace-king, ace-king-queen, or the king in a king-queen combination; (*c*) possible tricks, as kings, queens, or even lesser cards that can be saved while still lower cards are sacrificed. Surplus cards in a long side suit may also be possible tricks.

The sample hand bid by player *C* breaks down into the following:

Positive Tricks:	**Joker**	♢**J**	♡**J**
Probable Tricks:	♢**Q**	♢**8**	♠**A**
Possible Tricks:	♠**Q**		

Those are seven in all, so seven diamonds was a proper limit to the bid. However, the widow offered strong prospects, namely: a positive trick if it contained either the ♢**A** or ♢**K**; a probable trick if it contained the ♢**10**, ♢**9**, ♢**7**, ♣**A**, or ♡**A**. The ♠**K** in the widow would be a probable trick—and would enable the ♠**Q** (already in the bidder's hand) to become a probable trick as well. Several other cards would do for possible tricks, and the bidder actually picked up one of those, the ♣**K**, in the widow. But his failure to make good that possible trick caused him to lose the bid of eight diamonds.

AUCTION FIVE HUNDRED

In the original game of five hundred only one bid was allowed each player. This was not recognized as a serious limitation until the bidding system, already popularized in five hundred, was utilized in auction bridge, where, probably because thirteen tricks were involved instead of only ten, a continued or "repeat" form of bidding was required to raise the competition to the higher levels.

Whatever the precise reason, it was only logical that this unrestricted auction, having proved its worth in bridge, should have been borrowed back by five hundred. Actually it was, although no rule book or commentary on the game ever seems to have said so.

Most rule books state: "Only one bid is allowed each player," and that edict has never been rewritten because it wasn't necessary. Five-hundred players just crossed it out or ignored it as obsolete. When five hundred began to wane in popularity about the time of World War I, practically all devotees of the game were operating on the basis of an unrestricted auction.

In the original game of five hundred, bids were valued thus:

Trumps	6 Tricks	7 Tricks	8 Tricks	9 Tricks	10 Tricks
Spades	40	80	120	160	200
Clubs	60	120	180	240	300
Diamonds	80	160	240	320	400
Hearts	100	200	300	400	500
No-trump	120	240	360	480	600

Thus, a bid of seven no-trump beat ten spades. A bid of seven hearts equaled ten spades, but the latter took precedence because more tricks were required. There was nothing complicated about this; five-hundred players of the era regarded it as extremely simple.

They classed spades and clubs as inferior suits and aimed for bids in diamonds and hearts, much as bridge players of that period stressed "majors" and "minors." They considered it as rather "sporting" to go ten spades in order to beat out a bid of seven no-trump.

When the new evaluation now in vogue was first introduced, inveterate five hundreders wanted no part of it. They regarded it as highly efficient and therefore drab and uninteresting. So hardened were the die-hards that nobody has dared throw out the old evaluation, even to this day.

Yet the new count took over, for a very definite reason. It lent itself to unrestricted bidding, which everybody liked. You could start with six spades and climb on up to nine, maybe with a switch to clubs along the way, while you heard what others had to offer in diamonds, hearts, and even no-trump.

An analogy is found in pinochle, where bidding was originally limited in the three-handed game, yet became unrestricted in its later development as auction pinochle.

In five hundred unlimited bidding should be the rule, not only in the three-handed form just described but in the partnership game of

FOUR-HANDED FIVE HUNDRED

This game requires a forty-three-card pack, including joker, with red suits running from ace down through five; black suits, from ace down through four. Each player is dealt ten cards, with three over for the widow.

Opposite players are partners, and bidding begins with the player at the dealer's left, as illustrated in the following hand:

North
♠ K 7 5
♣ A Q
♢ A 10 7
♡ K 10

West
♣ J K 10 9 6
♠ Q 6
♢ K Q
♡ 9

Widow
♡8 ♡6 ♣7

East
Joker
♠ A 10 9 8 4
♣ 5
♢ 8 6
♡ Q

South
♡J ♢J ♡A ♡7 ♡5
♠ J
♣ 8 4
♢ 9 5
(*Dealer*)

For convenience, three of the hands are shown with the prospective trump suit at the top, the way many players place them before they start to bid. The other hand (North) has them in conventional order.

West opens with six clubs, indicating a long suit headed by a bower or the joker and some possible side help.

North has a good six no-trump as an ordinary opening bid, with top cards or blockers in at least three suits, including clubs, the suit bid by West. He could be asking his partner to bid his best suit or go seven no-trump if he holds the joker. North bids six no-trump.

East promptly makes a switch bid to the suit opposite his partner's bid, going seven spades. This is an almost unique feature of five hundred, the real gem of the game.

With joker and bowers interchangeable, East is telling West that he is long or strong in spades—perhaps both—but weak indeed in clubs.

South takes his partner's tip and bids seven hearts, showing one or both bowers but probably not the joker, though he could be bidding on a joker and a one-suit hand as East had just done.

The difference is that the joker, if held by South, would virtually clinch no-trump, even if North should be deficient in one suit. Contrarily, if South happened to hold a strictly poor hand, he could simply pass.

Now note this: In the old one-bid era this would have ended it. East and North would be bidding normally, but East's bid, instead of being informative, would have been final. His problem would have been that of making a sound seven-spade bid or overbidding his hand with eight spades in the hope of forcing South to overbid, as South's bid would have become final, too.

But with the bidding unrestricted, it goes into the second round, fully justifying the bids made so far.

Assuming that South's bid was seven hearts, West may either pass or go eight spades, switching to East's suit on the theory that it will prove stronger, which it is. Between them they will have nine out of a possible thirteen trumps (in spades) instead of only seven (in clubs).

West could practically call the shot on this, figuring East fairly long in spades and very short in clubs, whereas West has two odd and very helpful spades.

If West should pass, North could let South's bid go through, hoping to make a solid seven in hearts, or leaving it to South to supply a higher bid, particularly if West should go over the seven hearts. But should West go eight spades, North could afford to top it and might do so anyway, because, by a switch to eight diamonds North can announce that he has more diamonds than hearts, so South can stay with diamonds if he prefers it.

But also, North is leaving the door open for South to declare eight hearts if he prefers. In addition, North is avowing that he controls the diamond situation as well as clubs. Since South has strong hearts and only one spade (♠J), he can infer that North has a spade block, too.

South, then, could go eight no-trump if he held the joker. But South doesn't hold the joker, so let's suppose that the bidding either stopped at seven hearts or that South went to eight hearts, where it stopped.

In either case, South picks up the widow. Note, though, that if North had raised to eight hearts, he would have taken it, because the widow goes to the final bidder.

South picks up two small hearts, which practically assures him of eight tricks despite the absence of the joker. Discarding is a trifle ticklish, but South finally puts down ♠J ♣7 ♣4 and retains two small diamonds.

He does this because the other team bid clubs and spades both. He figures North surely has clubs stopped (because of North's no-trump bid over the clubs) and that the joker is in East's hand. This latter is neat reasoning:

West probably bid the low club on the strength of the right bower. North doesn't have the joker. East needed the joker or a black bower to go to seven spades. So he must have the joker because South himself held, and just discarded, the missing black bower (♠J).

If North happened to bid eight diamonds, pushing South to eight hearts, that's all the more reason for South to hold the two diamonds. But South discards the lone spade, figuring that when East takes the first trick with the joker, South can trump any spade lead that follows.

South's hand now stands:

♡**J** ◇**J** ♡**A** ♡**8** ♡**7** ♡**6** ♡**5**
♣ **8**
◇ **9 5**

South leads the ♡**J** (right bower), and the ♡**9** and ♡**10** fall, East winning the trick with the joker.

East leads his ♠**A** on a "hit-run" basis and South trumps it with the ♡**5**. The ♠**6** and ♠**5** fall.

There is no dummy hand in five hundred. North, as South's partner, plays his own hand, keeping it hidden, just like the opponents, West and East.

So South leads the ◇**J** (left bower), not knowing that a small trump lead would be taken by North with the ♡**K**. This lead clears the trumps (♡**K** and ♡**Q**).

South, confident that North holds either the ♣**A** or the ◇**A**, can now afford to risk a lead in either suit, trusting that if one fails, the other will work later.

South picks diamonds as the better choice because clubs was West's bid. He leads the ◇**9** and North takes it with the ◇**A**.

North then makes good with his ♣**A** and ♠**K**, South playing the ♣**8** and ◇**5** respectively.

South then takes in four remaining tricks with his trumps. His team scores 160 or 260 according to whether the bid was seven or eight hearts. The opponents get 10 points for one trick.

Note, in review, that if North had held ♣**K** and ◇**K** instead of ♣**A** and ◇**A**, his team would have lost another trick, which they could have spared. But this shows the importance of South's lead of the ◇**9**. He still retained an entry (◇**5**) if he needed it to play to North's ◇**K** later.

This shows the importance of discarding in the widow, a special feature in the intriguing game of five hundred, particularly when played on a partnership basis with unrestricted auction.

If North had made no diamond bid, with South going eight hearts purely on his own, some players would prefer to discard ♠**J** ◇**5** ♣**4** on the premise that North would surely have at least the guarded ♣**K** to have gone no-trump over West's club bid.

A slight difference, indeed, but enough to make or mar a close bid when the game itself is hinging on the outcome of a single hand.

FIVE-HANDED FIVE HUNDRED

This is a freak form of five hundred, yet it is the only version of the game utilizing the full standard pack of fifty-three cards, including the joker. That may explain how the five-handed game came into existence; with exactly enough cards for five players and a widow, it was inevitable that someone should someday tempt fate and try it out.

This problem was immediately encountered: one player would seldom have more than a slim chance of making a contract of six or better when opposing four others in the play. To solve the problem, the bidder was given a partner for that hand, to make it two against three.

That raised the question: who should be the bidder's partner? The rather ingenious answer was a method which may be termed

The High-Card Call

Each player bids and scores individually, as he would in the three-handed game. But after one wins the bid and picks up the widow, he is allowed to call for a partner, whose hand will provide him with a high card that will help in their combined effort against three opponents.

If the bidder does not have the joker, he usually calls for it, provided he does not find it in the widow. If he holds the joker, he calls for a high card such as an ace in a specific suit, or for a bower or some other important trump.

The player holding that card automatically becomes the bidder's partner. The best rule is to have him show it then and there, thus establishing his status. This has been varied by having the play proceed until the designated card appears in normal course, but it places an undue burden on the bidder.

In naming the joker, for example, the player might want immediate cooperation from his partner, yet he might also need to hold the joker in reserve until late in the hand. Not knowing who his partner was, would naturally impede the proper play of the hand. Any rule that produces such a result is obviously a bad one.

To avoid such blind play, a show of the called card is proper, unless the players prefer to use another system altogether, which is called

Naming the Partner

Here, the bidder chooses his own partner, without any reference to a particular card. In company where the bidding is spirited or somewhat reckless, this works nicely, because players gain an idea of one another's holdings from the bids they make.

A no-trump bid in such a game means that the bidder must hold the joker or he would be sunk. So a higher bidder would naturally pick the no-trump bidder as his partner. Similarly, a high bidder in diamonds would pick a hearts bidder as his partner, figuring that he would be holding one of the bowers good in both suits.

However, another factor arises: the score. A bidder with a really strong hand will pick the player with the lowest score to be his partner rather than give a free ride to a player who is better off or who might even "go game" if the bid should prove successful.

To push the bidding up, an optional rule is sometimes introduced whereby anyone bidding eight or better can pick two partners instead of only one. This can mean double trouble if two high-score opponents come in for a free ride. A bidder with a score of 100 could conceivably go ten no-trump on nothing and then pick as his partners two players with scores of 480 and 490 so as to drag them down below zero along with himself.

That would be like getting a fresh start in the game, except that the player would be laying himself open for similar treatment later. To avoid such situations, it is better to pick an unknown partner by the high-card call procedure.

In that case a player who has reached 480 and holds the joker may find it smart to pass rather than bid an easy six no-trump and give himself away.

There is no use delving further into the untouched intricacies of five-handed five hundred, which, after all the years of its existence, is still in an exploratory state. Even the rules are in a state of flux, which is all for the best, because it allows the introduction of

The Ghost Card

This was originally introduced into the three- or four-handed game in the form of an extra joker, but it was generally outlawed; it made the game topheavy with trumps and gave one player or team a decided advantage in no-trump when holding both super cards.

In the five-handed game, however, the addition of the extra joker may encourage higher bidding, while limiting the bidder to one partner, no matter how high the bid. This is on the basis of the successful bidder picking a player as a partner, not on the basis of calling for the holder of a specific card.

This is in keeping with the modern trend toward "wild" games that use the two jokers included in present-day packs of cards. It would also mean four cards in the widow, giving the bidder an additional slight advantage, which he would probably need.

Rather than rate one joker as higher than the other, both can be classed as top cards of equal value, but if both happened to be played on the same trick, the one first played would be the winner.

In scoring, as already mentioned, the player fortunate, or unfortunate, enough to be picked as partner by the bidder is scored the full amount of the bid—plus or minus, as it may turn out. The other players are credited ten points each for tricks that they take individually.

SIX-HANDED FIVE HUNDRED

This game requires the special sixty-three-card pack that contains four elevens, four twelves and two red thirteens. These form a highly imposing array, and their presence emphasizes the importance of trump length as a bidding factor.

There are eighteen trumps in either hearts or diamonds; although they still average about three to a player, it is actually possible for a bidder to hold an all-trump hand and still have eight higher trumps out against him. While such a holding would be very rare, it shows the trend of the game.

Strong trump prospects make it feasible to play six-handed five hundred with three teams of two players each, the partners being seated opposite. Here, high cards as well as length are essential toward successful bidding because of the heavy opposition, plus the fact that many widows are an almost total disappointment in the six-handed game.

The other–and preferred–type of game calls for two opposing teams of three partners each, the members of each team being in alternating positions; that is, Numbers 1, 3, and 5 opposing Numbers 2, 4, and 6.

This game gives a bidder two chances of finding a helpful partner–important in the six-handed game, as many hands are extremely weak, a point which many players are prone to overlook. Any card below a ten is practically chicken feed to be thrown onto winning tricks, except when it happens to form an addition to a long trump suit.

As in other forms of five hundred, the six-handed game is greatly improved by the use of an unrestricted auction which terminates only when all but one bidder have finally passed. Otherwise, when players with "almost" biddable hands hesitate at making an opening bid, it may go clear around to the dealer, enabling him to get by with an undeserved low bid. The moment one player has named a suit, the whole complexion of the hand may change, opening new vistas for unrestricted bidders.

The old rule restricting a player to a single bid included a pass in that same category, so that a bidder had only one chance to express himself in any way whatever. That, too, is rendered obsolete in unrestricted auction. As is customary in most games, players have the option of deciding on such rules beforehand.

Pitch and Auction Pitch

Pitch is a modern form of the old English game of all fours, which became popular in America as old sledge and seven-up, as well as high-low-jack-and-the-game, a title representing the four objectives that each player endeavors to attain. Auction pitch may be played by from two to seven, or even eight, participants, each playing on his own, without partners.

The regular pack of fifty-two cards is used and six cards are dealt to each player—usually three cards at a time—beginning with the player on the dealer's left, who has the first say as to which suit will be trump in the play that follows. In simple pitch the first player announces the trump by leading a card from the suit that he decides upon; this is called the "pitch."

The other players follow suit by playing trump cards if they can; otherwise they must throw on cards from an ordinary suit. The highest trump card takes the trick, and the winner makes the lead in the next trick, from whatever suit he wishes. The other players may either follow suit or trump the trick, even if holding a card of the suit that is led. That is, they are allowed to trump at any time. If out of the suit led, a player may trump or play a card of an odd suit.

The tricks themselves mean nothing in pitch, but certain cards that appear in the course of play are valued at one point each, as follows:

High: This point is scored automatically by the player holding the highest trump in play during that deal.

Low: This point is scored automatically by the player holding the lowest trump in play during that deal.

Jack: This point is scored by the player who takes a trick containing the jack of trumps, if the jack happens to be in play.

Game: This point is scored by the player whose tricks include the greatest total in high cards, which are counted thus: ace, four; king, three; queen, two; jack, one; ten, ten. These values apply to cards of all suits.

With only two or three players in the game, there may be much variance as to high and low, while the jack is often absent. It is also difficult to estimate the count toward game. This is illustrated by the following hand:

First Player	*Second Player*	*Third Player* (*Dealer*)
♡ **10 9 2**	♡	♡ **J 7**
♠ **10**	♠ **4**	♠ **K 5 3**
◊ **Q**	◊ **10 8**	◊ **7**
♣ **3**	♣ **Q 8 7**	♣

First Trick: The first player decides on hearts for trump, as he is sure of a point for low (the ♡**2**) and has more hearts than cards of any other suit. Being anxious to score a point for game, he leads or pitches the ♡**9** rather than risk losing the ♡**10** with its large count value.

The second player has no hearts and cannot follow suit, as one must always do, if possible, when trumps are led. So he discards the valueless ♠**4**.

The third player uses this opportunity to take the trick with the ♡**J**, thus scoring a point for jack.

Second Trick: The third player, as winner of the first trick, leads his strong ♠**K**.

The first player does not want to follow suit, as he would have to play his ♠**10** and lose its large count toward game. So he exerts his option of trumping the trick, using the ♡**10** to cash in its count value.

(The play of the ♡**10** at this stage is doubly advisable: the first player runs no risk of losing it, because he already knows that the second player holds no trump cards; but there is a chance that the third player is holding back a higher trump card than the ♡**J** and might use it later to take the ten.)

The second player discards the ♣**7** as a valueless card. He prefers to hold the ♢**8** as a safeguard for the ♢**10** in case a high diamond should be led.

Third Trick: The first player leads the ♣**3**, so that another player will take the trick and be forced to lead into the first player's stronger holdings.

The second player plays the ♣**Q**, hoping that the third player has the ♣**10** and will have to play it.

The third player has no clubs, so he discards the worthless ♠**3**. The second player wins the trick and takes the lead.

Fourth Trick: The second player, thinking that the first player may hold the ♣**10**, tries some strategy of his own. He leads the ♢**8**, hoping to coax out high diamonds and later make his ♢**10** good.

The third player follows suit by playing the ♢**7**, retaining his ♡**7** (trump) for later play.

The first player takes the trick with the ♢**Q**.

Fifth Trick: The first player leads the ♡**2** as the lesser of two evils. If another trump is out against him, it will at least be forced by such a play, whereas the ♠**10** would surely be lost, should an odd trump be at large.

The second player discards the ♣**8** rather than lose his ♢**10** on the ♡**2**. He is hoping that the ♡**2** will go through and that the first player will lead a small diamond next.

The third player takes the trick with the ♡**7**, which is his only play. With it, he gains the lead.

Sixth Trick: The third player leads his last card, the ♠**5**. He, too, hopes that the first player holds a diamond, as the ♠**5** will then be good.

The first player plays the ♠**10**, topping the ♠**5**. He has received the very break that he wanted, a lead in the suit of his lone card.

The third player plays the ♢**10**, and the first player, taking the trick, gains a count of twenty toward game in one swoop.

Summary: The first player made two points. One was the sure point for low, and the other was the hoped-for point for game with a count of thirty-five, as against the second player's two (from the ♣**Q**) and the third player's one (from the ♡**J**).

The second player made no points.

The third player made two points. One was for high and the other for jack. Oddly, he made them with the same card, the ♡**J**, which happened to be the highest trump in play and thereby rated as high, while by taking a trick containing the ♡**J**, he scored a point for jack.

Thus the score at the end of the initial deal, or round, stands: first player, two; third player, two; second player, zero.

The deal moves to the player at the left of the original dealer. New hands are dealt and a trump is declared in the same fashion as before. Scores are tabbed and the player who first reaches seven points is the winner, hence the name seven-up, which was used in an earlier version of the game.

The only points that must be scored in every hand are high and low, both of which are strictly automatic. The point for jack depends upon whether or not the jack of trumps appears in that particular deal, so that point is often missing. If two players are tied in their count toward game, it is not scored. This occurs occasionally when only a few counters happen to be in play.

Simple pitch is usually played by two, three, or four players. When four participate, they may play in partnership, each pair of opposite players forming a team. But the players are always on their own in the more modern and more popular form of the game known as

AUCTION PITCH

In this game, which often may include more than four players, the players bid for the privilege of pitching trump. The bidding is started by the player on the dealer's left and it continues around to the dealer.

The lowest allowable bid is two, which signifies that the player must make at least two of the possible four points represented by high, low, jack, and game. If unwilling to go that much, the player may pass. Should all players pass the bid, the cards are gathered, shuffled, and dealt again by the same dealer.

A bid of two may be topped by a later bidder's three, which in turn may be topped by a bid of four. When the bidding reaches the dealer, he may take it for the amount of the last previous bid. Thus the dealer may top a bid of three by simply bidding three himself.

The player who wins the bid may pitch whatever trump he pleases. He is the first to lead, no matter what his position at the table. Play proceeds in the usual manner, and if the bidder makes his required points or more, he is credited with them toward his score.

But if he fails to make his bid, he is set back that many points. They are subtracted from his score, even if they put him in the minus column, or in the hole. For example, suppose that the score in a five-handed game stands as follows:

A	*B*	*C*	*D*	*E*
0	4	1	5	1

Assume that player *C* bids three and makes three points consisting of high, jack, and game, with low going to player *D*. The score at the end of that round would then be:

A	*B*	*C*	*D*	*E*
0	4	4	6	1

Suppose, however, that player *C* had failed to capture the jack, which happened to be taken by player *A*, so that *C* made only two points (high and game), with low going to player *D*. Because of *C*'s inability to make his bid, the score would then have been:

A	*B*	*C*	*D*	*E*
1	4	−2	6	1

In this case, *C*'s bid (three) was subtracted from his existing score (one), putting him in the hole with minus two. The other players were credited with whatever points they made.

Generally, the opposing players combine their efforts to defeat the bidder. This is usually done by discarding counters on tricks that the bidder cannot take, thus preventing him from making game. There are times, however, when this is inadvisable.

For instance, with the score as originally shown above, it would be unwise for players *A*, *B*, and *E* to throw too many counters to

D at the expense of *C*. With *D* already registering a point for low, another point for game would bring his score to seven, making him the final winner of the entire game. In this case it would be better to let *C* make his bid than to have *D* go out.

In auction pitch the players often agree to set a higher figure than seven as the final goal. The commonest total is ten, but it can go to eleven, or even to twenty-one, if so agreed.

If the bidder makes enough points to go out, he is the winner, regardless of whether another player also manages to go out during the same deal. However, if two nonbidders go out in the same round, their points are counted in the order of high, low, jack, game, and the first to reach the required total is the winner.

Here is an example: Players *C* and *D* are tied at eight points each, with ten points the required total. Player *A*, the bidder, fails to make a single point, *D* makes high and game, while *C* makes low and takes the jack.

D scores first, one point for high. *C* then scores one point for low; next, one point for jack. *C* is the winner, having reached the required ten points. *D*'s one point for game is not counted.

Pointers on Bidding

Many beginners are apt to overbid their hands in auction pitch. This is often true in a three- or four-handed game, where fewer than half the cards are actually in play. Take, for example, this potential all-trump hand:

♡ **A K Q 10 8 6**

The only certain point is high, as represented by the ♡**A**, with game a strong probability, since the player is apt to take every trick. This warrants a bid of two, but no more.

If *any* of four cards, ♡ **5 4 3 2,** happen to be in another hand, as is very likely, some other player—not the bidder—will score a point for low.

If the jack is still in the pack—and chances are better than even that it is—it will not be counted as a point at all, and it would be impossible for the bidder to meet the requirements of three.

With a hand like this a player might risk a bid of three to prevent another player from bidding and going out. With five, six, or seven players in the game, the risk becomes proportionately less; there is correspondingly more chance that the jack will be in play, giving the bidder a strong opportunity to take it.

The nearest thing to an ironclad four-bid hand would be the following:

Bidder: ♠ A K Q J 10 2

Here, the bidder would cash ♠**A** for high, show ♠**2** for low, win a trick by playing ♠**J** for jack, pick up twenty counters toward game with his five top trumps. He could lose only one trick, the ♠**2**, if confronted by this hand:

Opponent: ♠ 9 8 7 5 4 3

However, in a four-handed game, the two other players could each throw a ten onto the opponent's trick, yet have no counters for the bidder to take. This would tie the game count at twenty each, and the bidder would lose that point, as it is nullified by a tie.

That, of course, could hardly happen; and, in general, luck favors the bidder where game is concerned, as his opponents count their own tricks separately and a split of counters may give the bidder the highest total, even though he lacks a majority.

In contrast to the powerful hand shown above, consider this one:

Bidder: ◊ J ♣ 3 2 ♡ 3 2 ♠ 2

Here, the bidder has low in three suits, but he could actually make *all four points* in the other suit–diamonds–if he were rash enough to bid it and lucky enough to have his opponents hold such hands as these:

Opponent A: ♣ 9 8 6 ♡ 7 ♠ 8 5

Opponent B: ♣ 7 4 ♡ 9 8 ♠ 9 6

With his pitch of the ◊**J**, the bidder would take high, show low, win jack, and gain game (with one counter), all in a single play. His opponents would get the remaining tricks to the tune of zero. It wouldn't happen, but it's worthy of note, as it illustrates the vagaries of auction pitch.

Here is a setup that could prove a real crusher:

Bidder: ♠ K J 3 ♡ A K ◊ 9

Opponent: ♠ A 10 2 ♡ 7 ◊ 8 ♣ 5

The bidder would go to three on his hand, figuring that he had either high or low–if not both–with an almost sure chance of cashing jack and a probable game to boot. But if the bidder should pitch the ♠**K**, hoping to force out the ace if it happened to be there, he might encounter trouble.

The opponent, figuring from the bid that the bidder must hold the jack, would let the king ride, simply showing the ♠**2** as low and playing it. That would be lulling in itself, as sometimes a player holds back on low rather than give away the fact that he has it.

If the bidder then led the ♠**J**, the opponent would take it with the ace and later make good the ♠**10**, winning all four points–high, low, jack, and game. If, instead, the bidder tried the ♠**3** as a "tester," the opponent would take it with the ♠**10** and lead back the ♠**A** on the hope of catching the jack, which he would.

Optional Rules in Auction Pitch

Among the optional rules that have been introduced into auction pitch, two of the most popular apply direction to the mode of bidding. They are:

The Dealer's Bid: By this option the dealer is forced to go higher than the previous bidder in order to gain the bid. This tends to lessen overbidding at the outset.

Smudge: This is a special bonus given to a player who bids four and makes it. As his reward, he receives sufficient extra points to win the game immediately, provided he was not in the hole.

Thus, assuming a player to have a score of two points, with eleven points the goal, a bid of smudge, if successful, would give him nine points. Failure to make the bid would set him back four points, making his score minus two.

With his score at minus two, a bid of four would not rate as a smudge. If successful, it would only give him four points, bringing his score up to two.

In some circles the winning of all four points in a deal constitutes a smudge, even though the bid was less. This option is not recommended, as it lays too much emphasis on luck.

Pitch with the Joker: In this modern innovation the joker is added to the pack and is rated at one point, which goes to the player who takes it.

The joker may be ranked as the top card of the pack, capable of taking the highest trump in play, but it is not scored as high.

Or it may be ranked just below the lowest trump in play, capable of taking cards in every other suit except trumps, but it is not scored as low.

If a bidder should decide to pitch the joker, as he very well might in games where it is ranked as top card of the pack, the joker must be accepted as a spade, making spades the trump suit.

In any case the joker adds a fifth point to the game, so the bids may go as high as five. With the joker in play, if two players go out in the same round, their points are counted in the order of high, low, jack, joker, game.

The smudge feature can be incorporated into auction pitch when the joker is included as an extra point; in this case smudge would require a bid of five, with the winning of all five points.

Taking Low: In most circles the player who takes the lowest trump in a trick is credited with a point for low, instead of having that point go to the player holding the low trump. This is particularly desirable when playing smudge, as it gives the bidder a better chance at capturing all four points (or five with the joker) and thereby makes the bidding more spirited.

CALIFORNIA JACK

This two-player game stems from the days of pitch, but it has a modern trend. The rules of pitch prevail, but trump is determined beforehand, by simply cutting the pack and accepting whatever suit is shown. The pack is then shuffled, six cards are dealt to each player, and the rest of the pack is turned face up. The opponent leads, the dealer follows, and whichever wins the trick takes the top card of the inverted pack, the loser taking the next card. This process is continued until the entire pack has been played, when each player's cards are counted and scored as in pitch.

SHASTA SAM

A game identical with California Jack, but with the pack turned face down, so that the players are drawing "blind," as in two-handed pinochle (see page 233).

Pedro and Snoozer

The various pedro games are an outgrowth of auction pitch, the general purpose being to simplify the play and to enliven it by the introduction of additional point cards. Bidding in every case is unrestricted; that is, it keeps going around the table until one player makes a bid that is followed by successive passes on the part of all the remaining players.

High, low, and jack count for one point each in pedro and its variants, but low must be taken in a trick, and it counts for the player thus winning it. Game also counts for one point when taken in play, but it consists of a single card, the ten of the trump suit. In addition, there are other trump cards with still higher values, from which the various games have derived their names, as follows.

PEDRO

In this early form of the game, one card is added to the point cards. That is the five of trump, known as the pedro, and it counts five points for the player who takes it in a trick. There are therefore nine possible points in a deal, and the total score required to win the game is twenty-one points. In case two players gain that total, the bidder's score is counted first; but when nonbidders are involved, the points rate in this order: high, one; low, one; jack, one; pedro, five; game (ten of trump), one.

Dom Pedro

The original game of this title is played exactly like pedro, but with the addition of still another point card, the three of trump, known as the dom, which counts three points for the player who takes it in a trick. There are twelve possible points in each deal, and the total score required to win the game is fifty points. In ties between nonbidders, points are scored in this order: high, one; low, one; jack, one; dom, three; pedro, five; game (ten of trump), one.

Pedro Sancho

This became the most popular of the pedro group, following the pattern of the previous games, but eliminating the three-point dom and introducing a new and bigger point card, the nine of trump, under the title of sancho, which scores nine points for the taker.

There are eighteen points in each deal, and the requirement for winning the game is fifty points or up to one hundred, according to agreement beforehand. In ties between nonbidders, points are scored in this order: high, one; low, one; jack, one; pedro, five; sancho, nine; game (ten of trump), one.

SNOOZER

In this, the ultimate in pedro games, all point cards are included from the other versions, with the addition of the joker, known as the snoozer, which is worth fifteen points to the player who takes it in a trick.

The joker rates as a trump card but is below the two of trump in value. It is not, however, regarded as low. That distinction goes to the lowest card of the actual trump suit that happens to be in play during the deal.

The point cards are counted in this order: high, one; low, one; jack, one; dom (three of trump), three; pedro (five of trump), five; sancho (nine of trump), nine; snoozer (joker), fifteen; game (ten of trump), one, making a total of thirty-six points per deal. The first player to reach one hundred points wins the game.

The joker was added to the game of pedro sancho before the three of trump was restored as a point card. Hence, the joker was known for a time as dom or dom pedro before being given the title of snoozer, which distinguishes it from the three of trump to which the name "dom" properly belongs.

While snoozer is generally played with six cards dealt to each player, as in auction pitch, it is customary in some circles to deal out the entire pack, as far as possible. This brings most of the potential point cards into play and thereby creates an incentive for higher bids.

In pedro sancho, a popular procedure is to remove the four threes, thus eliminating the dom entirely, and using the forty-eight-card pack to deal twelve cards to each player in a four-handed game. The same pack can be used to deal eight cards to each player in a six-handed game. Similarly a fifty-card pack (lacking two threes) will give each player ten cards in a five-handed game, while a forty-nine-card pack (lacking three threes) will give each player seven cards in a seven-handed game.

Note: In pitch, "game" is the last point scored in "going out," as it depends on the total of "counter" cards added after play has been completed. The joker, when used in pitch, scores ahead of game; so the same rule logically applies to the bonus cards used in various forms of pedro, when the ten of trump serves as substitute for game. However, since the ten is actually taken in play, it is generally regarded as a bonus card in its own right; and as such, it is scored immediately after jack, with any pedro bonus cards following it in the order listed. This rule should be used unless otherwise specified.

Pinochle: The Cards

A highly popular card game, pinochle is particularly intriguing because it utilizes a special pack, consisting entirely of high cards, which contribute unique features to the game and its play. There are forty-eight cards, comprising two cards of each value in all four suits, as follows:

♠	A	A	10	10	K	K	Q	Q	J	J	9	9
♡	A	A	10	10	K	K	Q	Q	J	J	9	9
♣	A	A	10	10	K	K	Q	Q	J	J	9	9
♢	A	A	10	10	K	K	Q	Q	J	J	9	9

Note that the ten ranks next in value to the ace, taking precedence over the king. Eights and sevens (two in each suit) are sometimes added to the pack, making sixty-four cards in all. If a regular pinochle pack is not obtainable, a pack can be assembled by taking cards of the required values from two standard fifty-two-card packs.

Pinochle is a trump game, in which one suit is declared as trump and takes precedence over the others. The cards are dealt as in other trump games, but during the course of play or as a preliminary to it, certain cards are drawn from the player's hand and placed face up on the table to form special combinations that add to the player's score.

This process is called melding and the cards themselves are termed a meld. Such melded cards are retained by the player or taken back into his hand. Rules on melding vary in different forms of pinochle, as will be discussed in the individual games.

In any case, whether the melds remain face up in front of the player or are added to his unshown cards, they are regarded as part of his hand; and they are led or played as in any other trump game, subject of course to the rules applicable to pinochle.

The fact that all cards in the pinochle pack are duplicated is somewhat puzzling to the beginner at the game, who wonders what may happen if one player leads a card such as the ◊**10** and another follows suit with its identical twin, the other ◊**10.**

Obviously, the higher card cannot take the lower, since both are equal in value. So the cards are rated in order of play, the one that is played first taking precedence over the other. Thus if player *X* leads the ◊**10** and player *Y* is forced to follow suit with the ◊**10** as the only diamond in his hand, player *X* wins the trick.

The same precedence applies when there are more than two players in the game. If the two highest cards in a trick are identical in value, the one played first in rotation is the winner.

Two-handed Pinochle

In this basic form of pinochle twelve cards are dealt to each player and the next card is turned up beside the pack to represent the trump. The opponent then leads any card from his hand and the dealer plays a card upon it.

Whichever player takes the trick has the privilege of melding certain combinations of cards from his hand by laying them face up on the table. He scores a specified number of points for such a meld, as will be explained further.

The winner of the trick then draws a card from the top of the pack to replenish his hand. The other player does the same. Then the winner leads another card and the other player responds as before. This continues until the pack is exhausted, each player being entitled to make another meld–if he has one–immediately after taking a trick.

When one player leads, the other is not required to follow suit at this stage of the game but may "throw," or discard, any card he chooses. He may, however, trump a lead at any time. Usually, he does so in order to make a meld.

The cards that are melded still belong in the player's hand, but they remain openly upon the table and may be led or played whenever desired. After the entire pack has been drawn, the dealer and his opponent take their remaining melds back into their hands.

From there on, they play out the hand, trick by trick, but now each player must follow suit if he can.

The old rule required the second player to take the trick whenever possible, meaning that he would have to play a higher card in the suit led, or trump the trick if out of suit.

That rule is now optional, but because its real purpose was to force out trumps, it has been modified in modern practice. A player must follow suit, but he may play a lower card of that suit. However, if out of suit, he still must trump if possible; and if a trump is led, he must play a higher trump when he has one.

This requirement has an important bearing on the game, because, in pinochle, players do not go after tricks but try to take certain cards that have point values and thereby rate as counters, which are added to the score along with the meld.

In two-handed pinochle, melds score as follows:

Trump sequence (**A 10 K Q J** of trump)	150
Dix, or Deece (**9** of trump)	10
Royal marriage (**K Q** of trump)	40
Plain-suit marriage (**K Q** in any one suit)	20
Pinochle (♢**J** and ♠**Q**)	40
Four aces of different suits	100
Four kings of different suits	80
Four queens of different suits	60
Four jacks of different suits	40

Besides these, there are certain optional melds that will be mentioned in due course.

Cards taken in on tricks during the play are counted according to the following point values:

Each ace, 11 points. Each ten, 10 points.

Each king, 4 points. Each queen, 3 points.

Each jack, 2 points. Each nine, 0 points.

For taking last trick of hand, 10 points.

Added up, these come to exactly 250 points, counted at the conclusion of the hand. Game, in pinochle, is 1000 points; often a player feels positive that he has taken in enough counters to go beyond that total. In that case he can declare himself out and call for a point count then and there.

If he is over 1000 he wins; if under, he loses. Often, this count can be the deciding factor in a close game, but in the earlier stages, in fact at the beginning of every hand, the players are generally "meld-minded" because in melding lie the quick-scoring opportunities.

A trick must be taken before melding, and only one meld may be made at that time. Once a card has been melded, it can be used as part of a totally different meld, as long as a new card is added from the hand to form it.

This is easily understood from a few examples:

Suppose a player melds a pinochle (40 points) with a ♢**J** and a ♠**Q**. Later, he cannot add another ♠**Q** from his hand to the ♢**J** on the table and call it another pinochle, because the ♢**J** has already figured in such a meld. Nor can he add another ♢**J** to the ♠**Q** already melded.

However, he can do any of the following:

Add jacks of the other three suits (♠**J** ♡**J** ♣**J**) to the original ♢**J** and score 40 points for four jacks.

Add queens of the other three suits (♡**Q** ♣**Q** ♢**Q**) to the original ♠**Q** and score 60 points for four queens.

Add a ♠**K** to the ♠**Q** and score 20 points for a marriage, or 40 points for a royal marriage when spades are trump.

In the last-named case, the player can make still another meld involving the ♠**Q**. He can add the ♠**A** ♠**10** ♠**J** to the ♠**K** ♠**Q** and form a 150-point trump sequence.

He can also meld the duplicate ♢**J** and ♠**Q** and count the combination as a new pinochle for 40 points in its own right.

On the contrary:

If a player melds a trump sequence to start, he cannot remove the ♠**K** ♠**Q** from the run and call the pair a royal marriage. Nor can he take the ♠**Q** from the sequence, add another ♠**K**, and form a royal marriage. That would be using a card from one sequence toward starting another sequence.

Similarly, a player cannot take an ace from a group of four to start another set of aces. The same applies with kings, queens, and jacks, once they have been melded as four of a kind.

While all that is rather obvious, a player runs into problems in situations like the following:

He has melded four queens and later four jacks. Now he wants to call his ♢**J** and ♠**Q** a pinochle and score his 40 points. He cannot do so without adding a card from his hand.

What he should have done was to meld his ♢**J** ♠**Q** before making the four jacks or four queens. Otherwise his pinochle is a goner unless he has another ♢**J** or ♠**Q** in his hand, or draws one to go with a card now on the table.

Another dilemma can arise if a player melds four kings for 80 and follows with four queens for 60. In so doing, he throws away four marriages, including a royal, unless he can add more cards from his hand; and then he may spoil chances for other marriages.

The correct procedure is to meld the four kings first; then form the marriages one by one, melding the royal as early as possible. But when he comes to the fourth marriage, he shouldn't meld it as such, as it is only worth 20 points. In putting down the final queen, he should add it to the other three queens and score it 60 for four queens.

In this way the scoring will go 80 for kings; 40 for a royal marriage; 20 for a marriage; 20 for another marriage; 60 for queens —a total of 220.

The nine of trumps, or dix, is a small yet important meld, which is handled in a special way. In melding the dix the player picks up the turned-up trump and puts the dix in its place, scoring 10 points for the action.

This in itself may be worth far more than the 10 points involved, as the player may acquire a card that will complete a sequence in trumps, or a card that may prove vital toward forming a group such as four aces.

After one dix has been melded in this fashion, a second dix is simply shown by the player who holds or draws it, whereby 10 points are added to his score. If a dix is turned up as trump during the deal, the dealer automatically gets 10 points. This happens rather frequently, as there are eight nines in the pinochle pack.

Here is a sample game, detailed play by play, showing how most of these things work out:

Opponent	*Dealer*
♣ **10 K Q**	♣ **A A Q J 9**
◇ **K Q 9 9**	◇ **10 J**
♠ **A 10 10**	♠ **Q J 9**
♡ **A K**	♡ **J 9**

Trump turned up: ♣**J**

Holding two ♠**10**s, the opponent decides to lead one, figuring that the dealer will let it ride rather than trump it or use an ♠**A** to take it and thus lose a chance for four aces, since the dealer can only be holding one ♠**A**, if any.

Opponent leads ♠**10**

Dealer plays ♠**9**

Opponent melds ♣**K** ♣**Q** *Score* 40

Opponent draws ♡**10**

Dealer draws ◇**Q**

With another meld to make, the opponent follows the same reasoning as before:

Opponent leads ♠**10**

Dealer plays ♡**9**

Opponent melds ◇**K** ◇**Q** *Score* 60

Opponent draws ♡**10**

Dealer draws ♠**9**

Although he has no more melds, the opponent decides to lead a ♡**10**, as he now holds two of them. Just as the opening ♠**10** lead did, it puts the dealer in a difficult situation.

Opponent leads ♡**10**

Dealer plays ♠**9**

Opponent draws ♣**10**

Dealer draws ◇**A**

The opponent now has a duplicate ♣**10** and can use one for trumping. He decides to hold a ♡**10** and simply throw away an odd ◇**9**, as he has no immediate melds.

Opponent leads ◇**9**

Dealer takes with ◇**10**.

This was a bad lead, as it opened a new suit in which the dealer was likely to be holding a ten–and he was. The dealer now cashes his dix (♣**9**) for the ♣**J** that was turned up as trump.

Dealer exchanges ♣**9** for ♣**J** *Score* 10

The dealer adds the ♣**J** to his hand and proceeds to meld four jacks, which is a better meld than a pinochle (◇**J** ♠**Q**) as it gives the dealer two playable jacks (♡**J** and ♠**J**) that are of no use in other melds.

Dealer melds ♣**J** ◇**J** ♡**J** ♠**J** *Score* 50

Dealer draws ♡**Q**

Opponent draws ♠**Q**

It is now the dealer's lead. He remembers that the opponent has twice led a ♠**10** and probably can't take a trick in spades.

Dealer leads ♠**J**

Opponent plays ◊ **9**

Having picked up a ♡ **Q**, the dealer now has four queens, good for 60 points, but he doesn't meld them. To do so would kill any chance of melding the ♠ **Q** with the ◊ **J** later. He melds the pinochle now:

Dealer melds ◊ **J** ♠ **Q** *Score* 90

Dealer draws ♡ **A**

Opponent draws ◊ **K**

The hands now look like this, the dix and melded cards still being in play:

Opponent		*Dealer*	
♣	**10 10**	♣	**A A Q J**
◊	**K**	◊	**A Q**
♠	**A Q**	♡	**A Q**
♡	**A 10 K**	*Melded:*	Exchanged dix (10)
Melded:	♣**K** ♣**Q** (40)		♣**J** ◊**J** ♡**J** *(40)
	◊**K** ◊**Q** (20)		♠**Q** (40)
			* ♠**J** melded and played

The dealer now tries another jack lead, using the ♡ **J** from the meld, but this time it doesn't work:

Dealer leads ♡ **J**

Opponent takes with ♡ **10**

Opponent draws ♣ **9**

Dealer draws ♡ **J**

Opponent *shows* dix *Score* 70

The opponent leads the ◊ **K** from the meld, as he has a duplicate of this card in his hand. The dealer needs a trick to meld, so takes it by trumping, using his duplicate ♣ **J** from the meld. Thus:

Opponent leads ◊ **K**

Dealer trumps and takes with ♣ **J**

Dealer melds ♣ **Q** ♠ **Q** ♡ **Q** ◊ **Q** *Score* 150

Dealer draws ♡ **9**

Opponent draws ♠ **J**

Again, the dealer leads a useless jack and the opponent responds accordingly:

Dealer leads ◊ **J**

Opponent plays ♠ **J**

Dealer draws ♠**K**

Opponent draws ♠**A**

Now, having nothing very much better that he can spare, the dealer leads his only nine. With the pack depleted, the opponent doubts that he will get four queens, so he throws the ♢**Q** that he has already melded.

Dealer leads ♡**9**

Opponent plays ♢**Q**

Dealer melds ♠**K** ♠**Q** *Score* 170

Dealer draws ♢**A**

Opponent draws ♠**K**

Having no need for the ♡**J**, the dealer leads it. The opponent's draw of the ♠**K** gives him four kings, which he must cash in fast. So he uses the ♡**A** to take the trick and thereby meld:

Dealer leads ♡**J**

Opponent takes with ♡**A**

Opponent melds ♠**K** ♡**K** ♢**K** ♣**K** *Score* 150

Opponent draws ♢**J**

Dealer draws ♢**10**

This new draw will give the opponent a chance to meld a pinochle (♢**J** ♠**Q**) if he can only take another trick! There are only a few more cards to draw from, and if one happens to be an ace of trump (♣**A**) he may have a chance. The dealer probably has at least one ♣**A**, so the opponent plays the ♣**Q** to force it.

Why lead the ♣**Q** when the dealer may be holding the ♣**K** as well as an ♣**A**? Because the dealer will have to save his ♣**K**, if he has one, to meld with his ♣**Q**, which is already on the table. So the dealer *must* use an ace of trump!

Opponent leads ♣**Q**

Dealer takes with ♣**A**

Dealer draws ♣**K**

Opponent draws ♡**K**

The dealer didn't have the ♣**K** after all, but he figured that the opponent had a meld to make, so he took the trick anyway, using the ♣**A**. What's more, he has another ♣**A**, and he leads it to prevent the opponent from melding. Also, he just drew the ♣**K** and is able to meld a royal marriage as a result.

Dealer leads ♣**A**

Opponent plays ♢**J**

Dealer melds ♣**K** ♣**Q** *Score* 210

Dealer draws ♡**Q**

Opponent draws ♣**9** (face-up dix)

By winning this trick the dealer was able to make the final meld, as this was the last draw from the pack. The dealer's lead of the top trump (♣**A**) made the trick sure, so the opponent threw on the ♢**J** knowing he would have no further chance to meld it.

After the dealer drew the ♡**Q**, the opponent picked up the face-up dix (♣**9**) and simply added it to his hand, like other draws.

Each player now takes up his own melds into his hand, so that each is holding twelve cards, ready to play out the deal as specified earlier. The hands now stand:

	Opponent		*Dealer*
♣	**10 10 K 9 9**	♣	**K Q J**
♢	**K**	♢	**A A 10 Q**
♠	**A A K Q**	♠	**K Q**
♡	**K K**	♡	**A Q Q**

The dealer leads the ♡**A** and the opponent follows suit with a ♡**K**. The dealer leads an ♢**A** and again the opponent must follow suit, with the ♢**K**. The dealer leads his other ♢**A** and the opponent trumps it with the ♣**9** (being out of diamonds).

The opponent then leads high trumps from the top down, clearing the dealer's trumps. The opponent does the same with his suit cards, making a clean sweep including the last trick.

The "takes" total thus:

Opponent			*Dealer*		
4 aces	44	points	4 aces	44	points
7 tens	70	"	1 ten	10	"
5 kings	20	"	3 kings	12	"
6 queens	18	"	2 queens	6	"
3 jacks	6	"	5 jacks	10	"
Last trick	10	"		82	"
	168	"			

These points are added to the opponent's score (150) and the dealer's score (210), to bring the totals to:

Opponent 318 Dealer 292

In recapitulation, it should be noted that although the opponent failed to make his final meld, he forced out the dealer's trump aces at low cost and gained trump domination with his tens. In short, by "going for counters" and getting them, one player may offset another's meld.

The fascination of two-handed pinochle lies in the fact that every hand is literally an adventure in itself. The game affords a vast array of problems and opportunities that resolve themselves into accepted patterns.

If you have some melds at the outset, with good prospects for others, you will have to get the melds down early or forget the prospects later. This necessity was emphasized in the game just shown, when the opponent immediately melded his royal marriage (**♣K ♣Q**) for 40 points and still had the cards available for a trump sequence if he could build to one later.

Similarly, the opponent had to meld his "forty jacks" before they cluttered his hand. Holding three jacks in hope of drawing a fourth is utterly futile if you have prospects of any other melds. Sometimes it is even better to break up four jacks without melding them than to sacrifice a key card to a future meld. It is also bad to throw tens (at 10 points each) to save four jacks or other small melds.

Each ten that you lose but could have taken means a 20-point margin in your foe's favor. Do that twice and your forty jacks will merely square the score, nothing more.

Holding back a big meld is sometimes good policy, as in the case of a trump sequence accompanied by an extra trump higher than the dix. This action encourages your opponent to go for a sequence himself, not knowing that you already hold one and have him blocked. Near the close of the draw you can take a trick with the odd trump, if need be, and meld your 150. Only then will your foe know how he hampered his hand.

Four aces are another sleeper that will worry your opponent, particularly if you have a duplicate ace in your hand. He may then try for a "hundred aces" himself, without being able to get them, meanwhile sacrificing other cards that he might have used in lesser melds.

Once your sequence or aces have been melded, they become powerful trick takers. When you have aces on the table, your opponent won't lead tens. If you have harbored a few tens of your own, you can use them to take the lower cards that he does lead. All this helps you to make further melds if you hold the cards for them.

Some players apparently ignore sly tactics and go after points in a blunt way. Suppose your opponent leads a ♠**10** and you are holding ♠**A** ♠**A**. You hit the ten with the spare ace, capturing two "brisques," as these high counters are sometimes called, and give yourself a melding opportunity.

Of course, you're practically telling your foe that he can't go for a hundred aces—but that can be a fooler too. Suppose you hold only one ♠**A** and no other aces at all. Your bold play of one ♠**A** may deceive your opponent into thinking you have both. He may then play aces in other suits, thinking he has no chance to meld a hundred aces.

Hands generally develop into meldable and counter types, and they should be played accordingly. When you hold kings and queens, go after all the melds you can, as the hand lacks playing power. When replete with aces and tens, you can often take tricks that your opponent needs for melds. Card count becomes your main objective.

The memory factor is important in two-handed pinochle, but it soon becomes second nature with most players. By comparing your opponent's meld with your own, you can often fill in missing links and analyze probabilities. By remembering the cards you play and closely watching what goes onto them, the mere association will enable you to recall your opponent's play as well.

There are certain optional melds in two-handed pinochle that should be checked before the game begins:

The Dix: According to an old ruling, the nine of trump must be melded separately to score its 10 points.

Thus, in the sample game shown, the dealer could have melded his dix (♣**9**) for 10 points, and saved his four jacks (40 points) for a later meld. Or he could have melded them with the dix, taking the 40 points then, but forfeiting the 10 points for the dix.

Another ruling, still generally accepted, is that the player holding the second dix must actually exchange it for the one showing beside the pack. This means he must take a trick to meld his dix, exactly as with the first dix.

Grand Pinochle: In the original game, this consisted of ♠**K** ♠**Q** ◇**J** and counted 80 points. Today it is regarded simply as a spade marriage (♠**K** ♠**Q**) and a pinochle (◇**J** ♠**Q**), but some players allow both to be melded at once. Such an arrangement requires agreement beforehand.

Double Pinochle: Also part of the original game, this allows two pinochles to be melded as a double for 80 points. By a fuller interpretation of the ruling, a player can meld a single pinochle (◇**J** ♠**Q**) for 40 points and add another later, calling it double pinochle for 80 points more.

This is much like melding a king-queen of trump for a royal marriage (40) and later adding an ace-jack-ten of trump to form a sequence (150). That, however, is standard practice, whereas double pinochle is no longer generally used. Hence, if included in the game, its exact status should be specified.

Point Counts: New styles of point counts have been introduced to the modern game and will be described under auction pinochle. Such counts can be used in two-handed pinochle instead of the standard count, if preferred.

Hands as Games: Some players prefer to score each hand as a game, rather than go for 1000 points or some other total. This means keeping a sharp watch on your opponent's melds, as you cannot afford to let him forge too far ahead while nursing your own prospects.

Auction (Three-handed) Pinochle

Originally styled auction pinochle with a widow, this is the three-handed game which has surged to such popularity that it has become synonymous with the word "pinochle" in many circles where it is played.

Its distinctive features are that the players bid for the privilege of declaring or naming the trump suit; and that the successful bidder gains the benefit of adding the contents of a three-card widow to his hand and discarding three other cards to replace them. These become part of the bidder's trick pile, and if he discards any counters they add to his score.

Only the bidder makes a meld, as the purpose of the opponents is simply to keep him from reaching the total of his bid, in melds and counters. In the play the opponents act as partners during that deal only, each deal or hand being played as if it were an individual game.

The standard pinochle melds given on page 234 are used. While the old standard point count still can be used—and is used—two newer forms have generally supplanted it:

The "10" Count		*The "5 and 10" Count*	
Each ace	10 points	Each ace	10 points
Each ten	10 points	Each ten	10 points
Each king	10 points	Each king	5 points
Each **Q J 9**	0 points	Each queen	5 points

If anyone asks "Which should we use?" the answer is simply "It doesn't matter." And the old standard count can be used as well. Actually, they add up so closely that to win or lose a bid because of a difference in the point count means that you shouldn't have made the bid in the first place. This we shall see.

First, let's describe the intriguing game itself.

Each player is dealt fifteen cards, and three are left over as a widow from the forty-eight-card pack. Call the players *A, B, C,* with *D* representing the dealer, because in the most refined versions of this highly sophisticated three-handed game four players participate, the fourth "dealing himself out" while the other three play the hand.

Starting with *A,* each player bids the number of points he thinks he can take, basing his estimate on three factors:

(*a*) The amount he can meld.

(*b*) The points he can take.

(*c*) How much the widow may improve his hand.

Usually, the opening bid must meet a required total, such as 250 or 300 points. Otherwise, the player must pass; and if all three pass, the hands are tossed in and the deal goes along to the next player.

By the original rules, once the bid is opened other players can raise it until two pass in succession; the bid then is final, there being no more competition. The more modern game, however, adds this proviso: if a player once passes, he cannot come back into the bidding. The game should be played under this new rule unless it is specified beforehand that the old rule is in force.

Having won the bid, the player turns up the three cards of the widow. He then names his trump and proceeds to lay down his entire meld–using the widow cards as needed–and adds the total of all the individual combinations that he thus puts on display.

This simultaneous meld has certain qualifications, namely: a royal marriage (**K Q** of trump) can be counted for its usual 40 points if melded individually, but if melded as part of a trump sequence (**A K Q J 10**) the king and queen merely go with the 150 points that such a meld represents. A completely separate royal marriage is needed to collect an additional 40 points.

However, if a player melds four kings and four queens, each of a different suit, he can include all the marriages as individual melds. Such a meld, in pinochle parlance, is a "round trip" or a "roundhouse." For convenience, it is sometimes classed as a meld on its own. It adds up thus: four kings, 80; four queens, 60; a royal marriage, 40; three plain-suit marriages, 60, or a total of 240 points.

Should a player meld both a trump sequence and a roundhouse, he loses the 40 points for a royal marriage, because it does not exist as such. He would score 150 for the sequence and 200 for the roundhouse, a combined total of 350, which is pretty nice.

After melding, the bidder discards three cards face down. These must come from his hand, never from the meld. Since he has taken the original widow cards into his hand, any of them that are not melded can be discarded. Often the bidder discards counters that were not needed in the meld and that look like losing tricks, because when play begins, he adds the discarded widow to any tricks he takes, getting the benefit of its count.

In play the bidder leads any card he wants. The other players must follow suit if they can, but they do not have to play a higher card. If out of suit, a player must use a trump if he holds one. The next player must do the same, but he does *not* have to overtrump if he can, though that was once a rule.

Only when a trump is led must the succeeding players go higher if they can. Otherwise, they simply follow suit and play a lower trump, or throw some other card if out of trump. This trump rule is usually helpful to the bidder, as it enables him to force trumps held by his opponents.

In contrast, the opponents may profit by throwing cards to each other in the form of counters on whatever tricks they take. The bidder's aim is to add sufficient points to his meld score to make the amount of his bid, while his opponents act together as partners for that hand only, in an effort to thwart him.

Frequently the contest is quite close, not just because a player is forced up in the bidding, but also because of his urge to reach a higher scoring bracket, as will be detailed later. For the present, let's study a sample hand:

♣ A A 10 K Q J 9
♡ A K K
♠ A 10 Q
◇ A J

This is a very fine hand. Its meld includes a trump sequence with dix in clubs (160), four aces (100), and a pinochle (40), for a total of 300 points. But the bidder can go a lot higher, depending on how many counters he can take during the play, as no great improvement is likely from the widow.

Two factors are important in taking tricks that bring in counters: first, high cards—aces and tens—which are counters in themselves; second, suit length, primarily in trump, but also in a side suit. Suit length helps to mop up loose counters, including the last trick.

Here is a simple system of estimating the probable number of counters that a hand is likely to take, the highest possible total being 250 in counters alone:

For each ace, count 10 points; for each ten, 5 points. Add 5 points extra for holding a second ace in a suit, and for each ten if the suit contains both aces.

Examples: ace-ace counts 10 + 10 + 5 = 25

Ace-ace-ten counts 25 + 5 + 5 = 35

Ace-ace-ten-ten counts 30 + 5 + 5 + 5 = 45

For each card over four in a suit, count 20 points.

By this method the hand shown above can be quickly rated as follows:

For the top three clubs, 35 points; for three single aces, 30; for one odd ten, 5. For three extra trumps, 60. Probable take in play: 130 points. These are added to the 300-point melding value of the hand.

That means the hand is biddable at 430 and should make it if properly played. Do not count on the widow for added playing strength, or even a small meld; you need it for insurance.

The very worst you could pick up from the widow would be ♡**9** ♠**9** ◊**9**—three nines, none of the trump, and therefore all losers. But by holding these, you could stow three counters in the discard, the ♠**10** ♡**K** ♡**K**, all cards that would almost surely be lost if you used them in play. So you would get the benefit of their count, letting your opponents take the worthless nines instead.

In playing this hand you would ordinarily lead the two aces and the ten of clubs, in order to clear out the trumps. This would work if one opponent held three clubs and the other held two. If one player happened to hold four or even all five of the clubs against you, it would be necessary to use a low trump to force out any still left, but you could afford the loss.

It would be nice to get such hands all the time, but when you don't, you have to take chances. Otherwise, your opponents would take too many easy bids. But just as you bid a solid hand close to its limit, so should you take a risk for all it is worth–if it is worth the risk at all.

That means that if you start bidding on prospects from the widow, hoping to fill an important meld, you must make sure there are enough such opportunities, not merely some attractive-looking long shots.

This point is illustrated by these comparative hands:

First Hand	*Meld*	
♠ 10 10 K Q J	Royal marriage	40
♣ 10 K K Q J	Plain marriage	20
♡ A J	Four jacks	40
◇ 10 10 J	Pinochle	40
	Total meld	140
	Winning counters	35
	Added suit length	40*
	Bidding value	215

* 20 in ♣ plus 20 in ♠

This wouldn't meet a 250 opening requirement, but it has possibilities from the widow. Either an ♣A or an ♠A will produce:

♣A		♠A	
Sequence	110*	Sequence	110
Added counter	10	Added counter	10
Added trump	20	Added trump	20
Total	140	Total	140
Original bid	215	Original bid	215
Possible bid	355	Possible bid	355

* 40 deducted for losing royal marriage

Second Hand	*Meld*	
♣ A J 9	Royal marriage	40
♡ 10 10 K Q J 9 9	Double dix	20
♠ A 9	Plain marriage	20
◊ A K Q	Total meld	80
	Winning counters	40
	Added suit length	60*
	Bidding value	180

* In hearts

But what a bonanza a single card will bring! All this hand needs to ride high, wide, and handsome is the ♡**A** from the widow. Then:

Trump sequence	110*
Four aces	100
Added counter	10
Added trump	20
Total	240
Original bid	180
Possible bid	420

* 40 deducted for losing royal marriage

Third Hand	*Meld*	
♣ A 10 Q 9	Four aces	100
♡ A K Q	Royal marriage	40
♠ A K J 9	Plain marriage	20
◊ A K Q J	Total meld	160
	Winning counters	45
	Added suit length	0
	Bidding value	205

This hand has these possible chances for improvement from the widow:

♣K	
Four kings	80
Marriage	20
Dix (by changing trump)	10
Added suit length	20
Total	130
Original value	205
	335
Possible bid	330

♠Q	
Four queens	60
Marriage	20
Pinochle	40
Dix (by changing trump)	10
Added suit length	20
Total	150
Original value	205
	355
Possible bid	350

◇10	
Sequence	110
Added counter	10
Added trump	20
Total	140
Original value	205
	345
Possible bid	340

Taking the lowest of the three potentials, the limit for bidding this hand is 330, if the bidder utilizes all three chances. (Bids must be made in multiples of ten.)

Now for the comparisons. Actually, there are none. The first hand, despite its neatly alluring potential of two nicely balanced possible trump sequences, will throw you for a loss two times out of three if you try to bid it up around 350. That would be the correct bid if you could fill the hand, but the chances are about two to one that you won't, with only two possible openings for improvement (♣A and ♠A).

The second hand is both a delusion and a snare. The delusion is the prospect of the trump sequence; the snare is the possibility of the hundred aces that you won't get when you miss your sequence. This is about a five to one shot against you.

Yet this is the glitter for which many pinochle players persistently strive, and the more you can urge them into going after such prospects the more you will profit by their loss. It isn't how much you can get if you do fill; what counts is the chance that you have of filling at all.

That is illustrated by the third hand, where there are three possibilities for a fill; the odds are about even–or slightly in your favor–that you will catch one of the cards you want. But make sure you gear your bid to the lowest of the trio, in this case ♣**K**, representing a prospect of 330. Either the ♠**Q** or the ♢**10** will give you a slightly stronger chance.

When you have four possible fills, it's better than three to two that you will come through if you take the lowest as your basis. But generally you won't find this number of openings offering more than 40 or 50 points additional. If they do, jump the bid to that notch first; then boost it higher if need be.

Incidentally, the widow that went with the three hands just given consisted of:

♠**Q** ♢**9** ♢**9**

That gave the third hand one of its fills–the ♠**Q** with its 150 improvement; but, by keeping diamonds as trump, it meant a double dix for 10 additional points, and those two little diamonds were worth 40 points in added trump length. That's the sort of cushion that enables you to coast home comfortably.

You will find that a hand heavy with kings and queens, the roundhouse type, like this one, is generally easy to play, because there is so little that it can take in the way of counters. Others can prove more difficult. But the question is when to go beyond sure limits and bid on a possible three-way fill.

That depends somewhat on the scoring schedule used. In three-handed auction pinochle each hand is generally scored on a plus-and-minus basis, according to the size of the bid, which comes within a specific scoring bracket. If the bidder wins, he collects a fixed number of points or tokens from each of the other players. If he loses, they collect from him.

In a game with 250 as the lowest allowable bid, and one chip as the stake, player *A,* as the winner of such a bid, would collect one chip each from players *B* and *C* or two chips in all. In some scoring schedules the minimum bid is 300. Here are examples of the schedules used:

Bracket	(*a*)	(*b*)	(*c*)	(*d*)	(*e*)	(*f*)
250–290	1	2	1	–	–	1*
300–340	2	3	2	1	1	3
350–390	3	4	4	2	3	5
400–440	4	5	6	4	7	10
450–490	5	6	8	6	10	15
500–540	6	7	10	8	13	20
550–590	7	8	12	10	16	25
600–640	8	9	14	12	19	30
650 . . .	9	10	16	14	22	35

*Used only if 250 minimum bid is allowable.

In the first schedule (*a*), which is perhaps the earliest used and definitely the simplest, player *A* would collect two chips each from *B* and *C* if the bidding reached 300. He would collect three chips from each if the bidding reached 350, and so on. Thus a bid of 300 would be as good as a bid of 340, so far as the amount won or lost is concerned.

The first two schedules (*a* and *b*) were once used almost exclusively, but most players today prefer one of the others, of which the final listing (*f*) is the steepest and therefore the most popular in certain circles.

In deference to the old schedule (*a*) it should be noted that many players used to jump it by fives upon reaching the 400 bidding level, so the modern version (*e*) is not too great a departure from tradition.

A paper-and-pencil score can be kept instead of using chips or tokens. Taking the final schedule (*f*) as an example, the score might run as follows:

	A	*B*	*C*	
First Hand	+10	− 5	− 5	*A* bids and makes 380
Second Hand	+ 7	− 8	+ 1	*C* bids and makes 330
Third Hand	+ 2	−13	+11	*C* bids and makes 360
Fourth Hand	−28	+ 2	+26	*A* bids 450 but gives up hand

If a bidder gives up a hand without attempting to play it, he is merely charged with the loss of the bid. This is illustrated in the fourth hand (above) where player *A* bid 450 and took a loss of thirty chips (paying fifteen each to *B* and *C*) rather than play out what looked like a sure losing hand.

However, if he elects to play it out and loses, the other players collect double. In the fourth hand shown, *A* would have gone down for sixty chips or units, if he'd tried to win his 450 bid but had failed. *B* and *C* would each have won thirty chips in that case.

Reverting to the third hand, if player *C* had barely missed making his bid of 360, he would have lost twenty chips, ten each to *A* and *C*, instead of winning only five from each for a gain of ten, as shown.

Naturally, a conservative bidder should always be sure of making his bid, but overcaution is often a mistake. Suppose you are holding a hand that is "sure" at 260, but that figure is either below the agreed minimum, or another player bids 320.

If your 260 hand has three possible fills enabling you to bid 360 on the chance of finding a needed card in the widow, do so. Your opponent may be forced to stretch a sure 320 to 370 on the hope of only two possible fills. You have about an even chance of outbidding his sure bid successfully, but if he tries to outdo you, the chances will be two to one against him.

In short, you match probabilities against an opponent's possibilities. If you don't fill, you toss in your hand, take a loss at the lowest cost, and forget it.

That brings up another factor: spades double. There is an almost universal rule in auction pinochle that if spades are declared trump, a bid counts double, win or lose. This means, in simple terms: if you bid 380 and win, you score plus ten and the other two players get minus five. But if you declare spades as trump and win, you score plus twenty and they go minus ten.

However, if you play a 380 bid and lose it, you go minus twenty; they get plus ten each. If you declare spades as trump and lose, you go minus forty, they get plus twenty each. But by tossing in your hand without declaring any suit as trump, you get by with a ten-unit loss, even though you were aiming for spades and its potential forty-unit gain!

The moral is obvious. Any time you have a three-way fill with spades as a possible trump, regard it as a choice prospect. You will gain double if you win, but if you don't fill, there is no need to risk a fourfold loss, or even a double loss. It just goes down as an ordinary hand that can't be played.

In some pinochle circles there is a still higher bid: hearts triple. This means that if you bid 380 and declare hearts as trump, you stand to make thirty units, while the other two players each lose fifteen. But if you lose, you go down sixty, while they rack up thirty units each on the plus side.

Again, you can simply throw in the hand if you see that you can't make it, and take a simple ten-point loss, with no trump declared. Even a hand with only two possible fills is a good one to bid if you can make hearts trump when playing the optional rule of hearts triple.

Before playing out a hand the bidder usually gets rid of cards from his short suits in the widow, so as to retain length in trumps and a single side suit. It is unwise, however, to retain only the ace of a short suit. You must then lead it to save it. That will give your opponents a clue to the situation. Hold a small card with it if you can. Play the small card on an ace led by an opponent; then make your own ace good later on.

The general plan is to clear trumps by leading them, then go into your strong side suit. To do this, you must be able to trump into suits that the opponents play back. If you are short on trumps, this can cause trouble. Suppose you have six trumps, headed by the ace ace, and find on the second play that the other six are distributed "five and one" against you, instead of a nice "three and three." What then?

You can go into your strong side suit. Take a couple of high-card tricks if you can and then force your more difficult opponent to trump such leads. You will be wasting cards from your side suit; he will be wasting trumps. The switch is generally to your advantage, however.

This is particularly true when you have been forced to name a five-card trump, because it gives you a sequence, as:

♡ A 10 K Q J

With this, you may hold a longer suit, as:

♣ A 10 K K Q 9 9

If you lead the ace of clubs and catch a queen and jack, a lead of a nine will force an ace or ten and perhaps a trump. The other nine, led later, is almost sure to force a trump card. Your plan is to force out your opponents' trumps before they can do that to you.

This brings up an essential feature of defensive play. If you are trying to beat the bidder, lead low cards in a suit when he is out of it, forcing him to waste valuable trumps. Be careful, though, not to draw trumps from the other player who is working with you as a temporary partner in a combined effort to defeat the bidder.

Another defensive weapon is the smear, or "schmear," which consists of slapping high counter cards on tricks that your temporary partner is sure to win. This keeps the bidder from capturing those counters with his trump or long suit. The smear is a must in smart pinochle.

If you lead an ace against the bidder, your temporary partner is supposed to throw on his own ace if he has one, smearing your lead and making the most of counters as quickly as possible. So don't lead an ace unless you hold a ten for the next lead; except when it is a lone ace that you must play or run the risk of losing.

There are times when you can beat the bidder by leading trumps yourself. Here, you are working on the simple theory that he doesn't want them led, or he would be leading them himself. That's the sort of play that puts the punch in pinochle!

When four players participate in a game of auction pinochle, the dealer is included in the scoring of each hand, even though he takes no part in the bidding or the play.

Thus, in a so-called "four-handed" game, if player *A* should bid and make 380, with schedule (*e*) in force, he would collect five chips each from players *B, C,* and the dealer, *D,* a total of fifteen chips. If *A* should lose the hand, *B, C,* and *D* would all collect from him.

A fifth player may also be included in the game. This means there is an extra (besides the dealer) in every hand. He is the first player at the dealer's left and he is also "dealt out" by the dealer, who skips him when dealing cards to the three active participants in that hand.

However, the extra player must pay or collect, just like the dealer. If player *A* should bid and make that same 380 in a five-handed game, he would collect five chips each from players *B, C,* the dealer (*D*), and the extra (*E*), or twenty chips in all. Should *A* give up the hand, he would pay five chips each to *B, C, D,* and *E.*

Double losses, spades double, hearts triple, all apply in these four- and five-handed games, increasing the risk proportionately, which has a definite effect on the bidding and the playing of a doubtful hand.

PARTNERSHIP PINOCHLE

Auction pinochle can be played four handed, by two teams of partners seated opposite. Eleven cards are dealt to each player, with four to the widow. After the highest bidder names trump, he and his partner meld separately but combine the total with points from tricks in play toward the score needed to make the bid.

Minimum bid is 200, and with a sure meld of 60 a player can safely open as a cue for his partner to raise by the amount of his own sure meld, or at least 20 points to give the initial bidder a final say. Example: South deals. West, with four aces (100) and a pinochle (40) opens for 200. North passes. East, with four queens (60) raises to 260. South passes. West, now knowing that he and East have a 200 meld between them (100 + 40 + 60), makes a final bid of 300 or more.

A player with a trump sequence (**A 10 K Q J**) should pre-empt with an opening bid of 300; or a responder with a sequence should jump a low bid by 160, using such figures as cues. By keeping safe bids in *even* totals, a player banking on widow possibilities can show it with an *odd* bid. Example: West holds ♡**A** ◇**A** ♣ **A 10 K Q J**. An ♠**A** from the widow would give him 140 (four aces and royal marriage), while a ♣**J** would mean 150 (trump sequence). West opens with 310, and East, with ♠ **K Q** ◇**J** (20 + 40 = 60), raises 50 to 360, letting West take it at 370 and pick up the widow.

Contract Bridge

From whist has evolved the game of bridge, first as bridge whist, then as auction bridge, and finally in the form of contract bridge, the most famous and widely played of modern card games.

In bridge the actual play of the cards resembles whist. There are two teams of opposing partners, and when one player leads, the others must follow suit if possible. The highest card of that suit takes the trick unless a player who is out of the suit plays a trump. In such instances the highest trump wins the trick.

Whoever takes the trick gains the lead. The main objective of each team is to take as many tricks as possible. From there, the games diverge. Perhaps the first difference to be noted is that while in whist there must always be a trump suit, it is possible to play a hand of no-trump in bridge. In such a case, as the term implies, there is no trump at all. If a player is out of a suit that is led, he can only throw cards from an odd suit; nothing more.

This stems from the fact that in bridge a card is not turned up as trump at the end of the deal. Instead, the players bid for the privilege of naming or "declaring" a trump suit. This bidding begins at one, which signifies that the player contracts that his team will take one trick more than its "book" of six, or seven tricks in all, and the bidding can go as high as seven, with the team contracting to win all thirteen tricks.

To facilitate this auction, from which the term "auction bridge" was derived, so that the highest bidder may essay to make his contract—which accounts for the name of the more modern game—the suits are scaled in value, too.

The lowest "one" bid is in clubs; next above is diamonds; above that, hearts; then spades, the highest suit; and topping all, no-trump. From one the bidding goes to two, so that two clubs is a notch above one no-trump. Next above two clubs is two diamonds, and so on to the topmost bid of all, seven no-trump.

In bridge the first bidder to name the trump suit, or declarer as he is properly styled, has two advantages. He has picked the trump suit—or no-trump if he prefers—and his partner's hand becomes a "dummy" which the declarer alone can play.

The lead comes from the opponent on the declarer's left. As soon as it is made, the declarer's partner places his hand *face up* on the table, arranging it in suits from ace down, and the declarer plays both hands; his own and the dummy's.

This gives the declarer a distinct advantage. He can fit the dummy's hand into his own, working back and forth between them. He can view all the twenty-six cards that they hold mutually —the ones in his own hand and those showing on the board—and therefore he knows exactly what cards his opponents hold, though he cannot immediately place them individually.

The opponents have factors in their favor, too. From the bidding they can often determine certain cards which the declarer or his partner should almost necessarily hold in order to bid so high. If those cards do not show up in the dummy hand, they know that the declarer must have them. The opponents can then play accordingly.

There are various devices or procedures in defensive play that may enable the opponents to defeat the contract of an unwary declarer who may have only slightly overbid his hand. So the play itself hinges on the bidding, much more so in contract bridge than in the now all but obsolete game of auction.

The fault with auction was that a hand that looked good for a "slam" of twelve or thirteen tricks could often be "bought" for a bid of one because the other players held inconsequential cards. No matter how low the bid, the declarer's team scored in full for whatever tricks the declarer took. In contract the trick points that count toward game are scaled to the size of the bid.

In auction expert players introduced informative bids when the competition became keen, thus suggesting ways to outbid the opposition. This highly intriguing feature is the very essence of contract bridge and it accounts for the popularity of bidding systems, which had their genesis in the auction period and have fully bloomed in contract.

In bridge, the bidding starts with the dealer, who may pass, which extends the bidding privilege to the player on his left; or he may bid and thereby commit himself to taking a specified number of tricks in a certain suit, or in no-trump.

Once the bidding has been opened, the next player may pass it on, or he may bid anything higher than the previous bid, such as one heart over one club, or three diamonds over two no-trump. The burden of taking those tricks is then upon the new bidder.

There is another option at this stage: a player may double a bid made by an opponent. If North should bid three spades and East should double it, North would still have to make his contract of three spades—by taking at least nine of the thirteen tricks—and if he manages it, he scores double in trick points and gets a bonus count besides. But if North should fail, East's team would score an additional bonus for setting North's team.

The next player may either pass or "overcall," which means to bid higher. If a player's bid is doubled, his partner can redouble, which doubles the trick points once again and also ups the bonus count, one way or the other.

Thus: North bids three no-trump. East doubles. South, if confident that his team can make the contract, might then redouble. Or if South should pass and West should also pass, North himself could redouble over the double made by his opponent, East.

Higher bids can still be made, in other suits, wiping out doubles and also redoubles along with all lower bids. After three passes in a row the bid immediately preceding them stands. The player who made it becomes the declarer, unless his partner originally named suit. In that case the partner becomes the declarer.

As an example, assume that North, as dealer, bids first:

North bids one spade. South bids one no-trump. North bids two diamonds. South bids three hearts. The bid stands and South becomes the declarer.

But if South had gone to three diamonds or to three spades, North would have become the declarer, because he named those suits originally.

Similarly, if North decided to up the bid to three no-trump and it should stand, South would become the declarer as the first member of the team to name no-trump.

Throughout the bidding, each player gains inklings as to his partner's holdings and thus the essential communication is established between the partners. The more in accord the partners, or the keener they are at sizing up each other's purposes, the more spirited and effective the bidding becomes.

When the bidding follows an accepted system—and there are several types and varieties of these—the picture may become still clearer. The opponents, through their acquaintance with such procedures, also form their own conclusions from the bidding, which adds to the zest of the game.

The scoring has a direct influence on the bidding and therefore should be carefully studied. The object is to win two out of three games of 100 or more points each, in order to win a "rubber" for which a team scores bonus points, as will be specified. The score for trick points which count toward game is as follows:

Tricks over Book of Six Tricks

Suit	1	2	3	4	5	6	7
Clubs	20	40	60	80	100	120	140
Diamonds	20	40	60	80	100	120	140
Hearts	30	60	90	120	150	180	210
Spades	30	60	90	120	150	180	210
No-trump	40	70	100	130	160	190	220

When doubled, tricks count double value

When redoubled, tricks count four times value

Game requires 100 trick points or more

This table may be reduced to simple terms and remembered thus: In minor suits (♣ and ♢) each trick over six counts 20 points. In major suits (♡ and ♠) each trick over six counts 30 points. In no-trump the first trick counts 40, succeeding tricks, 30.

These points are for bid tricks only and must be won by the team making the bid. They go *below the line* on the lower half of the score sheet and are the only points that count toward game. They are added hand by hand and when one team accumulates the necessary 100 points or more, that game is won and both teams start again from zero.

SAMPLE BRIDGE SCORE

We	*They*
(B) 50	(E) 700
(A) 30	(C) 30
(A) 90	(C) 130
	(D) 120
170	980
	−170
	810

(A) We bid three hearts and took ten tricks, scoring 90 below the line (for making contract) and 30 above for extra trick.

(B) They bid three no-trump but only took eight tricks, so we scored 50 above the line (for one undertrick).

(C) They bid four no-trump and took eleven tricks, scoring 130 below the line (for making contract) and 30 above for extra trick.

(D) They bid four spades and made it, scoring 120 below the line (for making contract).

(E) By winning two games they won rubber and gained 700 points above the line.

Deducting *we* total from *they* total leaves 810–the margin of points by which they won the rubber.

It takes a bid of five in a minor suit (♣ or ♢) to win a game in one hand, which means taking eleven out of a possible thirteen tricks. It takes only four to make game in a major suit (♡ or ♠) in only one hand, or ten out of thirteen tricks. In no-trump a team can "go game" with a bid of only three, making this a highly attractive bid that requires taking only nine of thirteen tricks.

A team is credited below the line only for the amount of its successful bid, regardless of how many additional tricks it may take, though extras are credited *above the line,* as will be specified. Only by scoring 100 points *below the line* can a team win a game.

As soon as a team wins two games, a rubber is completed. But after a team has won its first game, it is said to be "vulnerable," and this has an important bearing on *points above the line*. These are termed *premiums* and are scored through:

Overtricks: Extra tricks that a team makes beyond its contract. When a team is *not vulnerable,* these are counted at face value; 20 for each trick in a minor suit (♣ or ♢), 30 for each trick in a major suit (♡ or ♠), 30 for each trick in no-trump. If the bid has been doubled, each overtrick counts 100 points, regardless of suit. When redoubled, each overtrick counts 200 points. These go to the bidding team and are scored above the line.

Also, if a team makes its contract when doubled or redoubled, it is credited with an additional bonus of 50 points above the line, for fulfilling the contract.

Thus, a team bids three hearts and takes ten tricks. The team scores 90 points below the line, representing 30 for each of the three tricks over the book of six tricks. It also scores 30 points above the line for the single overtrick.

If doubled, the team would score 180 below the line–enough for game–and 50 above the line for making the doubled contract, plus 100 for the overtrick.

If redoubled, the team would score 360 below the line–also winning game–and 50 above the line for making the redoubled contract, plus 200 for the overtrick.

When the bidding team is *vulnerable,* it scores 200 points for each overtrick if doubled, or 400 for each overtrick if redoubled. The other scores remain the same when the team is vulnerable.

Undertricks: These are tricks by which the declarer falls short of making his contract. They are actually losses on the bidder's part. But instead of being deducted from his team's score, they are credited to the opponents, above the line.

Since the opponents have set the bidder, suits do not matter in this case. It is simply a question of trick shortage.

When a team is *not vulnerable,* for each undertrick the opponents score 50 points. If the contract is doubled, the opponents score 100 for the first undertrick; 200 for each additional undertrick. If redoubled, 200 for the first undertrick, 400 for each additional.

If the bidding team is *vulnerable,* each undertrick counts 100 for the opponents. If doubled, 200 points for the first, 300 for each additional. If redoubled, 400 for the first, 600 for each additional trick. Plainly, it usually doesn't pay to overbid a hand when vulnerable.

Besides these, there are special points that go *above the line* for honors, slams, and rubbers.

Honors consist of the ace, king, queen, jack, and ten in the declared trump suit. If a player holds four of these in his hand, his team scores 100 points. If a player holds all five, his team scores 150 points. Any player can claim honors in the declared trump suit.

In no-trump, aces alone rate as honors. If all four aces are held in one hand, the player's team scores 150 points.

Slams: These are of two types: a "little slam," wherein the player bids six and must take twelve tricks; and a "grand slam," which is a bid of seven and means that all thirteen tricks must be taken.

For a *little slam,* when bid and won, a team scores 500 points *above the line*. If the team is *vulnerable,* it scores 750 points.

For a *grand slam,* when bid and won, a team scores 1000 points *above the line*. If *vulnerable,* it scores 1500.

In neither case is there any penalty for failing to make the slam, other than the usual loss through undertricks, which can, of course, be heavy if a player keeps overbidding toward a hoped-for slam.

Rubber points are scored *above the line* for the team that wins a rubber. If a team wins two games out of two, it scores 700 points. If it takes two out of three–with the opponents winning the odd one–the team scores only 500 points.

If a team wins the first game of an unfinished rubber and play is terminated, the team scores 300 points for the game. If a team has made the only part score in an unfinished game, it is credited with 50 points.

Beginners should keep the foregoing scoring system handy until thoroughly familiar with it and should study sample scores as well. All this, of course, should be correlated in terms of actual bidding.

BIDDING IN BRIDGE

In days of yore much bidding in bridge was on a "by gum and by guess" basis with every player for himself and the declarer always hoping to be happily surprised by what his partner might lay down in the dummy.

Rather than trust to such sheer luck, veteran players would often come up with a "pre-emptory bid" such as three no-trump right bang at the start, so that nobody else had a chance even to speak.

That was all right in auction, where a three bid was considered pretty big even when holding a potential slam hand. But in contract such a bid would be a demand upon a partner to bid higher and informatively, so as to confirm a "fit" of hands and go for a slam.

This presupposes that two bridge partners have some method of mutually evaluating their hands. One of the simplest and most popular is known as the "point count." This does not refer to the points you expect to score from a winning hand. It is a system of evaluating the hand itself, by giving specific values to certain high cards and to extra cards in long suits.

In bridge all systems, including the point system and its variations, are largely an artificial means of simplifying the problem of reaching a contract. A good player will try to visualize his partner's hand, as well as those of his opponents, thus determining the strength of his team on offense or defense. Often a team can make more by setting the opponents than by going ahead with a bid of its own.

The general system of bidding as outlined here is only one example of the simpler procedures. There are many systems, some much more artificial than the point count, and unless a player's partner understands the system that he is using, there will be no communication between them and the bidding will be plain guesswork, often of the wrong kind. As a player progresses in his knowledge of contract bridge, he will become familiar with various systems, conventions, and other fine points, and can set his course according to his likes.

In the point-count system the high-card values are determined by noting the honor cards that you hold, and rating them, regardless of suit, as follows: ace, 4; king, 3; queen, 2; jack, 1; ten, 0. The ten, which was included in early versions of the point count, was reduced to a half point and finally to zero when the other values were whittled down proportionately. Still, it is a strong card in certain stages of play and its presence in a hand should be noted, if only for the satisfaction that no one else is holding it.

Basically, the point count applies to no-trump hands, which also require that the cards should be rather evenly distributed among the four suits, constituting what is often termed a "balanced" hand, as:

♠ A 9 3
♡ A 8 7
♢ A 9 7 2
♣ A 10 4

Note that the suits are distributed in a 4-3-3-3 ratio where the number of cards in each suit is concerned. The four aces represent one sure trick in each suit, which is important in no-trump. The aces add up to 16 points by the accepted system. This establishes 16 points as the minimum count for a one-no-trump bid, though four aces are regarded as worth an extra point because of their obvious strength.

This marks the hand as worth 17 points, and to be on the safe side the opening requirement usually is extended to include 18 points.

Here is another type of balanced hand:

♠ Q J 10 6
♡ K Q 7 3
♢ A J 5
♣ K 9

In this hand the suits are distributed in a 4-4-3-2 ratio. Its point count of ace (4), two kings (6), two queens (4), two jacks (2) meets the minimum requirement of 16. The ♢**A** is a trick taker and ♡ **K Q** is the same, because the ♡**K** can force the ♡**A**, making the ♡**Q** good.

Similarly, the ♠ **Q J 10** combination should be good for a trick, as the ♠ **Q J** can force the ♠ **A K**, making the ♠**10** good. In bridge parlance these are called "guards" or "stoppers" because they prevent the other team from running away with a suit.

The ♣**K** rates as a "guarded king" or "potential stopper" because its companion card (the ♣**9**) can be thrown off on the ♣**A** if the latter is led by an opponent. But there is a possibility that the ♣**9** might be lost to an opposing card lower than the king (as the ♣**Q**) which would leave the ♣**K** unprotected against the ♣**A**.

However, with a one-no-trump bid, a potential stopper is sufficient in a suit, as the bidder's chief purpose is to acquaint his partner with the fact that he (the bidder) has adequate no-trump holdings, except when this suit was bid by an opponent.

This is nicely illustrated in this third type of balanced hand:

♠ **A K**
♡ **10 9 7**
♢ **A Q 8**
♣ **K Q 10 9 6**

This shows a suit distribution of 5-3-3-2, which has only one two-card suit or doubleton, so it allows a one-no-trump bid, as its count of two aces (8), two kings (6), two queens (4) gives it 18 points.

It lacks a stopper in one suit, hearts, but the hand is so strong otherwise that such a bid is justified. If the point count came only to 16 and the hand had only one ace, the bid would have been doubtful. If the doubleton happened to be the weak suit, there should be no bid. (The bid can be made in suit–i. e., clubs.)

But the ♡ **10 9 7** will do if your partner has a fair supporting hand in no-trump with a heart stopper of his own. In fact, some experts bank on this to such a degree that they habitually bid one no-trump with stoppers in only three suits. Some also vary the count requirement, bidding on 15 points with a strong hand.

These practices are all right if your partner expects them, as the general purpose of an opening no-trump bid is to give your partner a fair picture of your holdings.

When the point count of a balanced hand totals 19, 20, or 21, it is generally conceded to be too high for one no-trump and not high enough for two no-trump. As an example:

♠ K J 9
♡ A K 7 6
◊ A 10 9
♣ K Q 2

The distribution is 4-3-3-3. All suits are stopped. But the count —aces (8), kings (9), queen (2), jack (1)—comes to 20. So the bid is one heart, the strongest suit. Later, you may be able to make a no-trump bid, and if you do, your holding will be nicely pin-pointed.

To make an opening bid of two no-trump, you follow this simple rule: since 18 points is the "top" for one no-trump, add 4 points to represent an ace or its equivalent, making 22 points the minimum for two no-trump. Again, there is a certain leeway, two no-trump being bid on a count of 22, 23, or 24.

Here is an example:

♠ Q 10 7
♡ K Q 9 4 2
◊ A K
♣ A K Q

This hand has 5-3-3-2 distribution, a point count of two aces (8), three kings (9), three queens (6), for a total of 23, with stoppers in all suits, which is a must when bidding two no-trump.

For a bid of three no-trump, only *one point more* than a two bid is required, so that the three bid falls into a bracket of 25, 26, or 27 points, as:

♠ Q J 10 8
♡ A K
◊ A K J 10
♣ A Q J

Here is a 4-4-3-2 distribution, a point count of three aces (12), two kings (6), two queens (4), three jacks (3), for a total of 25, with stoppers in all suits, calling for three no-trump.

Note that each of the three jacks is an almost certain trick taker, showing how a *single point* can turn a bid of two no-trump into a potential three no-trump, for by the time a count approaches 26 points, which is regarded good enough to make game, it must hold so many high point cards that the lower ones are promoted to the higher rank.

So much for the no-trump openers; now to consider suit bids. Here, the trump factor enters. Any type of distribution, balanced or unbalanced, is biddable, but the trump suit must contain at least four cards, preferably with a high-card count of 4 or more, which means that the suit must contain king-jack or better, though many players regard 3 as sufficient, and some even less. With a trump suit of five cards or more, no count is needed in trumps.

Special rating is given to extra cards in the trump suit or in long side suits, as they can often be turned into trick takers after opposing trumps are exhausted. These long suits are easily translated into point-count values, thus:

Each card over four in a trump suit, 1 point.

Each card over three in a side suit, 1 point.

These are called distributional points to distinguish them from high-card points, but all are counted together in determining the point count for most trump bids.

Opening requirements will vary with different situations, for example, vulnerability and part score, so these should be given due consideration as they occur.

Naming trump gives a player a definite advantage. The average point count of a balanced hand is 10, so 4 more points—or the equivalent of an ace—should give a hand the added strength for a one bid in a specified suit. By remembering that, you have the required figure for such a bid: 14 points.

Here is an example:

♠ 9 6
♡ A Q 9 8 5
◇ A 4
♣ Q 10 9 7

The point count includes two aces (8), two queens (4), and 2 distributional points, one in trumps (hearts) and one in the long side suit (clubs). The bid, of course, is one heart.

Note: Instead of adding points for extra cards in long suits, it is common practice to count 1 point for *each card under three* in a *short suit*. In the hand shown, each doubleton (♠ and ♡) would be counted as 1 point instead of the long suits (♡ and ♣). These "long" and "short" counts work out the same, so either will do. The long count is preferable in that the long suits contain the cards that may prove to be actual trick takers.

If there is any doubt as to the bidding quality of a 14-point hand, it can be settled by checking the high cards or combinations which may take tricks on the first or second lead of a suit. Known as "quick tricks," these are:

Ace-king of the same suit	2 quick tricks
Ace-queen of the same suit	1½ " "
An ace, with no other honors in its suit	1 quick trick
King-queen of one suit	1 " "
King and any other card of its suit	½ " "

Generally, a hand needs two quick tricks or better to become a sound "one" bid in a suit. If it falls short of that qualification, a player can pass it. In contrast, if a hand with a 13-point count shows two and a half quick tricks, it may be worth a bid of one.

The hand shown above has two and a half quick tricks (♡ **A Q** = 1½ and ◇ **A** = 1) and if you substitute the ♣**J** for the ♣**Q**, reducing its point count from 14 to 13, it will still have two and a half quick tricks and should be worth a bid of one heart.

Also, the experienced bridge player looks for such sleepers as a king-jack-ten, which is almost as good for one quick trick as the king-queen of a suit; or a queen-jack-odd, which may be a safer half trick than a king-odd. Use judgment in evaluating individual hands, remembering that circumstances may alter cases. The purpose of an opening bid is to give your partner some idea of your holdings. Passing a doubtful hand may mean passing up an opportunity, but bidding it may bring disaster.

When the first two bidders pass, the third hand may open on as low as 11 points, if the hand shows special merit, say with all its strength and most of its point count in a single suit headed by ace-king-jack. You don't need two quick tricks when bidding a fairly good hand in third position.

The logic is this: if none of the first three hands are worth a normal opening bid, the fourth hand may be packed with strength. As third hand, you may as well speak your piece, because the fourth hand is due to open anyway. An opening suit bid may mean a holding as high as 25 points, and you alone know how weak your hand really is. Your third-hand bid may not help your partner, but he may be helpless anyway. What it can do, is confuse the opposition, causing them to shy from the suit you bid, perhaps passing up a potential no-trump contract.

Fourth hand as opening bidder usually follows the conventional pattern, but many players rigidly adhere to a count of 14 points plus two quick tricks. Remember, here, that a pass will bring a new deal, which may be the best answer; whereas a risky opening bid may start a sequence that will prove a boomerang, enabling the opponents to garner a part score.

However, strength and concentrated point count in a single suit may warrant an opening bid, just as with the third hand, provided it is in a major suit (♠ or ♡), as this may pave the path to a game contract.

Choice of Suit for Opening Bid

Choosing the suit for the opening bid is often a very simple matter, the rule being to bid the longest suit; whether it contains any point cards (jack or better) does not matter, provided the suit contains at least five cards.

Thus there is no doubt about the opening bid with:

♠ K 8
♡ A K
◇ 10 9 7 6 5 2
♣ Q J 3

This hand has a point count of 15, consisting of ace (4), kings (6), queen (2), jack (1), and distributional points (2), which can be counted either as two extra trumps (♢) or two doubletons (in ♠ and ♡). It has two and a half quick tricks (♡ **A K**, 2; ♠ **K** 8, ½). The long suit (♢) contains six cards.

The bid is *one diamond.*

With a hand containing two long suits of equal length, the usual procedure is to bid the suit of higher rank first. No hand can hold two seven-card suits, and hands with two six-card suits are rare; but those with two five-card suits are frequent, as:

♠ Q J 9 8 2
♡ A 8
♢ A Q J 7 5
♣ 9

This hand has a point count of 17, consisting of aces (8), queens (4), jacks (2), and distributional points (3) from one extra trump and two extra cards in a side suit; or the heart doubleton (1) and the club singleton (2). It has two and a half quick tricks (♢ **A Q**, 1½; ♡**A**, 1).

The bid is one spade, the higher-ranking five-card suit; but the other five-card suit, diamonds, may be bid later as a "rebid" at a higher level than one. Actually, leeway is allowed for two intervening bids, one no-trump and two clubs, before bidding two diamonds.

When the hand contains spades and clubs as its two five-card suits, most players bid one club first, as that allows the same leeway of two intervening bids, one diamond and one heart, before rebidding the other long suit, which in that case would require only one spade.

When a hand has two four-card suits as its two longest, it is a good plan to go by the rule that a suit must have a minimum count of 4 points in order to be biddable. Some players may rightfully go along with queen-jack, queen-high, or even less, but by eliminating such hands, the opening bid is simplified.

Often, only one four-card suit will qualify, as:

♠ A 5
♡ K Q 9 8
♢ J 10 7 3
♣ A 9 6

This hand is the balanced type (4-4-3-2) but its high-card count is only 14 points—aces (8), king (3), queen (2), jack (1)—so it is short of the 16-point requirement for a one-no-trump opener.

For a suit bid, it adds 1 distributional point, giving it a count of 15. But only in one long suit, hearts, is there a point count of 4 or better, the ♡ **K Q** adding up to 5. The hand has three quick tricks (**A**, 1; **A**, 1; **K Q**, 1) and is therefore a healthy bid at one heart.

Where there is a choice of two four-card suits, some players bid the higher, as with two five-card suits, provided the two suits are next to each other, or "touching," as they say in bridge parlance. If a short suit intervenes, they bid the long suit below it. Here are comparative examples:

♠ **10 8 6**
♡ **K Q 7 2**
♢ **A Q 9 8**
♣ **K 8**

Point count, 14 for high cards—ace (4), kings (6), queens (4) —plus 1 for distributional point, total 15. Hand has three quick tricks (**A Q**, 1½; **K Q**, 1; **K 8**, ½). In suits, hearts has high-card count of 5 (**K Q**) and diamonds has 6 (**A Q**). Hearts is the higher of the two adjacent suits, so bid one heart.

♠ **K Q J 5**
♡ **8 6 3**
♢ **A Q J 7**
♣ **J 10**

Point count, 14 for high cards—ace (4), king (3), queens (4), jacks (3)—plus 1 for distributional point, total 15. Hand has two and a half quick tricks (**A Q**, 1½; **K Q**, 1). In suits, spades has high-card count of 6 (**K Q J**), and diamonds 7 (**A Q J**). A suit (hearts) intervenes, so bid the lower four-card suit, one diamond.

With a hand containing *three* biddable four-card suits, one plan is to bid the highest-ranking suit below the singleton. For example:

♠ **K J 8 4**
♡ **A Q 8 7**
♢ **9**
♣ **A Q 10 2**

This hand has a high-card count of 16 points—aces (8), king (3), queens (4), jack (1)—but the singleton kills it as a one no-trump. Add 2 points for distribution, making a strong 18. There are three and a half quick tricks (**A Q**, 1½; **A Q**, 1½; **K J**, ½).

The bid is the suit below the singleton, one club.

Bidding Shorter Opening Suits

Modern bidding favors high-card strength in an opening suit, with passing of even slightly doubtful hands allowable. So the bidding of a shorter suit as opener has gained some vogue. A strong five-card suit may take precedence over a weak six-card suit, though such hands are generally rare. Usually, the choice falls between a strong four-card and a weak five-card suit, as:

♠ **A 8**
♡ **A K Q 10**
◇ **J 8 6 5 3**
♣ **9 7**

Here, the strength is in hearts, the four-card suit. With a point count of 16—aces (8), king (3), queen (2), jack (1), distributional (2)—the hand calls for an opening one bid, with hearts preferable to diamonds. However, some conservative players are reluctant to open with a four-card major suit (♠ or ♡) at all. They would prefer one diamond.

The Forcing Two Bid

Since the purpose of the one bid is to encourage the partner's response, an opening bid should be kept at that level, unless the bidder has an unbalanced hand with sufficient point count to make a "game-forcing" two bid. With such an opener the bidder signifies that his hand is so strong that he expects his partner to keep on bidding until they reach a game-winning contract.

For simplicity, a suit bid of two can be placed in the same point-count bracket as two no-trump (22, 23, 24), but with these provisos:

With 22 points a strong seven-card suit is needed.

With 23 points a strong six-card suit is needed.

With 24 points two strong five-card suits are needed.

With a higher count one strong five-card suit will do, but the hand must necessarily have over-all strength.

The minimum count may be shaded with a specially strong hand, but it is better to be on the conservative side, as some experts feel that a 24-point minimum is desirable with most hands.

A checkup of quick tricks helps to evaluate a forcing two bid. Again, there is a question of minimum. With some hands four quick tricks may be enough, but four and a half would be a safer figure. As the trump suit shortens, more quick tricks are desirable, five and a half being a good figure.

The hand must be strong enough to go for game almost on its own. The bidder *wants* help and *demands* that his partner make some response, but the bidder should *not* bank on such help.

Here is a hand with a seven-card suit with a count of 22 points:

♠ **A K**
♡ **A K Q 9 7 5 3**
◇ **K 10 8**
♣ **5**

Quick tricks total four and a half (**A K**, 2; **A K**, 2; **K 10**, ½), but in actual play the bidder may make all his hearts good, with two sure spades and the ◇**K**, for a total of ten tricks and game on a four-hearts contract. So his forcing bid of two hearts is simply a lead up to that goal.

Consider this example of a hand with only one five-card suit and a count of 26 points:

♠ **A K Q 9 7**
♡ **A**
◇ **A Q 8**
♣ **K Q 7 2**

High cards are aces (12), kings (6), queens (6), distributional points (2). Quick tricks total five and a half (**A K**, 2; **A Q**, 1½; **A**, 1; **K Q**, 1).

In actual play the bidder is sure of three tricks in trump (♠), with single tricks about certain in each of the other suits. If he can cash in his two smaller trumps and pick up an extra trick with each queen (in ♢ and ♣) he will have the four tricks required for game in spades.

Pre-emptive or Shutout Bids

Opening bids of three or four are often made in suits when the hand contains seven or more good trumps, usually without the ace, and lacking support in other suits. These are called pre-emptive or shutout bids, because they prevent the opponents from making informative bids at lower levels.

Point count figures in such hands, but somewhat in reverse. The more points that the opponents may hold, the more reason for a shutout bid. So the bidder's hand should contain only 10 points, or less, to warrant a three bid. At the same time it needs enough playing strength to take at least six tricks and in some cases, seven.

Here is a sample hand:

♠ 8
♡ K Q 10 9 8 7 3
♢ 10
♣ Q 9 8 7

There are only 7 points in high cards, but hearts, as trumps, should take five tricks and possibly six, while the ♣ Q is good for another. Thus with six tricks sure, the hand can be bid at three hearts.

If things go badly against the bidder, with his partner coming through with no help at all, the team may be set by as many as three tricks in hearts. But that is worth the risk, because the opponents could well have been shut out from a high bid of their own that they would probably have made but for the pre-empt.

However, when a team is vulnerable, three tricks are too great a risk. The player should be sure or nearly sure of seven tricks before making a three bid, which would require taking nine. In the hand shown, the chance of making the extra trump would encourage many players to bid three even when vulnerable.

The same hand, with one more small heart (making an eight-card suit) instead of the lone spade or the lone diamond, would be worth a shutout bid of four hearts. This would give the bidder a chance at game and at the same time force the opponents to go still higher in any effort to outbid him.

With a count of more than 10 in high-card points, or more than one and a half quick tricks, a bid of one is usually a better opener than a three or four shutout bid. With a one bid, distributional points would also be counted, bringing the hand up to the required 13 or 14 points required for most one bids. So it would be better to announce it in its proper category.

Responding to Opening Bids

An opening bid is an invitation or a demand for the bidder's partner to chime in with his side of the story. With an opening no-trump bid, it gives the partner a good over-all picture of the opener's hand, so that a response is sometimes almost automatic.

An opening one no-trump specifies a balanced hand with 16 to 18 high-card points. With the minimum 16, there are 24 in other hands, making up the total of 40, so the responder needs 8 points to meet his quota.

So with a balanced hand of his own, and 8 or 9 high-card points, the partner can respond with two no-trump. If he has 10 to 14 points, he can go to three no-trump, as that means a minimum of 26 high-card points for the partnership, a figure that usually produces game. With 15 to 16 points he can go to four no-trump. With 17 to 18 there is a jump to six no-trump, and with 21 points a towering seven no-trump.

Remember, these are high-card points, the only kind that apply in no-trump bidding, and the hands are balanced (with suit distribution of 4-3-3-3, 4-4-3-2, or 5-3-3-2). If the responder's hand is unbalanced, he should bid two in a five-card suit, with anything less than 8 points in his hand, to show where his length lies. This rule, however, has one exception, namely, the responder should never bid two clubs with less than 8 high-card points in an unbalanced hand. The two-clubs bid is reserved for use in a "two-clubs convention," one form of which is known as the "Stayman convention" after the expert who developed it.

The two-clubs convention works thus:

With a hand containing 8 high-card points or more and a major suit (♠ or ♡) with four cards, the responder may bid two clubs. This calls upon the original bidder to bid two in a four-card major suit of his own, if he has one. From the opener's rebid, the responder may find a "four-four fit" in a major suit, he and his partner holding eight (or more) cards of that suit between them.

Here is a type of hand that calls for a two-clubs conventional response following an opening bid of one no-trump:

♠ K J 9 8
♡ A J 7 5
♢ Q 10 9 6
♣ 5

Note that clubs, the suit named in the bid, just doesn't figure at all, as an actual holding. The opener gets the responder out of it by rebidding two diamonds if he is unable to show a worthy major suit; or occasionally by some other bid.

When the responder's hand contains 10 high-card points, with a five-card suit or longer, there is another prospect. Here, the responder can jump to three in a long major suit, if he has one; otherwise, a long minor suit may do.

Usually, such a hand should have a full point count (high-card and distributional) of 12 or 13 toward a suit bid, and this can go still higher. In any case the opener knows that the responder has the point count for three no-trump but prefers the suit bid because of concentrated strength.

Such a bid is called a "take-out." With a really long suit, with only 10 high-card points or less in the entire hand, the responder can take out the opener with a four bid in a suit. This is similar to a shutout bid.

When the opener originally bids two no-trump, the responder, if holding a balanced hand, needs only 4 high-card points to raise to three no-trump. With 9 points he can jump to four. With 11 points, to six. With 15 points, to seven.

After an opening bid of two no-trump the responder can go to three in a suit; but he does not need 10 high-card points to do it. A five-card major suit, topped by jack or better, will swing it if the hand contains 6 points in all (high-card and distributional). With a six-card major, anything goes for a three bid in that suit.

An opening three-no-trump bid can be raised to four with 7 points; to six with 8 points; and to seven no-trump with 12 points. Any long suit (five cards or more) is worth a take-out bid of four in that suit, provided the hand contains 5 points in high cards.

Responses to Suit Bids

Responses to suit bids are of three general types. Assuming that your partner has opened with a one bid in a suit, a bid that allows a very wide point range, you can respond by:

(*a*) Making a bid in no-trump.

(*b*) Switching the bid to a new suit.

(*c*) Raising your partner in his own suit.

Taking these in order:

If you hold a balanced hand containing 6 to 10 points inclusive, in *high cards* only, the usual response is one no-trump. This gives your partner a fair idea of your hand, but does not force him to a further bid, as your holdings are admittedly weak. This bid is sometimes optional.

With a balanced hand containing 13 to 15 high-card points, with stoppers in all suits except the one bid by your partner, respond with two no-trump. This gives a good picture of your hand and its possibilities.

With an ideal balanced hand (4-3-3-3 in suit distribution) containing 16 or 17 high-card points and stoppers in the three unbid suits, your response should be three no-trump. This gives a still sharper picture of your hand.

In switching to another suit you have an advantage if your partner opened with a bid of less than one spade, as this gives you a chance to deliver the cheapest of responses:

The One over One

Assuming that your partner opened with one diamond, you can bid one heart or one spade without raising the level of the bidding. For this, you need only 6 points in high-card and distributional points combined. To be biddable, a four-card suit should be headed by the queen at least; but any five-card suit is biddable at one over one.

For example, your partner has bid one diamond. In your hand you hold:

♠ 10 9 7 6 3
♡ 8 7 5
◇ K 9
♣ Q 10 7

Your hand contains 5 high-card points, which is not enough for a one no-trump, even though the hand has a balanced distribution (5-3-3-2). However, the 1 additional point for an extra card in trump (spades) brings the total to 6 points.

Even with a higher count, this could still be a better spade than no-trump bid; in fact, you can bid a one over one with a count up to 18 points, as it is still a cheap way to tip off your partner to your suit holding, and you can usually boost your bid later. But with stronger hands, you can often respond with:

The Two over One

This refers specifically to a response of two in a lower suit after an opening bid of one in a higher suit. To go two over one, you need 10 to 18 points with a biddable suit.

Your partner has opened with one heart and you hold:

♠ K 10 8 7
♡ 7
◇ A Q 9 8 5
♣ 9 3 2

The hand has 11 points–ace (4), king (3), queen (2), extra cards in suits (2)–with diamonds as a strong five-card suit. This warrants a bid of two diamonds.

If it lacked a little strength in diamonds (◇ **K J** instead of ◇ **A Q**), a one-over-one bid in spades would be justifiable, even though the suit has one less card than diamonds.

Like an opening one bid, a one-over-one or two-over-one response allows a lot of leeway and room for judgment as well.

Raising Partner's Suit Bid

This is an important type of response, particularly when your partner has opened with a major suit (♠ or ♡), and it allows a special appraisal of your hand, provided you can furnish sufficient suit strength, which consists of three cards, headed by a high card (jack or better) or simply four low cards of the bid suit. With 6 to 10 points you raise from one to two.

As an example, your partner bids one heart. Your hand consists of:

♠ 8
♡ Q 9 8 7
♢ K 8 5 3
♣ 9 7 3 2

Normally, the count would be 7 points: 3 for the king, 2 for the queen, and 2 for extra cards in side suits (or 2 for the singleton spade). However, since you are bidding your partner's suit, this rates as a dummy hand. So you can add 1 point because of the high card in hearts. (This is allowable until such cards reach a total of four.) Also, you add 1 extra point for a singleton; and 2 extra for a blank suit. With only three trumps, subtract 1 point.

In this hand you add 1 for the ♡**Q** and 1 for the singleton spade. This makes a total of 9 points, which is in the 6- to 10-point bracket, making the bid two hearts.

With 11 or 12 points by this stepped-up count, you bid another suit, hoping to bid your partner's suit later. With 13 to 16 points and a four-card trump suit, you can raise his one to three. Say your partner has bid one heart and you have:

♠ Q 9 3 2
♡ K 8 7 5
♢ 8
♣ A J 9 2

High-card points total 10 plus 1 for the high trump (♡**K**). Distributional points total 2 plus 1 for the singleton (or simply 3 for the singleton). This makes 14, putting the hand in the 13-to-16 bracket, making the bid three hearts.

If the hand contains *five trumps,* with a *singleton* or *blank suit* and *fewer than* 10 high-card points, you can make a shutout bid of four. The hand shown would qualify if it had one more small trump (say the ♡**3**) instead of a high card (such as the ♣**J**). You should have at least 11 or 12 points, however, counting distributional points on the "stepped-up" basis.

Raising a partner's bid in a minor suit is usually bad business when it can be properly avoided. Sometimes a bid in another suit or no-trump may offer a reasonable alternative.

Responding to an Opening Two Bid in a Suit

When your partner opens with a two bid in a suit, he is forcing you to bid until game is reached. In return you must give him a negative or positive response.

A bid of two no-trump is the negative cue. It means that you have less than 6 high-card points and probably not even one quick trick. You might have length in an odd suit, but if you do, you can furnish that information later.

With 6 or more high-card points and preferably one quick trick or better, you can make a positive response. This consists in naming a biddable suit–either your partner's or your own–much as you would after an opening one bid.

In this case, however, since your partner opened with a two, you will either have to go two in a higher-ranking suit (for example, two spades over your partner's opening two hearts) or bid three in a lower-ranking suit (as three diamonds over three hearts) or simply raise your partner's suit bid from two to three.

If you have 8 high-card points and one or one and a half quick tricks in a hand with balanced distribution, you can go to three no-trump. Such a bid is positive, in contrast to the negative two no-trump.

Rebidding the Hand

After a player makes an opening bid and hears his partner's response, he gains a partial idea as to the fit of their hands, as well as their mutual point count. The opener considers those factors in his next bid, or "rebid," as it is termed.

First, he checks his own point count as closely as possible. To that the opener adds the probable point count of the responder, according to the range of the latter's bid. From that the opener makes his rebid, his magic number, so to speak, being 26, for if the combined points reach that total, the team should make game.

Since the commonest type of opening bid is one in a suit, this will be considered first, with the various responses. An opening bid may range from 11 to 24 points, but usually it can be placed in one of three convenient brackets, namely:

13 to 15, representing any opening bid under 16 points.

16 to 18, a strong hand, usually an unbalanced type.

19 to 21, a powerful hand, with occasional higher counts.

Though the opener can pinpoint his count exactly, these brackets are helpful, because they allow for variations due to the make-up of the hand, such as the distribution of high cards, which no point count can fully cover. Also, they are valuable to the responder, for after hearing the opener's rebid, he can gauge the opener's hand according to its bracket.

Opening bid: one in suit. *Response:* two in same suit.

This shows 6 to 10 points in responder's hand, with at least three trump cards. Opener can add 1 point for a fifth trump in his hand; 2 points for each trump beyond that, if he raises suit in his rebid.

With hand in the 13–15 bracket: total short of game. *Pass.*

In the 16–18 bracket: game possible. Bid three in original suit, or switch to two no-trump with a balanced hand, or make a game-forcing bid in a new suit.

In the 19–21 bracket: total sufficient for game. Jump to game in original suit, or bid new suit.

These brackets represent the *total value* of the *rebid hand,* consisting of the original count, plus points for extra trumps which are added when opening bid, response, and rebid are all in the same suit. An example follows.

As a sample hand, consider:

♠ 4
♡ A Q 10 7 5 2
◇ Q 10 8
♣ A 7 3

Opener bid one heart with 12 high-card points plus 2 distributional points, a total of 14. Responder bid two hearts, indicating 6 to 10 points. Opener adds 1 plus 2 points for fifth and sixth hearts, making his count 17. Adding responder's 6 to 10 makes a total of 23–27, or possible game. Opener rebids three hearts.

Opening bid: one in suit. *Response:* three in same suit.

This shows 13 to 16 points in responder's hand. Opener adds values to his own hand, as described, if he raises suit in rebid. If opener's hand is only in 13–15 bracket, the total calls for a bid of four in the original suit, or three no-trump. When the opener's hand is in a higher bracket, he can try for a slam.

The next category includes:

Opening bid: one in suit. *Response:* one no-trump.

Again, this shows 6 to 10 points in responder's hand, but all in high cards and with a balanced hand.

In the 13–15 bracket, with a *balanced hand,* the opener should pass. With an *unbalanced hand* he can rebid his original suit at two or rebid in a new suit.

In the 16–18 bracket the same applies; but with a count of 18 in *high cards only,* the rebid can be two no-trump.

In the 19–21 bracket a bid of three can be made in a new suit, or if the count is in high cards only, the right bid is three no-trump, preferably with all suits stopped in a balanced hand.

Opening bid: one in suit. *Response:* two no-trump.

This shows 13 to 15 points in the responder's hand, with all suits stopped, which forces the bidding to game, as well it might. It tells the original bidder to rebid thus:

In the 13–15 bracket, rebid three no-trump with a balanced hand, unless it is a 5-3-3-2 distribution with a five-card major suit, which can be bid instead. With an unbalanced hand, make a rebid in a suit.

In the 16–18 bracket the same applies, with a try for slam advisable at 18 points.

In the 19–21 bracket a slam becomes a must.

When the original bidder opens with one in a suit and the responder bids in another, we have:

Opening bid: one in a suit. *Response:* one in another suit.

From the one over one, the opener knows that the responder has a count of 6 to 18 points in the new suit named. This gives the opener great leeway.

In the 13–15 bracket the opener can show balanced distribution by bidding one no-trump.

He can rebid his own suit at two, valuing a fifth trump at 1 extra point, additional trumps at 2 each, as already stated.

He can raise his partner's suit, treating it as if the responder were the original bidder. This allows the opener to add dummy values to his hand, in terms of partner's trump.

The opener can rebid in a new suit, if it is strong enough.

In the 16–18 bracket the bidding may follow the same pattern. If the opener holds six trumps in his own suit, he can jump to three. Or with four of the responder's trumps he can often jump that suit to four. Otherwise, bid as in the lower bracket.

In the 19–21 bracket the opener can rebid a balanced hand at two no-trump. If the hand is very strong in the unbid suits, he can go to three no-trump. If strong in his own suit, opener can jump to game; if strong in partner's, he can jump it to game.

If over 21 points, the hand further justifies such bids, and also calls for a jump bid in a new suit as the best of all, as the show of new strength can often lead to a slam.

Opening bid: one in a suit. *Response:* two in a lesser suit.

Though similar to the one over one, this two over one indicates that the responder has at least 10 points in his hand, and perhaps as many as 18. This affects the opener's rebid thus:

In the 13–15 bracket, with a combined count of from 13 plus 10 to 15 plus 18, there are prospects for game. The opener should rebid at least two of his own suit, if he has nothing else.

To show balanced distribution and a blocker in one or both of the unbid suits, the opener can make a rebid of two no-trump. But if he can show a good unbid suit at the two level, the opportunity should be taken. Or he can raise his partner's bid by one.

In the 16–18 bracket the opener can rebid as he would after a one-over-one response, but with more surety.

In the 19–21 bracket: the same as with one over one.

When the original bidder opens with one no-trump, his hand is definitely pegged as the balanced type in the 16- to 18-point bracket. Similarly, the responder's bid defines his hand sharply, as with:

Opening bid: one no-trump. *Response:* two no-trump.

Opener has 16 to 18 points; responder, 8 or 9. Total, 24 to 27. Opener should usually pass with 16 points; raise to three no-trump with 17 and strength in all suits; raise to three no-trump with 18 points.

Opening bid: one no-trump. *Response:* two in suit.

Opener has 16 to 18 points, responder less than 8, so opener should pass unless he has 18 points and strength in the responder's suit. The opener can then bid three in that suit.

There is one special exception: after an opening bid of one no-trump and a response of two clubs, the opener *must* bid two in a major suit (♠ or ♡) if he has such a suit containing four cards headed by the jack or higher. Lacking that, he bids two diamonds to show only 16 or 17 high-card points, or two no-trump to show 18.

This is known as the Stayman convention and both the responder's two clubs and the opener's rebid of two diamonds (when used) are termed "artificial" bids. Both partners should be conversant with this convention for it to be used.

Rebidding by the Responder

When the bidding again reaches the original responder, he may have a fairly close idea as to the make-up of the opening bidder's hand, including its point count. If the original opener's rebid is forcing to game, the responder must comply with some rebid of his own, as best he can.

Otherwise, he may estimate his partner's count, add his own

exact points in the light of a prospective bid (if any), and figure how far his team can go toward game (26 points) or slam (33 points).

Take this example:

The opener bid one heart, showing a count of 13 plus.

The responder bid two hearts, showing 6 to 10 points.

The opener rebid three hearts, normally a 16- to 18-point holding.

Now ready to make his own rebid, the responder figures that the opener has 18 points and wants to know if the partnership can make game, which is 26 points. So:

With 6 or 7 points the responder passes $(18 + 7 = 25)$.

With 8 or 9 points he bids four hearts $(18 + 8 = 26)$.

A single rebid is the normal limit by the responder when his hand is in the 6–10 bracket; but with 11 or 12 points, he may make two rebids, if he avoids forcing his partner to game. With 13 plus he should go after game, as the opener is usually working on a 13-plus basis, too. With 18 plus the responder should go after a slam.

Bids for Slam

A bid of six constitutes a small slam and requires that the team take all the tricks but one; while a bid of seven or grand slam means that all must be taken. Obviously, the bidders require strong hands; but even with a combined count of 33 points in a suit bid (which includes distributional points), there is a chance that the opponents may be holding two aces.

Even one ace can prove a "sinker" if the opposition takes another trick; and often one partner needs to know whether or not the other holds a particular ace, or which suit happens to be his strongest or best for an immediate play.

In fact, the slam bid may hinge on such information, and one approach is to name an ace by a "cue-bid" in its suit. Here is an illustration:

The opener bid one heart. The responder jumped to three hearts. In revaluing his hand in hearts the opener finds he has 19 points. A mere 7 or 8 in the responder's hand would be sufficient for the opener to bid four hearts and game; but the responder's jump in hearts indicates the 13–16 bracket.

So the opener aims for slam. He happens to be holding the ♡**A** and the ♢**A**. He also has a singleton club, so the ♣**A** would be very helpful. The opener makes a cue-bid of four diamonds. His bid announces the lowest suit in which he has an ace, namely the ♢**A**. Since diamonds is a higher suit than clubs, it also states that the opener does *not* have the ♣**A**.

The responder recognizes the purpose of this otherwise meaningless bid. If his hand held no aces, he would simply bid four hearts, thus expressing his weakness and pegging the bid at game. But the responder happens to be holding the ♣**A**, so he takes the opener's cue and responds with a cue-bid of his own, five clubs, stating that he has the ♣**A**.

Since that is all the opener needs in order to go for slam, he can then bid six hearts. If the opener had *not* been satisfied with the ♣**A**, he could have stopped at five hearts.

Instead of using cue-bids to show individual aces, many players prefer the "Blackwood convention," which gives the number of aces in a partner's hand and can be extended to include kings as well. The Blackwood convention operates as follows:

When a player's hand and the trend of the bidding indicate that his team should go for slam in a suit, the player jumps the bid to four no-trump. This special bid calls upon the partner to state *how many* aces he holds, according to the following schedule of fixed bids:

A bid of *five clubs* signifies either no aces or all four.

A bid of *five diamonds* signifies one ace.

A bid of *five hearts* signifies two aces.

A bid of *five spades* signifies three aces.

The first bidder then knows how many aces the team has between them, by counting his own and adding the number stated by his partner. If they have only one or two aces between them, the first bidder keeps the bid at five in their established suit; while with three between them, he can bid six for a small slam.

If, however, they have all four aces, the first bidder can announce it by bidding five no-trump. This allows his partner to state how many *kings* he holds, as follows:

A bid of *six clubs* signifies no kings.

A bid of *six diamonds* signifies one king.

A bid of *six hearts* signifies two kings.

A bid of *six spades* signifies three kings.

A bid of *six no-trump* signifies four kings.

The original bidder can then bid seven for a grand slam knowing exactly what aces are in his partner's hand and how many kings his partner holds.

DEFENSIVE BIDDING

When one team opens the bidding, the opposing side is often put on the defensive. The nature of their bids is then influenced by the known competition, and in some cases a player's own bidding thunder may be stolen before he can use it.

For convenience, we will term one team South and North; the other, West and East. Assume that the bidding has begun with South as the original opener, and that the first defender to bid is West. Since West's bid must be over South's, it is termed an overcall.

If South opens the bidding with one in a suit, an overcall of one no-trump by West would be the closest to the usual form.

Such an overcall is almost identical with an opening of one no-trump. West requires the same number of high-card points (16, 17, 18) and a hand with balanced distribution (4-3-3-3, 4-4-3-2, or 5-3-3-2) and stoppers in at least three suits.

But one of those must be the suit bid by South, and its stoppers must be sure for West to make the overcall.

If South makes an opening bid in a suit, as one diamond, and West makes an overcall in another suit, as one spade, the situation widens. Again, point count figures—as do quick tricks—but on a lesser scale than usual. The emphasis swings to suit strength and playing tricks.

South, opening with one diamond, should have a minimum of about 13 points in high cards, which puts the other hands at $9 + 9 + 9 = 27$. So West, to be above average, needs 10 or 11 points—

both high-card and distributional—when making an overcall of one spade. The hand should also have one and a half quick tricks.

Most of those points, however, should be concentrated in the trump suit, spades, which should be strong enough to be rebiddable. In such a hand, playing tricks must offset lack of point count. The opener has points; the overcaller needs tricks.

As an example:

♠ K Q J 9 8 3
♡ 8
◇ 6 4 3
♣ K 10 9

This hand has a count of 9 high-card and 2 distributional points, a total of 11. But most important, with 6 points for high cards and 2 for trump length all in spades, West should be good for at least four tricks in trumps alone.

That means he can come within three tricks of making his one, which gives this hand some similarity to a pre-emptive bid. In that way it may discommode the opposing bidders, as well as offer a chance for a response by West's partner, East. If nothing else, it will give East good information toward defense play, if the other team makes the final bid.

Enough more strength is needed to take an extra trick or so, if making an overcall at the two level; for example, West going two diamonds with an overcall after South's opening bid of one heart. This may require 12 or 13 points.

A jump overcall is truly pre-emptive and consists of going one trick higher than is necessary, as when two spades are overcalled by West after South's opening one heart. The jump can go to a still higher level, if preferred. This is a fine bid with a hand of 18 points or higher, with a long strong trump suit and a high-card side suit:

♠ A K J 10 9 7 5
♡ 8 7
◇ 6
♣ A K J

Unfortunately, such hands don't crop up too often in the face of heavy opposing bidding, so there is a tendency to make weak pre-emptive overcalls as a substitute. A hand with seven solid trumps from king down, but with nothing else, still could take six tricks and therefore would be worth a jump to three under some circumstances.

The Take-out Double: Originally known as the informatory double, this is one of the best of all defensive bids. Assume that South has opened with one spade and that West holds:

♠ 9
♡ K Q 9 7
◇ A K 8 2
♣ K J 10 5

West cannot overcall with two as he lacks a strong suit. But his hand should fit with any good holding of his partner, East. So West proceeds to double South's bid of one spade.

While informatory, this cannot be termed an artificial bid, for West could gain very little by doubling South's low bid of one. East recognizes it as calling for a bid of a new suit, so East bids his longest, even though it may be weak. That ends the double and West picks up the bidding later.

A player must make a take-out double *before* his partner has made any bid; he should make it at his first chance to double an opponent's suit; and he should double only bids of one or two and nothing higher. Otherwise, his partner may take it to be a penalty double, or "business" double, as it is termed, and may let it ride, to the doubler's chagrin.

Responding to Overcalls

Assuming that South has bid one heart and that West has overcalled with one spade, West becomes the original bidder for his team and it is up to East to act as the responder. East by then has a partial picture of both hands.

He knows that South has 13 points or more, with a biddable heart suit of at least four cards. He knows that West may have fewer points, but that his minimum spade strength may be stronger.

Also, either South or West—or both!—may have some really strong holdings.

So East should not expect too much from his own hand. If he holds 7 points or more, he can raise West's suit with as few as three small supporting trumps, or only two trumps, topped by queen or better. West is bidding on trump strength more than points, so he is apt to need more side-suit help.

With 11 or 12 points, game is probable if East has any support for West's suit; but it is best to let West go for it himself, following an encouraging bid, unless East's own hand is very strong.

If East has little or nothing in West's suit, East can go into no-trump if he has all other suits stopped. (He should have a good double stopper in South's suit, since South sits behind him.) Otherwise, East must pass or come up with a new suit. To bid in a new suit, East needs about the same minimum that West required to make his overcall, though East can shade it a bit, knowing that West's hand is strong in trick value. But East will need his own strong, long trump.

Free Bidding

When South makes an opening bid and West overcalls it, South's partner, North, becomes a free bidder. That means he does not have to keep the bidding open by responding with various poor or low-point holdings, as South is sure to have another chance to bid.

Often, when North does make a response despite West's raise, it is more than ordinarily helpful to South, because he knows that North's response is a solid one and not just something that he supplied through necessity more than urge.

Assume that South opened with a bid of one diamond and that West overcalled with one heart. Normally, North might make a one-over-one bid of one spade on the strength of only 6 points, both high-card and distributional. But as a free bidder, North should up that count to 9 or even 10 points, showing South something better than a bare minimum.

Similarly, if North's hand happened to be strong in clubs instead of spades, there would be the question of a two-over-one response. Ordinarily, 10 points, high-card and distributional, would do for two clubs. But as a free bidder, North should look for 12 points in his hand.

To respond with one no-trump, North would ordinarily want 6 to 10 points in high cards only, in a balanced hand. As a free bidder he should have 11 or 12 such points and a stopper in hearts, the suit named in West's overcall. This gives South something tangible to work on.

With jumps to two or three in no-trump, North, as a free bidder, can use the regular point count for those levels, but there should be added strength in the opposing suit (in this case hearts) in the form of *two* stoppers.

When raising his partner's bid, North again needs more points in the suit named by South (◇), so he should up the range from the 6–10 bracket to that of 8–12.

Behind these higher minimums is the logic that South (as opener) may have less than average point count because West (the overcaller) has better than average. So it will help if North (the responder) can help boost the team count.

The Opening Lead

In bridge, the opening lead is made by the member of the defending team just to the left of the declarer. After the defender leads, the dummy hand is shown; the declarer plays from it and play continues around to the declarer, who plays the fourth and final card of the trick.

Assume that you are the defender making the opening lead and that your partner has not made a bid, so you are leading blind. What is your proper opening lead?

The answer depends first upon whether the contract is in no-trump or in a trump suit.

In no-trump you have the same purpose as the declarer; namely, to establish a strong suit–if your team has one!–and to take whatever tricks you can in it. Very often the best lead is from your longest suit, consisting of four or more cards. But the first rule is *not* to lead the ace, if you have it, except in a rare instance where you hold the ace, king, jack, and four or more additional cards.

Then, your ace announces that you hope to sweep the suit, and your partner must immediately throw on his highest card–especially the queen, if he has it–so that you can keep on leading from your suit.

Otherwise, hold back the ace. You can use it later, and meanwhile the declarer will be worried about it. Sometimes with ace-king as the top cards, you can lead the king, but often it is good to hold back both.

The lead of your highest card is wise when it happens to be an honor (**K**, **Q**, **J**, or **10**) heading a three-card sequence at the top of your long suit. For example:

Holding ♠ **K Q J 2,** lead the king.
Holding ♠ **10 9 8 2**, lead the ten.

A similar lead may be made with the top card of a broken sequence which has a single space between the two lower cards of the trio, as:

Holding ♡ **Q J 9 3 2**, lead the queen.
Holding ♡ **10 9 8 3 2**, lead the ten.

Such holdings will do with a four-card suit, but five cards are better. The same is true with the lead of the top card of an inner sequence. Here, the suit contains a high honor, a space, then a lower honor followed by the card next below it in value. For example:

Holding ♢ **K J 10 4 2**, lead the jack.
Holding ♢ **A 10 9 4 2**, lead the ten.

If your long suit contains no such honor sequences, in which the lead of a well-backed honor will force out high opposing cards but still leave you with playing strength, the most promising lead is the fourth highest of your longest and strongest suit. There are many holdings of this type. Consider these:

Holding ♣ **Q J 7 5 2**, lead the five.
Holding ♣ **A Q 9 6**, lead the six.
Holding ♣ **J 8 7 3**, lead the three.

This opens your long suit without sacrificing your higher cards, but there is sometimes a question whether your higher cards are worth saving, as with a holding like ♣ **J 8 7 3.** In such cases, it is sometimes better to lead from a shorter suit. If you have a three-card suit headed by two adjacent or "touching" honors, as ♣ **Q J 5**, you can lead the higher honor (♣**Q**). But with only one honor, as ♡ **K 8 3**, it is better to play the lowest card in hope of saving the honor (♡**K**).

With three small cards in a suit, as ♣ **9 6 4**, some players prefer a "top-of-nothing" lead, as they term it, which means the ♣**9**. Others like the lowest (♣**4**) as a lead. Two partners should certainly be in accord on which it is to be, and perhaps they will decide to dispense with such a lead entirely.

With a lead from a doubleton, as ♡ **9 4**, there is no question. Lead the higher card.

All these leads against a no-trump declarer are tempered by a suit bid that your partner may have made. Assuming that your partner bid spades, your lead is no longer blind. It should be made in your partner's suit, unless you have good reason for a different lead.

If you have a sequence of two honors (as **K Q**) topping your partner's suit (♠) you should lead the higher, whether you hold four, three, or only two cards of that suit.

Otherwise, lead your fourth highest in your partner's suit, or the lowest from a three-card holding in his suit. With a doubleton, lead the higher card in his suit, though here it is sometimes better to lead from a stronger suit of your own.

Against a trump-suit contract the defensive opening lead takes a different aspect. The establishment of a long suit may be futile. The declarer or dummy, having few in that suit, often can win the second or third round by trumping in, shortness in your suit being one of the reasons behind their bidding.

So it is often wise to get what you can while you can get it. This means that when a suit is headed by two honors in sequence, they furnish a good opening lead; and sometimes, the shorter the suit the better, as there is less chance of declarer or dummy being out of it.

A suit headed by the ace-king comes into this category and is one of the best of leads, as it may mean two quick tricks for the defense. One rule is to lead the king first, then the ace, except when you hold only those two cards. Then, a lead of ace-king in that order will inform your partner of your special holding, and later he may lead a small card in that suit, enabling you to trump it.

However, if you hold a long suit headed by the ace-king and suspect that your partner may be void in that suit, it is better to lead the ace first. Otherwise, your partner may trump your king lead, thinking that the ace is in the declarer's hand.

With top holdings of king-queen or queen-jack or jack-ten, the lead of the higher honor may make the next one good, and usually it should be done in a hurry. If your partner has bid the suit, your lead from top honors in sequence is good; and many players lead the ace of the partner's suit, no matter how feeble the remaining holdings; again, the idea being to cash it before the dealer puts his trumps to work.

With a doubleton in your partner's suit, lead the top card of the pair. With a singleton, lead it. Either way, your partner may make a long suit good against long holdings by the opponents; if he falters, you can trump the opposing high cards of the suit.

When holding four or more of your partner's suit, without an ace or two top sequence honors, the lead of fourth best is in order and enables your partner to use the "rule of eleven."

By this rule, he deducts the *value* of the card you lead (say **♠6**) from eleven. The result (11 − 6 = 5) tells him the *number* of *higher* cards (above the **♠6**) held by himself, the dummy, and the declarer.

Thus, if he holds **♠ A Q 9 5** and in the dummy he sees **♠ J 8 3**, he accounts for *all five* cards above the **♠6** and knows that the declarer has *none*. Since your lead tells that you have *three* cards above your fourth-best **♠6**, your partner *knows* that they must be **♠ K 9 7** and that the declarer cannot be holding anything more than the **♠ 4 2**.

Thus, if the **♠3** is played from the dummy, your partner can safely top it with the **♠5**. If the **♠8** is played, he can take it with the **♠9**. If the **♠J** is played, he can take it with the **♠A**.

There is one other type of opening lead, namely, that of leading the opponent's trump. When bidding indicates that the declarer is hoping to trump or ruff some of your high cards in other suits, forcing out his trump will help you to establish a side suit, much as in no-trump.

Once the opening lead is made, the dummy is laid face up, and its disclosure helps shape the pattern of the ensuing play. Sometimes a defender may take a trick and find himself in such doubt that he must revert to a type of procedure listed under the opening lead. Often, however, he will find a more fitting play.

As an example of the dummy's revealing nature, assume that West leads the ♣**5** and the dummy (North) shows ♣ **J 10 3**. South, as declarer, decides to follow the old whist practice of "second hand low" by playing the ♣**3** from dummy.

If East happens to be holding ♣ **Q 9 8** and wants to counter with the whist principle of "third hand high," he does not have to waste his ♣**Q** to force South higher. Noting the ♣ **J 10** in the dummy, East can accomplish his purpose by playing the ♣**8** as the equivalent of "high."

Other whist truisms are applicable to bridge, but with many modifications or extensions, since bridge, with its bidding and the disclosure of the dummy, is a much more volatile and intriguing game. The play of the hand in bridge involves many fine points and unusual situations that can be recognized only through actual experience or detailed study.

Volumes have been written on that phase of the game alone, a fact that goes far toward accounting for the popularity of bridge and the never-ending interest that it affords its dedicated followers.

Glossary-Index of Card Games and Terms

Abandon: Give up a hand.
Above the line: *Bridge*. A premium score.
Adversary: Principal opponent.
Age, or Edge: Player to dealer's left.
Announce: Name a trump or a game.
Ante: Preliminary bet. To make a preliminary bet.
Anything opens: Form of *Draw Poker*. 156
Any value wild: Variant of *Draw Poker*. 129
Around the world: Form of *Poker*. 141
Assist: *Euchre*. Order up trump. 187
Auction: Bidding to make trump.
Auction bridge: Forerunner of *Contract*.
Auction five hundred. 197
Auction (three-handed) pinochle. 233
Partnership pinochle. 245
Auction pinochle counts. 233
Auction pinochle scoring schedule. 241
Auction pitch: Modern form of *Pitch*. 210
Automatic lowball: Variant of *Draw Poker*. 156

Back in: *Poker*. Bet after checking.
Back to back: *Stud Poker*. A hole card and first upcard of same value.
Balk: *Cribbage*. Give cards to the crib that may not help the dealer.
Banker: Player who sells and buys chips.
Baseball: Wild form of *Draw Poker*. 163
Bate, or Bete: *Pinochle*. Failure to win bid.
Beat your neighbor: Form of *Draw Poker*. 167
Below the line: *Bridge*. Entries of trick scores.
Best bower: *Five Hundred*. The joker.
Bet: Stake placed on play to come.
Bete: See *Bate*.
Bicycle: Lowest hand in *Lowball*. (5 4 3 2 A).
Bid: Offer to take specific number of tricks.
Bidder: Player making a bid.
Big Cassino: *Cassino*. The ♢10.
Black Lady, or Black Maria: *Hearts*. The ♠ Q. 82
Blackwood convention: *Bridge*. A way to use cue-bids to reach slams.
Blank suit: A suit totally missing from a hand.
Blind: An ante. Also a widow.
Block rummy: A form of *Rummy*. 27
Bluff: *Poker*. Play a poor hand as a good one.
Boathouse rummy: A form of *Rummy*. 28
Bobtail flush: *Poker*. Four cards of a suit.
Bobtail straight: *Poker*. Four cards of mixed suits in sequence.

Contract bridge (*cont'd*)
  Rebidding the hand. 272
  Rebidding by the responder. 275
  Bids for slam. 276
 Defensive bidding. 278
  A jump overcall. 279
  The take-out double. 280
  Responding to overcalls. 280
  Free bidding. 281
  The opening lead. 282

Convention: *Bridge.* Bid or play in accordance with a system.

Count: Value given to certain cards when bidding or playing.

Counter: Card with special point value. Also, a chip or token.

Counting out: Keeping score of points or tricks when going for game.

Court cards: Face cards (K, Q, J).

Cover: Play a higher card on trick.

Crib: *Cribbage.* Extra hands formed from discards.

Cribbage. 67

Criss-cross: A form of *Crossover.* 143

Crossover: A variety of *Poker.* 142

Cross-ruff: *Bridge.* To trump alternating leads back and forth.

Cross the suit: *Euchre.* To change trump to suit of opposite color.

Cross widow: *Criss-cross* plus *Crossover.* 143

Cue-bid: *Bridge.* One that reveals that the bidder controls a suit.

Cut: To put lower portion of pack on upper.

Cutthroat: A game in which each participant plays for himself.

Dead card: One that has been played, discarded, or rendered unavailable.

Dead hand: One that is out of play.

Deadwood: *Rummy.* Leftover cards in a hand.

Deal: Distribution of cards, chiefly as hands to players; plus action that follows.

Dealer: Person distributing the cards; also applied to banker.

Dealer's choice: *Poker.* Hand in which dealer names type of game he wants played.

Deal out: To exclude a player from a deal.

Deck: A pack of cards.

Declare: To name a trump suit (or no-trump).

Declarer: *Bridge.* Bidder originally naming the suit finally chosen (or no-trump) and thereby playing his own hand and dummy.

Defender: *Bridge.* Member of team opposing the declarer.

Defensive bid: *Bridge.* Bid made to force opponents to bid higher.

Defensive strength: *Bridge.* Cards helpful against opposing contract.

Demand bid: *Bridge.* One calling on bidder's partner to respond with another bid unless an opponent bids ahead of him.

Deuces wild: Special form of *Poker.* See *Draw Poker with Deuces Wild.* 121

Diamond jack: *Hearts.* ♢J as bonus card. 82

Dillinger: *Seven-card Stud.* Hand with two sixes as original hole cards.

Discard: Elimination of unwanted cards, often in exchange for others. In trump games: Throw off from an odd suit.

Discard pile: *Rummy* and *Canasta.* Face-up pile from which players can draw.

Distribution: Division of cards in player's hand, by suits.

Group: *Rummy.* Three (or four) cards of one value (9 9 9), in contrast to a sequence (J 10 9).

Guards: *Bridge.* Low cards protecting one of higher value, in the same suit (as ♡ Q 8 7; the Q is "guarded" by the 8, 7). 175

Hand: The cards dealt to a player. Also, the equivalent of "deal."

Hands as games: Way of scoring *Pinochle.* 232

Hearts. 81
- Black Lady (♠Q). 82
- Bonus card (◇J). 82
- Take all hearts. 85
- Pink Lady (♡Q). 86
- The widow. 86

Hearts triple: *Pinochle.* Special score. 243

Heinz: Form of *Seven-card Stud.* 163

High: *Pitch.* The highest card dealt. Also, a point for holding same.

High card: *Poker.* Top in "no pair" hand. 106

High, low, jack, and game: Points in *Pitch.*

High-low poker. 145
- High-low draw poker. 145
- High-low five-card stud. 147
  - Additional options. 148
- High-low seven-card stud. 148
  - Declaring for high or low. 148
  - Declaring for both high and low. 149
  - Optional valuation of cards in high-low poker. 150
- Other forms of high-low poker. 151

High spade split: Special form of *Draw Poker.* 156

His heels: *Cribbage.* Jack turned up as "starter" in suit. 69

His nobs: *Cribbage.* Jack matching the "starter" in suit. 68

Hold 'Em: *Poker.* Form of *Omaha.* 166

Holding: Cards forming a player's hand.

Hole card: *Stud Poker.* Any card dealt face down.

Hole-card stud: Variant of *Five-card Stud.* 160

Honors: *Whist.* Top five trumps (A, K, Q, J, 10). *Bridge:* Same, with four aces honors in no-trump.

Hundred aces: *Pinochle.* A meld of four aces of different suits for 100 points.

Improve: *Poker.* Better a hand by a draw.

Index: The upper corner of a playing card, showing its suit and value.

Informatory double: *Bridge.* A false double that tips off the bidder's holding to his partner.

Inside straight: *Poker.* Four cards needing an in-between value to make a straight (example: 10 9 8 6 needs a 7).

In the hole: *Five Hundred.* A minus score. Applicable to other games.

Introduction to trump games. 173

Jack: *Pitch.* Point scored for taking jack of trumps.

Jack pots: *Poker.* By popular interpretation, a hand requiring a pair of jacks—or higher—to open the betting.

Joker: A card added to the standard 52 pack, making 53. Today, most packs have an extra joker, making 54. By combining two packs, a joker quota can be increased to four; with three packs, to six.

Joker poker: *Poker*. Any game with the joker as a wild card.

Joker wild: *Poker*. The joker or jokers wild. 127

Jump bid: *Bridge*. A bid beyond the conventional pattern.

Kicker: *Poker*. An odd card retained during a draw.

Kitty: A pool, or portion thereof. Also, a widow.

Knave: Former term for a jack.

Knock: To end a hand by rapping the table.

Knock rummy: Cross between *Rummy* and *Gin*. 38

Last: Scoring for the last point in *Cribbage*, or the last trick in *Pinochle*.

Lay away: To make discards in a crib or widow.

Lay down: To make a meld or reveal a winning hand.

Lay off: *Rummy*. To dispose of cards on an opponent's meld.

Layout: *Russian Bank*. Cards as dealt on the table. *Michigan:* Extra cards from a spare pack, indicating pay-offs.

Left bower: *Euchre*. The jack of the same color as the right bower.

Light: *Poker*. Drawing chips from the pot to show how many a player owes.

Limit: *Poker*. The ceiling placed on bets.

Little cassino: *Cassino*. The ♠2.

Little slam: *Bridge*. Taking twelve tricks.

Long game: One in which the whole pack is dealt to start.

Long suit: Predominant suit in a hand, or any suit exceeding normal quota.

Low: Any low card or hand.

Low: *Pitch*. Lowest trump in play. Also, a point scored for holding or taking it.

Lowball: Low-hand *Poker*. 152
  Lowball with the bug. 153
  Lowball with wild cards. 153

Low card wild: A form of *Draw Poker*. 129
  With *Five-card Stud*. 161

Lurched: To be beaten before reaching half the score for game.

Make: To name trump, also to win amount bid.

March: *Euchre*. To win all five tricks.

Marriage: *Pinochle*. K and Q of a suit.

Meld: To lay combinations of cards face up and score their value.

Mexican low card: Form of *Mexican Stud*. 161

Mexican stud: *Five-card Stud* with choice of hole card. 160

Mexican wild: *Mexican Stud* with wild cards.

Michigan. 18
  Spinado. 22
  Additional boodle cards. 23

Misdeal: To deal cards incorrectly; usually, this demands a new deal.

Mistigris: Another name for *Joker Poker*.

Mouth bet: *Poker*. Promise to put chips in pot.

Muggins: *Cribbage*. A special penalty call. 80

Multiple Klondike. 39

Natural: *Poker* and *Canasta*. Combination made without using "wild" cards.

Newmarket: Early form of *Michigan*.

New York stud: *Canadian Stud*.

Nine-card stud poker. 159

No draw: Straight *Poker* without the draw.

No low cards: A form of *Five-card Stud*. 161

No-trump: In a trump game, a hand played without a trump.

Nullo: A hand in which a player tries to lose all tricks or points.

Odd trick: One giving a player a majority.

Oklahoma gin: Variant of *Gin Rummy*. 37

Old sledge: A name for *Seven-up*.

Omaha: *Poker*. Form of "dealer's choice." 166

One-card poker. 169

One card wild: Variant of *Draw Poker*. 128

One-end straight: *Poker*. An A K Q J or 4 3 2 A.

One-eyed jacks: Chiefly *Poker*. The ♡J and ♠J.

One pair: *Poker*. Lowest combination of cards. 105

One suit wild: Very wild *Draw Poker*. 129

One wild card: *Draw Poker*. Player's choice. 128

Open: First bid or first bet.

Open-end straight: *Poker*. A bobtail straight.

Openers: *Poker*. Cards required to open a pot (as pair of jacks).

Opening bid: First bid in an auction.

Open poker: Game with cards dealt face up (as *Stud*).

Option: Feature of *High-Low Five-card Stud*.

Order it up: *Euchre*. Acceptance of turned-up card as trump, by non-dealer. 185

Ordinary suit: Any non-trump suit.

Original bidder: Player making first bid.

Original hand: A hand as first dealt.

Other variations of "dealer's choice." 166

Overbid: Bid too high to win.

Overcall: Bid higher than the previous bid.

Overtrick: One more than needed to win.

Overtrump: To play a higher trump on a trick already trumped.

Pack: All cards used in a game.

Pair: Two cards of the same value.

Pairs royal: *Cribbage*. Three of a kind. 68

Partnership pinochle: With four hands. 245

Pass: To refuse to bid or bet. Also, to swap cards with other players.

Pass the garbage (or trash): A form of *Poker*. 167

Pat hand: *Poker*. A hand that a draw will not improve, as a straight or a flush.

Pedro: *Pitch* with the five of trump (called "Pedro") as an extra counter. 217

Pedro and Snoozer. 217
- Pedro. 217
  - Dom Pedro. 217
  - Pedro Sancho. 218
- Snoozer. 218

Pedro Sancho: Elaboration of *Pedro* with the nine of trump ("Sancho") as an extra counter. 218

Peek poker: Early form of *Seven-card Stud*.

Peg: *Cribbage*. To score points on a board.

Penny ante: *Poker* with one-cent limit.

Picture card: A face card.

Pink Lady: *Hearts*. The ♡Q. 86

Pinochle: A game with a special, 48-card pack. 220. Also, the ◇J and ♠Q.

Pinochle: The cards. 220
Two-handed pinochle. 222
Melds and other scores. 223
Auction (Three-handed) pinochle. 233
Newer forms of counts. 233
Scoring schedules. 241
Partnership pinochle. 245

Pinochle poker: *Poker* with a pinochle pack. 157

Pistol, or Pistol Pete: *Hole-card Stud.*

Pitch and auction pitch. 207
Pitch scores: High, low, jack, game. 207–8
Auction pitch. 210
Pointers on bidding. 212
Optional rules in *Auction Pitch.* 214
The dealer's bid. 214
Smudge. 214
Pitch with the joker. 214
Taking low. 215
California jack. 215
Shasta Sam. 216

Plain suit: An ordinary suit.

Play on or off: *Cribbage.* 75

Player: Participant in a card game.

Point: Scoring unit in various games.

Point count: *Bridge.* Bid evaluation. 253

Poker. 102. See also: *Draw Poker; Draw Poker with Deuces Wild; Five-card Stud Poker; Seven-card Stud Poker;* Poker Variations; Poker Today; *High-Low Poker; Lowball;* Special Forms of Poker.

Poker: The hands. 102–6. The royal flush–The straight flush–Four of a kind–The full house–The flush–The straight–Three of a kind–Two pair–One pair–High card.

Pone: Non-dealer in two-handed game.

Pool: Common fund of chips or tokens.

Pot: Same as pool. In *Canasta,* the discard pile.

Pot limit: *Poker.* Restriction of a bet to the amount already in the pot.

Pozo: *Canasta.* The pot.

Pre-emptive bid: One that prevents opposing team from bidding. 265

Premiums: *Bridge.* Scores above the line. 251

Prize pot: *Canasta.* One containing a wild card.

Progressive jack pots: *Poker.* Raising requirements for openers after a passed bid. 110

Psychic bid: *Bridge.* An unconventional bid to bluff or deceive opponents.

Push poker: Same as *Take It or Leave It.*

Quick trick: *Bridge.* High-card holdings. 259

Raise: To bid higher or put more chips in pot.

Rank: Relative value of a card.

Rebid: A new bid by a former bidder.

Renege: Failure to follow suit or play a required card, often resulting in a penalty.

Renounce: Discard on the suit led.

Response: *Bridge.* Support for a partner's bid. 266

Revoke: Same as renege.

Ride along: *Poker.* Keep calling bets.

Right bower: *Euchre.* The jack of trump.

Rob: Exchange a card for a turned-up trump.

Roodles: *Poker.* A round of hands with stakes increased according to agreement.
Round: A series of hands in which everyone deals.
Roundhouse: *Pinochle.* Meld of four kings and four queens. 234. Also called "round trip."
Round-the-corner straight: *Poker.* Special hand. 171
Royal flush: *Poker.* A K Q J 10 of same suit. 102
Royal marriage: *Pinochle.* K and Q of trump.
Royal straight flush: Same as royal flush.
Rubber: To win two out of three games.
Ruff: Trump a lead from another suit.
Rummy: Standard game. 24
  Block rummy. 27
  Boathouse rummy. 28
Run: A sequence of cards.
Russian bank. 88

Samba and Bolivia. 62
Samba (description). 62
  Bolivia. 64
Saratoga: Variant of *Michigan.*
Schmear: Defensive play in *Pinochle.* 244
Score: Total tricks or points won.
See: *Poker.* To call a bet.
Set: To lose a bid.
Set back: Deduct from a score.
Seven-card flip: Extension of *Mexican Stud.* 164
Seven-card mutual: *Seven-card Stud* with common upcards. 165
Seven-card stud poker. 134
  Seven-card stud with deuces wild. 136
  Also see: Special forms of *Seven-card Stud.* 163
Seven-five reverse. 164
Seven-up: Another name for *Pitch.*
Shasta Sam: *Pitch* with a draw. 216
Shifting sands: *Mexican Wild Poker.*
Short game: A game in which only a portion of the pack is dealt.
Short suit: A suit with fewer than average cards for the hand.
Shotgun: Form of *Draw Poker.* 157
Show: To meld or display certain cards.
Showdown: *Poker.* Disclosure of all hands.
Shuffle: To mix the pack before dealing.
Shutout: To keep opponent from taking points or tricks. *Bridge:* To pre-empt.
Shy: Said of a player owing chips to pot.
Side bets: *Poker.* Any bets apart from the main pot.
Side strength: High cards other than trumps.
Side suit: An ordinary suit.
Signal: Conventional bid or play in partnership game.
Singleton: *Whist* and *Bridge.* Lone card of a suit in a player's hand.
Six-card stud: Popular form of *Poker.* 159
Six-handed five hundred. 205
Sixty queens: *Pinochle.* Meld of four queens of different suits for 60 points.
Small slam: Same as "little slam."
Smear: Same as schmear.
Smudge: Bonus in *Auction Pitch.* 214
Snoozer: *Pedro* with all extra counts. 218
Spades: *Cassino.* A 1-point score for having most spades.
Spades double: Special score in *Pinochle.* 242
Spade cassino: Variant with each spade counting 1 point. 11

Special forms of *Poker*.
Special forms of *Draw Poker*.
Special forms of *Stud Poker*.
Special forms of *Five-card Stud*.
Special forms of *Seven-card Stud*.
Other variations of "dealer's choice."
Poker with fewer than five-card hands.
Freak poker hands.

Spinado, or Spin: *Michigan* with ◇A wild. 22

Spit in the ocean: *Poker* with wild card in middle. 140

Spite and Malice. 98

Split openers: *Draw Poker*. To break a required opening combination (as a pair of jacks or better) to draw for a higher hand (as a straight).

Spot card: Any card from A up to 10.

Spot hearts: Variant of *Hearts*, each heart counting according to its spots from ace (1) up to king (13).

Squeeze: *Bridge*. Series of plays forcing opponent to throw a winning card.

Stand, or Stand pat: To play a hand as held.

Stay: *Poker*. To call.

Stock: Cards not yet dealt.

Stopper: A card high enough to keep an opponent from winning an entire suit.

Stops: Games such as *Fan-tan* and *Michigan*.

Straight: *Poker*. A sequence of mixed suits. 104

Straight flush: *Poker*. Sequence in one suit. 103

Striped straight: *Poker*. Freak hand with alternating colors. 172

Stripped pack: A pack with low cards removed.

Sweep: *Cassino*. Clear the board for 1 point.

Sweeten: *Poker*. Feed the pot.

Table stakes: *Poker*. Limiting a player's bets to his immediate funds.

Take all hearts: To win them all. 85

Take in: *Cassino*. To gather the last cards. 4

Take it or leave it: Special *Five-card Stud*. 162

Tenace: *Bridge*. Honor cards with a gap between, as A–Q (major) or K–J (minor).

Ten-card stud: *Ten-card Stud Poker*. 159

Tenth card: *Cribbage*. K, Q, J, 10. 75

Texas Tech: *Poker*. *Double-barreled Shotgun*.

Three-card monte: *Three-card Poker*.

Three-card poker: A special game. 169

Three of a kind: *Poker*. Hand with three cards of identical value, as J J J. 104

Three out of five: *Five-card Stud*, but with players finally choosing their best cards for *Three-card Poker*. 169

Throw, or Throw off: To make a discard.

TNT: Offshoot of *Draw Poker*. 157

Touching: *Bridge*. Suits next in value.

Trail: *Cassino*. To lay down an odd card.

Trey: A three-spot.

Trick: Cards played singly by each player, forming a group that one wins.

Trick score: *Bridge*. Points for tricks bid and won, going below the line. 251

Tripleton: *Bridge*. Only three cards of a suit in a player's hand.
Triplets: Three of a kind.
Trump: Card of a special suit that ranks higher than the others. 174
Also, to play such a card.
Trump suit: A suit named as trump.
Twin beds: Elaboration of *Cincinnati*. 166
Two-card poker. 169
Two pair: *Poker*. Hand with two pairs of different value, with an odd card (as J J 8 8 10). 105
Two-suiter: A "long game" hand composed chiefly of two suits.

Undercut: *Gin Rummy*. To finish with hand with lower count than knocker's. 32
Under the guns: Player to dealer's left.
Unmatched: *Rummy*. An odd card.
Up: *Poker*. Raise a bet. Also, top cards in "two pair" (10 10 3 3 Q = "tens up").
Upcard: *Stud Poker*. A card dealt face up. *Rummy* and *Canasta:* Top card of discard pile.
Utah: Another name for *Cincinnati*.

Variations of "dealer's choice." 166
Void: A blank suit.
Vulnerable: *Bridge*. A team with one game toward rubber.

Whangdoodles or Rangdoodles: Roodles.
Wheel: *Lowball*. Any 5 4 3 2 A. 152–53
Widow: A special deal of extra cards.
Wild: A card representing any other.
Wired: *Stud Poker*. Cards "back to back."

Yarborough: A hand with no "honor cards."

Zebra: *Poker*. A striped straight.
Zsa Zsa: A very lovely hand.